D1076217

MARVEL
ENCYCLOPEDIA

MARVEL ENTERPRISES, INC.

CEO & GENERAL COUNSEL	Allen Lipson
CHIEF CREATIVE OFFICER	Avi Arad
CHIEF INFORMATION OFFICER	Gui Karyo
PRESIDENT CEO, TOY BIZ	Alan Fine
CHIEF FINANCIAL OFFICER	Ken West
EXECUTIVE SALES V.P.-TOY BIZ	Ralph Lancelotti
V.P.-HUMAN RESOURCES	Mary Sprowls

ADVERTISING—PROMOTION—RETAIL SALES

EXEC. VICE PRESIDENT CONSUMER PRODUCTS, PROMOTIONS, AND MEDIA SALES	Russell A. Brown
DIRECTOR OF ADVERTISING	Jeff Dunetz
TRADE BOOK SALES MANAGER	Jennifer Beemish
ADVERTISING SALES	Sara Beth Schrager

PUBLISHING GROUP

PRESIDENT AND COO PUBLISHING, CONSUMER PRODUCTS & NEW MEDIA	Bill Jemas
EDITOR IN CHIEF	Joe Quesada
MANAGING EDITOR	David Bogart
PRODUCTION DIRECTOR	Dan Carr
DIRECTOR OF MANUFACTURING	Sangho Byun
MARKETING COMMUNICATIONS MANAGER	Michael Doran
PUBLISHING BUSINESS MANAGER	Chet Krayewski
SENIOR MANUFACTURING MANAGER	Fred Pagan
MANUFACTURING MANAGER	Christine Slusarz
MANUFACTURING REPRESENTATIVE	Stefano Perrone, Jr.

WRITERS/EDITORS	Mark D. Beazley and Jeff Youngquist
WRITER	Matt Brady
COPY EDITOR	Sarah Fan
ART DIRECTOR	Matty Ryan
DESIGNERS	John Roberts and Tim Smith III
COVER	Alex Ross

Special Thanks: **Axel Alonso, Seth Biederman, Tom Brevoort, C.B. Cebulski, Nanci Dakesian, Andrew Goletz, Victor Gonzalez, Jen Grünwald, Hi-Fi Design, Kelly Lamy, Nick Lowe, Andrew Lis, Ralph Macchio, Mike Marts, John Miesegaes, Mike Raicht, Wilson Ramos, Dan Reilly and the *Wizard* staff, Raphael Riche, Bill Rosemann, Peter Sanderson, Andy Schmidt, Cory Sedlmeier, Brian Smith, Marc Sumerak, Flo Steinberg, Jeof Vita, Lynn Yoshii and Joe Zerbo.**

MARVEL ENCYCLOPEDIA. Second printing 2003. ISBN# 0-7851-0984-6. Published by MARVEL COMICS, a division of MARVEL ENTERTAINMENT GROUP, INC. OFFICE OF PUBLICATION: 10 East 40th Street, New York, NY 10016.

$29.99 per copy in the U.S. and $48.00 in Canada (GST #R127032852); Canadian Agreement #40668537.

Printed in Canada. STAN LEE, Chairman Emeritus. For information regarding advertising in Marvel Comics or on Marvel.com, please contact Russell Brown, Executive Vice President, Consumer Products, Promotions and Media Sales at 212-576-8561 or rbrown@marvel.com

10 9 8 7 6 5 4 3 2

TABLE OF CONTENTS

ALEX ROSS

INTRODUCTION

Thousands of years ago, ancient story-tellers gathered around a fire to regale the tribe with stories of the great hunters and the great hunt.

On hillsides overlooking marble white temples, great Greek and Roman fablers awed their audiences with tales of warriors of battles past and mighty gods of legend who walk amongst us.

In 1961, Stan Lee, Jack Kirby, Steve Ditko and many others continued this great tradition. Within the confines of newsprint and nine-panel grids they have handed us a new legacy of stories of great warriors, hunters and gods.

To this day we continue this tradition at the modern Marvel. With the most fruitful minds in all of the entertainment world we create, on a daily basis, the myths and legends of tomorrow. This book you hold in your hands barely scratches the surface...

...but it's a great place to start!

See ya in the funnybooks!

JQ
EEK!

AVENGERS

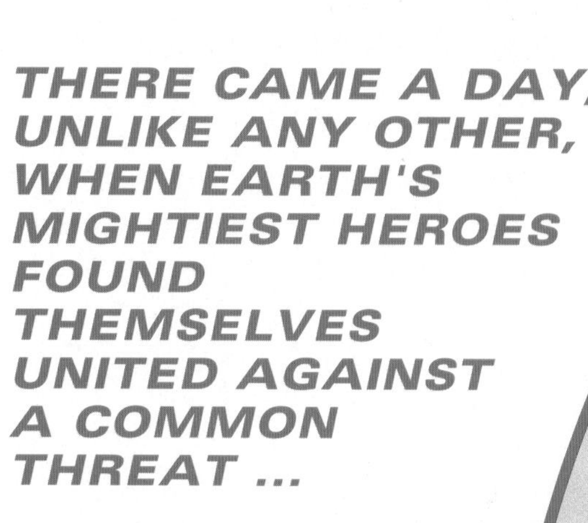

THERE CAME A DAY, UNLIKE ANY OTHER, WHEN EARTH'S MIGHTIEST HEROES FOUND THEMSELVES UNITED AGAINST A COMMON THREAT ...

A handful of the planet's foremost superhuman adventurers were drawn together by chance when the Asgardian trickster Loki attempted to set the Hulk on a collision course with his heroic foster brother Thor. Hulk's sidekick, Rick Jones, sent out a distress call that was answered by Iron Man, Ant-Man and Wasp. Together with Thor, the three heroes tracked down Hulk and uncovered Loki's plot.

On that day, the Avengers were born—to fight the foes no single hero could withstand.

The newly formed team assembled a short time later at the midtown-Manhattan mansion of industrialist Anthony Stark, Iron Man's alter ego. Stark donated the mansion for the Avengers' exclusive use and established a foundation to cover all operational expenses incurred by the non-profit team.

The squad's roster has expanded since its inception, undergoing numerous changes. And while the team has faced countless challenges through the years, both internal and external, the Avengers always have risen to the occasion—meeting and defeating any and all threats to the planet.

Art by Alex Ross

ANT-MAN

Real Name:	Scott Edward Harris Lang	**Weight:**	190 lbs.
First Appearance:	*Marvel Premiere* #47 (1979)	**Eye Color:**	Blue
Height:	6'	**Hair Color:**	Reddish-blond

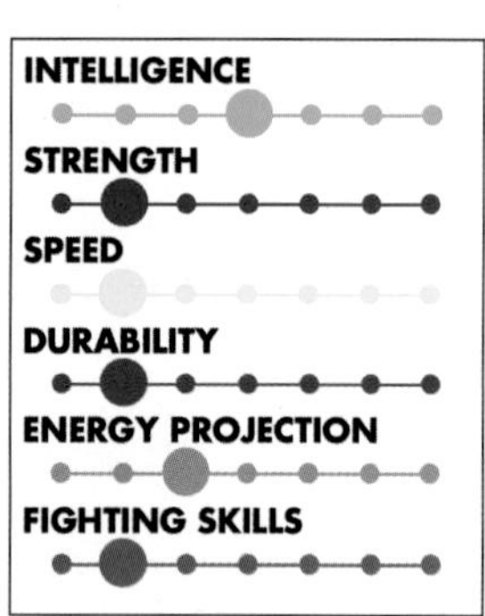

POWERS/ WEAPONS

- Size reduction to sub-atomic levels
- Telepathic communication with insects via cybernetic helmet
- Maintains the strength of a normal-sized human at reduced height
- Disruptor blasters in gloves

ESSENTIAL READING

- *Fantastic Four: Into the Breach TPB*
- *Avengers Vol. 1: World Trust TPB*

Unable to provide for his daughter through conventional means, Scott Lang turned his talents to burglary. After being arrested, the electronics expert furthered his studies in prison. Following an early release for good behavior, Lang went to work in the design department at Stark International, the corporation owned by Iron Man's alter ego Tony Stark.

A model employee, Lang impressed Stark with his schematics for advanced security systems. But while work was important, Lang's daughter Cassie was his life—and his world crumbled when she was diagnosed with an inoperable heart condition. Cassie's health continued to deteriorate, and even salary increases from Stark International couldn't stem the tide of medical bills. Almost without conscious thought, Lang began to case certain wealthy neighborhoods—reluctant to return to his criminal ways, but seeing few other options.

Cassie's only hope was surgeon Erica Sondheim, who had pioneered advanced techniques in critical-focus laser surgery. But when Lang visited the Sondheim Institute, he witnessed the doctor's abduction by Darren Agonistes Cross, president of the multinational conglomerate Cross Technological Enterprises. The ailing industrialist required Sondheim's expertise to correct his own heart condition, and was unwilling to wait in line for her specialized services. Leery of the law, Lang planned to hire sufficient muscle to force his way into the Cross compound and rescue the doctor.

Desperate for the cash needed to finance such an endeavor, he returned to one of the houses he'd cased, where he had noted an array of extremely sophisticated detection devices and assumed they were protecting valuable goods. In reality, Lang had stumbled upon the home of Hank Pym. Inside, he discovered the super hero scientist's original Ant-Man costume, along with several canisters of shrinking gas. Intending to free Sondheim by himself, Lang stole the equipment.

Pym observed the theft, but chose not to reveal himself. Instead, he followed Lang to his destination as Yellowjacket, curious to ascertain Lang's intentions. Garbed as Ant-Man, Lang rescued Sondhiem, who later operated successfully on his daughter. He planned to return the Ant-Man outfit to its owner, but Pym let Lang keep the costume—provided he put it to lawful use.

As Ant-Man, Lang assisted Iron Man and others, always willing to shrink to the occasion when duty calls. When Mr. Fantastic was believed dead, Lang worked with the Fantastic Four for a short period. A fount of intellect and invention, he served as a valued stand-in for the elastic inventor, and has since returned to aid the team as needed. For years, Lang considered himself a part-time crimefighter. Now a member of the Avengers, he strives to make the world a safer place for his daughter—and seeks to rise above his reputation as a poor man's Hank Pym.

Art by Joe Jusko

Art by Stuart Immonen

BLACK PANTHER

Real Name:	T'Challa	**Weight:**	185 lbs.
First Appearance:	*Fantastic Four* #52 (1966)	**Eye Color:**	Brown
Height:	6'	**Hair Color:**	Black, shaved bald

Art by Mark Texeira

ESSENTIAL READING

- *Black Panther Vol. I: The Client TPB*
- *Black Panther Vol. II: Enemy of the State TPB*
- *Essential Avengers Vol. III*
- *Essential Fantastic Four Vol. III*

A powerful, cultured and noble monarch, T'Challa succeeded his father as king of the small, reclusive African nation Wakanda. Following his father's murder, T'Challa was educated at the finest schools in Europe and America. He returned to his homeland with a degree in physics, eager to assume the mantle of leadership. To do so, he was required to defeat six of Wakanda's greatest warriors in unarmed combat, and then obtain the secret heart-shaped herb that grants the country's chieftains their great physical strength and enhanced senses. Successfully carrying out the dual challenge, T'Challa donned the ceremonial garb of the Black Panther, totem of the Wakandan people. As chieftain of the country's Panther Clan, he is the latest in a long line of warrior kings steeped in tradition, tribalism and a deeply rooted sense of honor.

Under T'Challa's leadership, Wakanda has become one of the wealthiest and most technologically advanced nations on the planet. The country is home to the world's only deposit of Vibranium, an extraterrestrial metal capable of absorbing all sonic vibrations. After meeting Captain America, the Panther was offered membership in the Avengers. Given the potential threat such superhuman beings posed to his kingdom, accepting their invitation afforded T'Challa the opportunity to investigate their motives and intentions.

Taking a leave of absence from his royal duties, the Panther served among Earth's mightiest heroes for a lengthy interval, acquainting himself with American methods of crimefighting. Although his initial intentions were somewhat self-serving, T'Challa has come to consider the Avengers true friends and valuable allies.

T'Challa eventually returned to Wakanda, only to find the nation in turmoil after his prolonged absence. After regaining his people's respect, he worked to bring his country out of isolation from the rest of the world. He now must stand forever vigilant against those inside and outside Wakanda who would usurp the throne and plunder its riches. Always, T'Challa's owes his primary allegiance to his people, and his actions are driven by their continued well being.

A cunning creature of the night, the Panther manipulates global events with chilling ease and seeming emotional detachment, careful to remain one step ahead of his adversaries at all times. He is secretive and appears aloof, to the chagrin and bewilderment of friends and super hero allies. Due to his responsibilities of state, T'Challa has denied himself the worldly pleasures his vast wealth would allow—and the happiness of life with his true love, American social worker Monica Lynne. To protect his kingdom, no price is too high for the enigmatic and unflappable king.

Art by Joe Quesada

POWERS/ WEAPONS

- Enhanced senses, strength, speed and agility
- Accomplished gymnast and acrobat
- Expert tracker
- Master of various African martial arts
- Bulletproof Vibranium bodysuit
- Impact- and sound-absorbing Vibranium-soled boots
- Retractable Vibranium claws
- Energy dagger

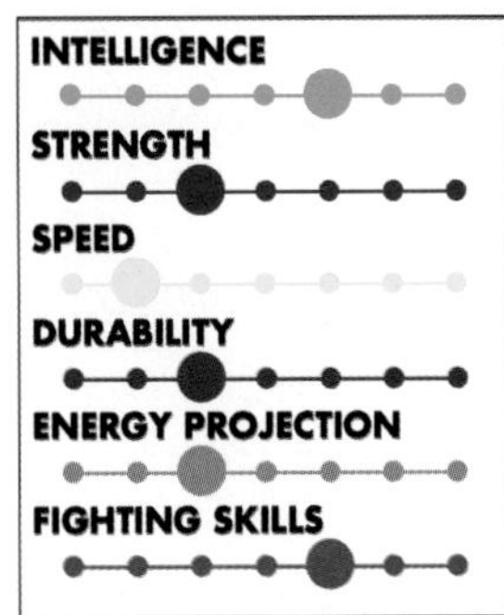

CAPTAIN AMERICA

Real Name:	Steve Rogers
First Appearance:	*Captain America Comics* #1 (historical, 1941), *Avengers* (Vol. 1) #4 (modern, 1964)
Height:	6'2"
Weight:	240 lbs.
Eye Color:	Blue
Hair Color:	Blond

Art by Travis Charest

Born during the Great Depression, Steve Rogers grew up sickly and frail in New York City. Despite his economic and physical limitations, Rogers worked hard to support himself. As World War II newsreel footage from Europe made its way back to the United States, he was horrified by scenes of the Nazis overtaking Europe and persecuting those who opposed them. Inspired to join the Army, Rogers was rejected due to his physical infirmities.

Captain America Comics #1, March 1941

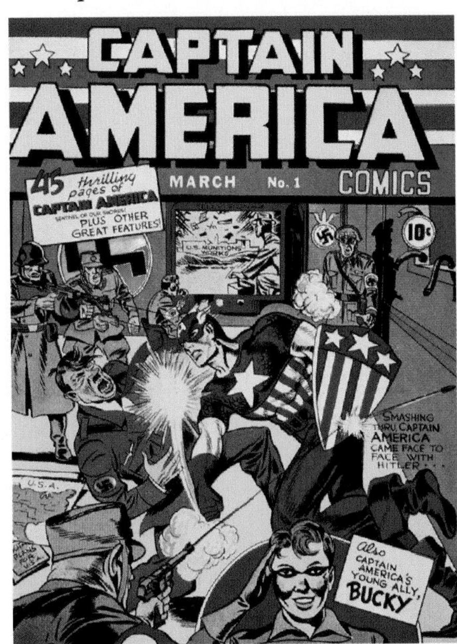

Overhearing Rogers' protests, General Chester Phillips offered him a place in a top-secret biological experiment, Operation: Rebirth. Determined to make a difference in the war effort, Rogers eagerly accepted the offer; after weeks of tests and training, he was injected with the experimental Super-Soldier Serum and exposed to low-level radiation to enhance the formula's effectiveness. Rogers emerged from the treatment with a perfect body. Following extensive combat training and extreme physical conditioning, Rogers was deemed fit for active duty as the Army's ultimate weapon—and the single-minded embodiment of America's fighting spirit.

The military first deployed Captain America to the European Theater of Operations. Serving as an Army private, Rogers transferred from base to base, going wherever Captain America was needed. Opposing Hitler, the Red Skull and Axis forces at every turn, he led his fellow soldiers into battle and served selflessly as a living, breathing symbol of a nation. When a teenager named Bucky Barnes discovered Rogers' secret identity, Captain America accepted him as an ally.

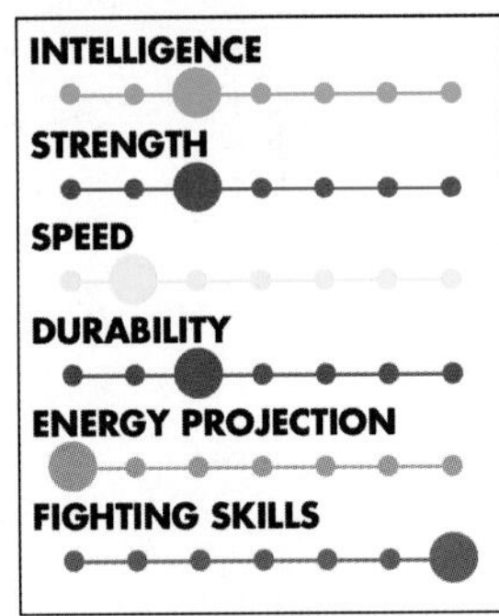

During the waning days of World War II, a bomb-loaded drone plane launched by Nazi scientist Baron Heinrich Zemo exploded with Cap and Bucky aboard, killing the youngster and hurling his mentor unhurt into the icy Arctic Ocean. The Super-Soldier Serum, combined with the extreme cold of the water, enabled Cap to survive for years in a state of suspended animation. Rescued decades later by the Avengers, he quickly became a cornerstone of the new team of costumed heroes.

POWERS/ WEAPONS

- Peak physical condition
- Heightened endurance, strength and reaction time
- Expert hand-to-hand fighter
- Virtually indestructible metal shield

Since emerging in the present day, Cap has been embraced by the American people. But the country is different than the one he knew. As the nation has undergone political and social upheavals, Rogers has been forced to re-evaluate his role. For a brief period, he even cast off the mantle of

CAPTAIN AMERICA

Captain America, unable to fight for a dream in which he no longer believed. Rogers later reclaimed his heroic identity to prove to the world that the American ideals are greater than any governmental body.

Captain America's modern-day missions most often have involved individuals and groups that would see their philosophies supersede democracy, including the Red Skull and Hydra. Cap's allies through the years have included the Falcon and Nick Fury of S.H.I.E.L.D. Drawing on his own history and his unflagging moral compass, Captain America has led the Avengers and other adventurers through countless crises. Younger heroes look up to him, while seasoned veterans often seek his counsel.

As Cap has come to represent the United States in the minds of the American people and citizens the world over, certain government agencies and politicians have attempted to assert authority over the hero. But Cap stands for people more than politics, the preservation of the American dream rather than one political party's views.

Re-energized in his belief in America and what it stands for since terrorists attacked New York and Washington, D.C., Captain America has realized he is needed now more than ever to stand up to those who would see his country in ruins.

ESSENTIAL READING

- *Essential Captain America Vols. I & II*
- *Captain America: Operation Rebirth TPB*
- *Captain America: Man Without a Country TPB*
- *Captain America: Red, White & Blue HC*
- *Captain America Vol. I: The New Deal HC*
- *Captain America: The Classic Years Vols. I & II*
- *Essential Avengers Vols. I-III*

Art by John Cassaday

Art by John Cassaday

CAPTAIN MARVEL

Real Name:	Genis-Vell	**Weight:**	195 lbs.
First Appearance:	*Silver Surfer Annual* #6 (1993)	**Eye Color:**	Blue
Height:	6'2"	**Hair Color:**	Blond; turns white when cosmically aware

Art by Alex Ross

ESSENTIAL READING

- *Avengers Forever TPB*
- *Captain Marvel: First Contact TPB*
- *Captain Marvel Vol. I TPB*

Linked by circumstance to human teenager Rick Jones through the atom-exchanging Nega-Bands, the exiled Kree warrior Mar-Vell forged a reputation as a legendary intergalactic protector. Rick would summon the original Captain Marvel in times of danger by banging the Nega-Bands together, thus trading places with the hero. But in the end, Mar-Vell was stricken by the one enemy he could not defeat: an incurable systemic cancer.

Rick slowly began to move on with his life, eventually marrying. But Mar-Vell's lover, Elysius, felt more alone than ever. Using Titanian super-science, she sampled Mar-Vell's genetic structure to conceive a child, Genis-Vell. To protect him from his father's enemies, Genis was aged to maturity through artificial means, implanted with false memories of his upbringing and sequestered on an isolated world. Although it had all been done for his own good, Genis-Vell emerged from a technological womb aged 18 years without the experience to bear the weight of his family's heroic responsibilities.

Upon discovering his true lineage, Genis donned Kree Nega-Bands similar to those worn by his father, determined to carry on Mar-Vell's legacy. Eager to uphold the tradition of heroism set forth by his father but naïve to the ways of the world, Genis learned that power could be used wisely—abused easily. Plagued by doubts and insecurities, he agonized over how Mar-Vell would have approached any given situation. But ultimately, he realized that what his father would have done didn't matter. He had to start deciding how to live life on his own terms. Genis had finally begun to understand what it takes to be a hero. Formerly known as Legacy, he renamed himself Captain Marvel, after his father.

Rick and Genis later became pawns in the Destiny War, a time-spanning conflict. At the height of the battle, Captain Marvel found himself unwillingly merged with Rick—a process that triggered Genis' latent Cosmic Awareness. Now, Captain Marvel carries on his father's crusade for universal justice—while sharing space with a well-traveled, well-meaning former teenage sidekick. Linked by destiny to Rick, he is driven to seek out and eliminate those forces that threaten the galaxy.

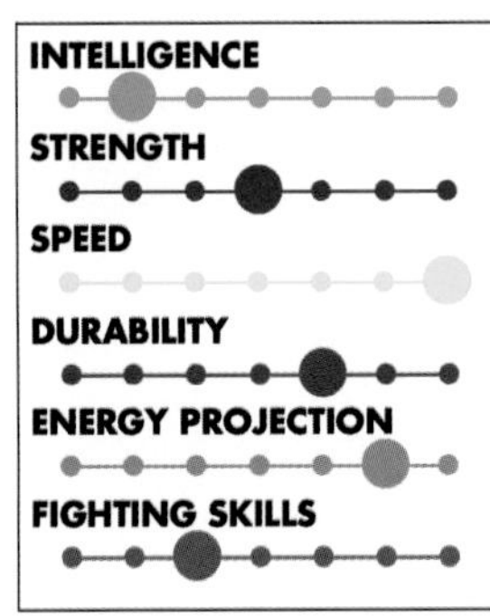

POWERS/WEAPONS

- Cosmic Awareness—allowing him to perceive objects, individuals and cosmic threats cloaked by invisibility or illusion throughout the universe
- Ability to absorb cosmic energy, converted into increased strength by Nega-Bands
- Increased resilience, interstellar flight and the ability to survive unprotected in outer space due to Nega-Bands

Art by Alex Ross

FALCON

Real Name:	Sam Wilson	**Weight:**	240 lbs.
First Appearance:	*Captain America* #117 (1969)	**Eye Color:**	Brown
Height:	6'2"	**Hair Color:**	Black

POWERS/ WEAPONS

- Telepathic link to his falcon, Redwing, allowing him to "see" through the bird's eyes
- Vast knowledge of multiple fighting styles
- Jet-powered, cybernetically controlled glider wings

INTELLIGENCE
STRENGTH
SPEED
DURABILITY
ENERGY PROJECTION
FIGHTING SKILLS

ESSENTIAL READING

- *Essential Captain America Vol. II*
- *Avengers Vol. I: World Trust TPB*

Art by Kieron Dwyer and Rick Remender

When his parents were murdered, upstanding community volunteer Sam Wilson gave in to his grief and anger. Severely depressed, his personality shifted, and he became a self-serving racketeer.

On a mob assignment involving the minions of the Red Skull, Wilson recognized the error of his ways and reclaimed his lost idealism. Wilson joined with Captain America to defeat the Skull's forces. Recognizing the Falcon's potential, Cap took him under his wing, and Wilson eventually became the legendary adventurer's partner. He also established himself as a hero of the people—always accompanied by his pet falcon Redwing.

Early in the Falcon's career, the Black Panther presented the novice hero with a new costume and jet-powered wings based on Wakandan technology. Shortly thereafter, the Falcon joined the Avengers, but resented the fact that he was made a member merely because he fulfilled a government-mandated minority quota. The Falcon left the Avengers for a time, preferring to work only with Cap.

Motivated by a strong desire for ordinary people to help themselves and one another, the Falcon sees himself as an enabler rather than a costumed icon. Armed with a strong sense of community, he believes being a hero starts at home, and so remains close to Harlem. There, he can act as both a role model and protector of the people.

The Falcon devotes nearly as much time to his work out of costume as he does to his super hero activities. Shuttling between his job as an urban planner in New York City and active membership in the Avengers, the Falcon focuses his efforts on making a positive difference in the world.

Art by Kieron Dwyer and Rick Remender

HAWKEYE

Real Name: Clinton Francis Barton
First Appearance: *Tales of Suspense* #57 (1964)
Height: 6'3"
Weight: 230 lbs.
Eye Color: Blue
Hair Color: Blond

POWERS/ WEAPONS

- Expert archer with near-perfect accuracy, keen eyesight and exceptional reflexes
- Trained aerialist and acrobat
- Seasoned hand-to-hand combatant
- Custom-made bows, including a longbow, regular bow and compound bow
- Gadget-laden "trick" arrows

INTELLIGENCE
STRENGTH
SPEED
DURABILITY
ENERGY PROJECTION
FIGHTING SKILLS

ESSENTIAL READING

- *Avengers: Celestial Madonna TPB*
- *Avengers: Clear and Present Dangers TPB*
- *Avengers/Defenders War TPB*
- *Avengers Forever TPB*
- *Avengers: The Morgan Conquest TPB*
- *Avengers: The Kree/Skrull War TPB*
- *Avengers: Supreme Justice TPB*
- *Essential Avengers Vols. I-III*

Art by Patrick Zircher

Clint Barton's parents were killed in an automobile accident when he was 8 years old, and the youngster was placed in a state orphanage. At 14, Barton ran away to join a traveling carnival, where he apprenticed himself to the show's star attraction, the mysterious rogue known only as the Swordsman. Recognizing Barton's natural flair for archery, the Swordsman agreed to tutor him in the art. For years, Barton practiced with the bow and arrow eight hours a day. Soon, he became a good enough trick-shooter to perform professionally under the name Hawkeye the Marksman.

Avengers: Clear and Present Dangers TPB

Witnessing **Iron Man** in action, Barton attempted to emulate the hero by donning a colorful costume and employing his archery skills to fight crime. During his first public appearance, Hawkeye was mistaken for a thief by police and found himself actually fighting Iron Man, the adventurer who had inspired his efforts. Weeks later, Barton's attraction to the **Black Widow** led him to actually commit criminal acts. But even when he was getting away with it, Hawkeye knew deep down he had strayed from his quest to become a hero. When he approached the **Avengers**, Iron Man sponsored his membership on the team.

Hawkeye lives life on the edge, straddling the fine line between right and wrong with a battle-ready swagger that masks an inner struggle for acceptance. For years he served as a valued member of the Avengers, his archery skills complementing his associates' superhuman powers. But Barton's bravado in battle and stubborn refusal to accept orders at face value frequently put him at odds with **Captain America**, an old-school Army man not used to subordinates questioning his commands in the field.

Dissatisfied with his role, the master marksman parted ways with the Avengers to join the Thunderbolts, one-time super-villains seeking redemption for past crimes by proving themselves as heroes. Having walked a mile outside the law himself, Hawkeye empathized with the Thunderbolts' plight—and the former criminals' state of mind. In leading the wayward adventurers, he hoped to lend credibility to their efforts. Hawkeye was lucky enough to find a better life, and he thinks others can do the same. All they need is someone who's willing to show them the way.

Heroes are expected to play by the rules, and Hawkeye does—his own. And he's willing to live with the hard choices and moral compromises his anti-authoritarian philosophy entails.

HULK

Real Name: Robert Bruce Banner
First Appearance: *Incredible Hulk* #1 (1962)
Height: 5'9" as Banner, 7' as Hulk
Weight: 128 lbs. as Banner, 1,040 lbs. as Hulk
Eye Color: Brown as Banner, green as Hulk
Hair Color: Brown as Banner, green as Hulk

ESSENTIAL READING

- *Essential Hulk Vols. I & II*
- *Incredible Hulk Vol. I: Return of the Monster TPB*
- *Incredible Hulk Vol. II: Boiling Point TPB*
- *Incredible Hulk Vol. III: Transfer of Power TPB*
- *Startling Stories: Banner TPB*

Bruce Banner had a tragic childhood. When he was a boy, his alcoholic father finally murdered his mother after years of beatings. Suppressing his pain and rage, the highly withdrawn, intellectual Bruce threw himself into science, where he felt safe from the chaos that ruled his life. A genius in nuclear physics, Bruce went to work after college at the U.S. Defense Department nuclear-research facility at Desert Base, New Mexico, under General Thaddeus "Thunderbolt" Ross. There, Bruce designed and oversaw construction of the first gamma bomb, a nuclear weapon with a high gamma-radiation output.

As the countdown commenced for the first detonation of the gamma bomb, teenager Rick Jones entered the testing site on a dare. Bruce saw him and knew he would be killed in the blast. Heedless of his own safety, he rushed onto the grounds and shoved Rick into a protective trench. Before Bruce could follow, the bomb detonated, bathing every cell of his body in high-intensity gamma radiation.

The Incredible Hulk #1, May 1962

Miraculously, Bruce survived the blast—but his world would never be the same. Thereafter, the radiation would cause him to transform during times of extreme stress into the dark personification of his long-repressed rage and fury. A savage brute: The Hulk lashes out at his tormentors with an anger unmatched by any creature on Earth and the strength of a thousand armies. And the angrier he becomes, the stronger he gets. The most powerful creature ever to walk the planet, the Hulk has ravaged cities and towns from coast to coast, smashing any object that stands in his way. When his temper tantrums subside, the Hulk is a gentle, childlike man-monster who wants only to be left alone.

Bruce managed to keep his condition secret for years, but his strange affliction eventually became public knowledge. As a result, he spent years wandering the country as a fugitive—plagued by recurring, uncontrollable transformations into the Hulk. Hounded by the authorities, the Hulk repeatedly has eluded the Army and Thunderbolt Ross, his most dogged pursuer.

Bruce's time as the Hulk has exacted a heavy toll on the bookish physicist. So far, his alter ego has resisted virtually every attempt to effect some measure of a cure. Certain treatments have appeared to work for a time, but they always come undone, including extensive psychotherapy by Doc Samson aimed at repairing the damage done during Bruce's childhood.

Art by Dale Keown

HULK

One of the few bright spots in Bruce's life was his true love Betty Ross, daughter of General Ross. The two shared a mutual attraction from their first meeting at Desert Base and ultimately married. Despite Bruce's condition, Betty loved him deeply, and she remained faithful even through the most trying times. But, the Abomination murdered Betty, removing one of the few calming influences in Bruce's life.

Growing increasingly resigned to his condition, Bruce has endeavored to better himself through the use of meditation and yoga. As a result of such introspective practices, he has arrived at a new realization: Bruce has come to count on the Hulk to get him out of trouble, and calmly collects the shattered pieces of his life once he reverts to human form—awaiting the return of the monster. Theirs is a dangerous relationship of human will struggling to control the raging anger of a seven-foot monster.

INTELLIGENCE

STRENGTH

SPEED

DURABILITY

ENERGY PROJECTION

FIGHTING SKILLS

POWERS/ WEAPONS

- Superhuman strength, endurance, speed and healing factor

Art by Joe Jusko

Art by John Romita, Jr.

IRON MAN

Real Name:	Anthony Stark
First Appearance:	*Tales of Suspense* #39 (1963)
Height:	6'1"
Weight:	225 lbs.
Eye Color:	Blue
Hair Color:	Black

POWERS/ WEAPONS

- Superhuman strength and durability due to armor
- Genius-level intellect
- Flight via jet-boots
- Repulsor blasts in gauntlets
- Chest-mounted uni-beam

INTELLIGENCE

STRENGTH

SPEED

DURABILITY

ENERGY PROJECTION

FIGHTING SKILLS

ESSENTIAL READING

- *Essential Avengers Vols. I-III*
- *Essential Iron Man Vol. I*
- *The Power of Iron Man TPB*
- *Iron Man: The Mask in the Iron Man TPB*

Art by Ariel Olivetti

The son of a wealthy industrialist, Tony Stark was an inventive mechanical engineering prodigy. He inherited his father's business at age 21, transforming the company, Stark International, into one of the world's leading weapons manufacturers. While field-testing a suit of battle armor in Asia that would enhance a soldier's combat capabilities, Stark was struck in the chest by a piece of shrapnel and taken prisoner by the warlord Wong-Chu. He was ordered to create a weapon of mass destruction—only then would he receive the operation needed to save his life.

Tales of Suspense #39, March 1963

Along with fellow prisoner Ho Yinsen, a Nobel Prize-winning physicist, Stark began work on a modified exoskeleton equipped with heavy weaponry. Yinsen designed the armor's breastplate to sustain the industrialist's wounded heart. Stark donned the suit in an attempt to escape captivity, but Professor Yinsen was killed in the resulting melee. He gave his own life, buying Stark time to charge the armor.

Overcoming the warlord's forces, Stark returned to America and redesigned the suit. Inventing the cover story that Iron Man was his bodyguard, he embarked on a double life as a billionaire industrialist and costumed adventurer. At first little more than a glorified security guard, Iron Man's early opponents included industrial spies and foreign agents, all intent on stealing Stark's defense and military secrets. Over time, Stark ceased simply protecting his own interests. He expanded the scope of his activities to include threats to national and international security. Iron Man even helped found the Avengers, and Stark became the team's corporate sponsor.

Despite his vast wealth, Stark's life is not perfect. He must wear some form of his armor's breastplate at all times to prevent the inoperable shrapnel from further damaging his heart. Stark is also a recovering alcoholic, and his personal life is often a shambles. In many ways, Iron Man is both Stark's release and a shell he wears to keep the real world out.

Iron Man's enemies have taken a variety of forms, from would-be world conquerors and corporate rivals to super-villains and foreign agents who have emulated or stolen his technology. As Iron Man's opponents and needs have changed, so has the hero's armor. One suit in particular was so advanced it gained sentience and attempted to replace Stark as Iron Man. Armed only with his wits, Stark severely damaged the artificially intelligent Sentient Armor. Seeking to die like a man, to know the meaning of sacrifice, the suit self-terminated—leaving its creator with a new, mechanical heart fashioned from its power source.

IRON MAN

Stark has grown to feel more responsible for the use of his technology throughout the world. He has realized that by and large, his legacy is one of destruction and warfare as nations employ his early inventions to oppress and kill. Stark Enterprises broke off its relationship with the U.S. government, refusing to manufacture any weapons and focusing instead on technology that would enhance human life.

Taught as a youth to give back to those who help him live such a comfortable life, Stark has established numerous charities and foundations. With his growing sense of responsibility, he has achieved a new level of maturity. Seeing his secret identity as more of a liability than an asset, Stark chose to reveal to the world that he is Iron Man. The weight of a double life off his shoulders, Stark finds himself in unfamiliar territory as one of the planet's few public heroes.

Art by Michael Ryan

Art by Kia Asamiya

HANK PYM

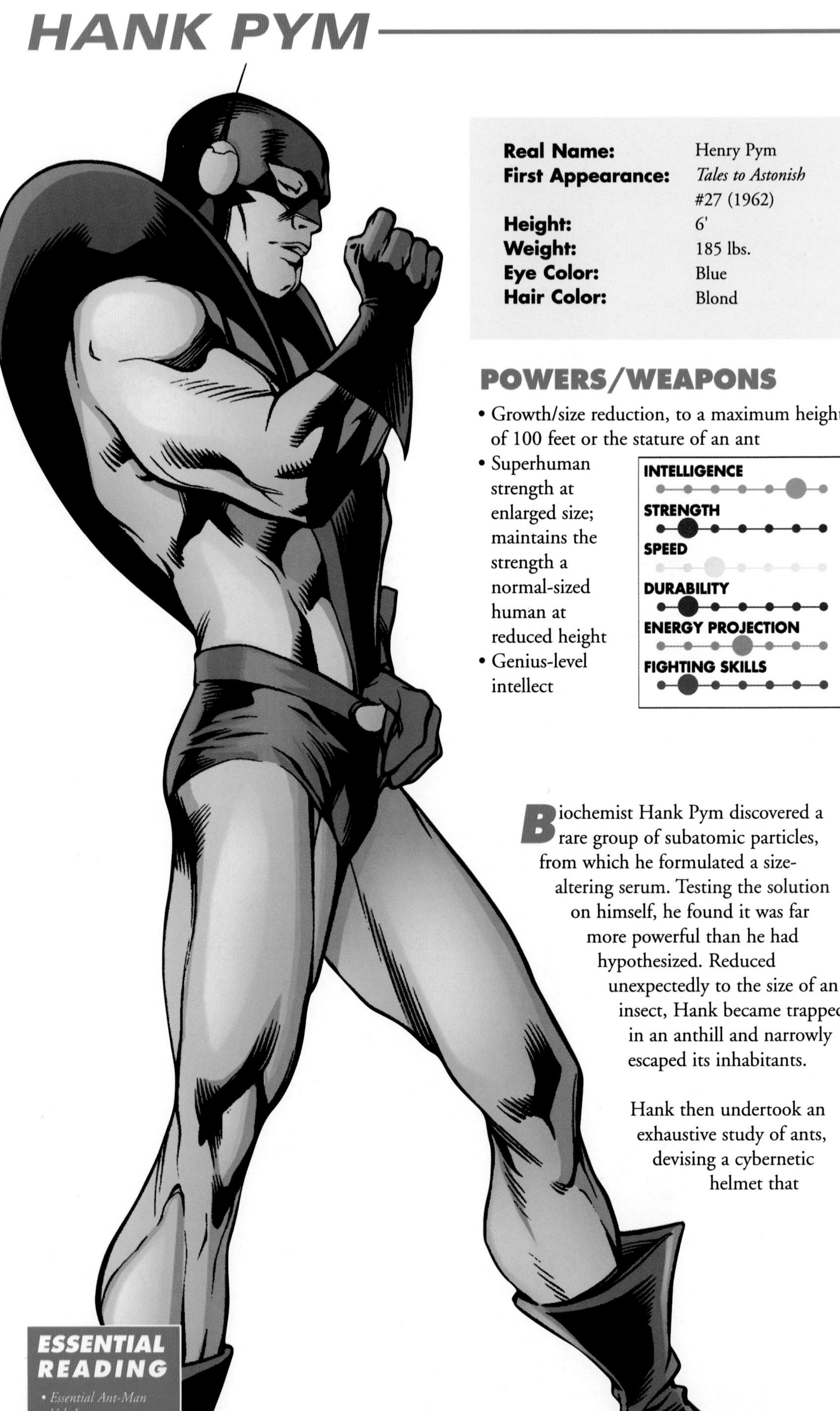

Real Name:	Henry Pym
First Appearance:	*Tales to Astonish* #27 (1962)
Height:	6'
Weight:	185 lbs.
Eye Color:	Blue
Hair Color:	Blond

POWERS/WEAPONS

- Growth/size reduction, to a maximum height of 100 feet or the stature of an ant
- Superhuman strength at enlarged size; maintains the strength a normal-sized human at reduced height
- Genius-level intellect

INTELLIGENCE
STRENGTH
SPEED
DURABILITY
ENERGY PROJECTION
FIGHTING SKILLS

Biochemist Hank Pym discovered a rare group of subatomic particles, from which he formulated a size-altering serum. Testing the solution on himself, he found it was far more powerful than he had hypothesized. Reduced unexpectedly to the size of an insect, Hank became trapped in an anthill and narrowly escaped its inhabitants.

Hank then undertook an exhaustive study of ants, devising a cybernetic helmet that

ESSENTIAL READING

- *Essential Ant-Man Vol. I*
- *Essential Avengers Vols. I-III*
- *Avengers Forever TPB*

Art by Carlos Pacheco

enabled him to communicate with insects. Forced to employ his size-changing serum and new invention to prevent the theft of his research, Hank was inspired to embark on a career as the costumed adventurer Ant-Man.

When one of his colleagues was murdered, Hank shared the secret of his double life with the man's daughter, Janet Van Dyne, and empowered her to avenge her father's death. As the Wasp, Janet helped Ant-Man bring the killer to justice. The duo continued their partnership, and Hank and Janet eventually fell in love, and later married. After Ant-Man and the Wasp helped found the Avengers, Hank developed a second serum that enabled him to grow to greater-than-normal heights and adopted the guise of Giant-Man, and later Goliath. Eventually, Hank learned he and Janet no longer required the formula to use their powers due to years of exposure to the size-altering properties of Pym Particles.

Art by Carlos Pacheco

As Hank's abilities fluctuated between growth and size reduction, he remained an intellectual at heart. But his single-minded pursuit of scientific excellence resulted in the scientist's greatest failure: the self-aware, artificially intelligent android Ultron. Possessing the capacity for creative thought, Pym's creation set out to wipe humanity from the face of the Earth, replacing organic life with robotic life. Turning against its creator, Ultron became one of the Avengers' most formidable adversaries. Years later, it was revealed that Hank had based Ultron's brain patterns on his own: Ultron is Hank stripped of conscience and morality.

Ultron plagued Hank for years, pushing him to the brink of insanity and beyond. Wracked with guilt and haunted by the actions of his rogue creation, Hank spent years attempting to atone for the lives destroyed by Ultron. His psyche further splintered by a freak laboratory accident, Hank adopted yet another costumed identity, that of the swashbuckling Yellowjacket. Ultimately, his intense feelings of remorse over the invention of Ultron and increasing emotional instability destroyed Hank's marriage to Janet.

After Ultron decimated the Eastern European nation of Slorenia, exterminating every living being in the country, Hank pummeled the robot into submission, finally putting the past to rest. His scarred psyche began to heal, and Hank settled on the identity of Yellowjacket to symbolize his new mental state. He and Janet are once again romantically linked, but have no immediate plans to remarry. Having achieved equilibrium in his life, Hank now strives to balance his responsibilities as companion, scientist and Avenger.

QUICKSILVER

Real Name:	Pietro Maximoff
First Appearance:	*X-Men* #4 (1964)
Height:	6'
Weight:	175 lbs.
Eye Color:	Blue
Hair Color:	Silver

INTELLIGENCE

STRENGTH

SPEED

DURABILITY

ENERGY PROJECTION

FIGHTING SKILLS

POWERS/ WEAPONS

- Superhuman speed

ESSENTIAL READING

- *Avengers: The Kang Dynasty TPB*
- *Avengers: The Morgan Conquest TPB*
- *Essential X-Men Vol. I*
- *Essential Avengers Vols. I-III*

Art by Derec Aucoin

Orphaned at birth, Pietro and Wanda Maximoff were raised by gypsies. As adolescents, the twins discovered they possessed unusual superhuman abilities. Wanda could cause strange phenomena to occur, and Pietro moved faster than the blink of an eye. When their adoptive father stole food to feed his starving family, enraged villagers attacked the gypsy camp. Using his incredible speed, Pietro took flight with his sister. For the next few years, they wandered Central Europe, living life on the run.

Visiting a small village, Wanda accidentally caused a house to burst into flame with her uncontrollable hex-casting abilities. Despite Pietro's attempts to defend his sister from superstitious townspeople, the siblings soon were overpowered. They were about to be killed when Magneto arrived on the scene and rescued the young mutants. Fearing the charismatic subversive's wrath, the Scarlet Witch and Quicksilver served their new master out of obligation. As members of Magneto's Brotherhood of Evil Mutants, they aided and abetted his terrorist campaign against humanity.

When the Brotherhood disbanded, Pietro and Wanda recognized the error of their ways and sought redemption for their actions. No longer pawns in a madman's quest for power, they successfully petitioned for membership in the Avengers. Only later did they discover the truth regarding their parentage. Hoping to sway Pietro and Wanda to rejoin his crusade against humanity, Magneto confronted them with the revelation that he was their true father, but they denounced him and his cause.

Gifted with the ability to think and move at superhuman speeds, the quick-tempered Pietro is uncomfortable standing still. Plagued by impulsive decisions and rash actions, Quicksilver strives to achieve a semblance of equilibrium in his life. So far, such balance has eluded him. Undermined by neglect and infidelity, Pietro's marriage to Crystal of the Inhumans was doomed to fail despite repeated attempts at reconciliation and the birth of their daughter Luna.

Art by Derec Aucoin

Pietro bears the heavy burden of his father's legacy—and his own shortcomings as a man, a husband and a father. Still, Quicksilver continues to forge ahead—seeking direction, purpose and a life outside Magneto's shadow. Often considered arrogant, unlikable and overconfident, he does not care how others perceive him. His father's son, Pietro has inherited Magneto's poise, confidence and strength. Although sometimes frightened by what he sees in the mirror, he is a reflection of the man his father once was—and would have been, had he not given in to the hate and anguish that eventually corrupted his soul. Pietro's has been a turbulent life, but he has made peace with who and what he truly is; an honorable man and a hero at heart.

SCARLET WITCH

Real Name:	Wanda Maximoff
First Appearance:	*X-Men* #4 (1964)
Height:	5'7"
Weight:	130 lbs.
Eye Color:	Blue
Hair Color:	Auburn

INTELLIGENCE
STRENGTH
SPEED
DURABILITY
ENERGY PROJECTION
FIGHTING SKILLS

POWERS/ WEAPONS

- Mutant ability to control chaos magick and affect probability fields

ESSENTIAL READING

- *Avengers: Celestial Madonna TPB*
- *Avengers: Clear and Present Dangers TPB*
- *Avengers/Defenders War TPB*
- *Avengers: The Kang Dynasty TPB*
- *Avengers: The Morgan Conquest TPB*
- *Avengers: Supreme Justice TPB*
- *Avengers: Ultron Unlimited TPB*
- *Essential X-Men Vol. I*
- *Essential Avengers Vols. I-III*

Wanda Maximoff and her twin brother Pietro, the children of Magneto, were born without their father's knowledge in the mountains of Eastern Europe. Abandoned by their mother, they were adopted by a gypsy couple. Born the night of a supernatural storm, Wanda was imbued from infancy with mystical potential, which would affect her latent mutant abilities and allow her to channel chaos magick in a number of useful ways. Chief among these are her probability-altering hex-spheres—finite pockets of reality-disrupting, psionic force that cause random disturbances in the molecular-level probability fields surrounding their targets. As a result, unlikely phenomena occur. With time to prepare, Wanda can cast her hex power to garner specific results.

As Wanda and Pietro reached adolescence, they both manifested their mutant powers, and soon were forced to flee their adopted family. During their early teens, the twins wandered Central Europe. They were often the targets of persecution, with the superhumanly fast, self-assured Pietro defending his quieter, meeker sister.

During one such encounter, a mob of superstitious villagers would have killed Wanda and Pietro were it not for the intervention of Magneto. Unaware he was their natural father, they joined his Brotherhood of Evil Mutants as the Scarlet Witch and Quicksilver. They knew their terrorist actions were immoral, but served out of a sense of obligation—and because they feared Magneto's wrath.

After the Brotherhood's dissolution, Wanda and Pietro sought redemption for their transgressions. They petitioned for membership in the Avengers and were inducted to replace a pair of departing founders. With the Avengers, Wanda slowly emerged from her shell. She became close friends with many of the teams' members, forging strong bonds that endure to this day. Whereas Magneto viewed Wanda merely as a means to an end, the Avengers valued her for her abilities.

Seeking the stability that life had denied her thus far, Wanda fell in love with and married the Avengers' "perfect man"—the synthetic humanoid known as the Vision. Fate intervened, however, and their marriage crumbled when the U.S. government dismantled the android, viewing him as a threat to world security. To carry on, Wanda was forced to find her own inner strength.

Art by George Pérez

Reserved, emotional and intense, Wanda has matured among the Avengers—attaining a greater degree of control over her unpredictable abilities, and often taking on a leadership role. But given her history, she can still feel like an outsider on occasion. The Avengers are her family, providing the only real security and stability Wanda has ever known. Taken in despite her troubled past, she will always be grateful for their trust and unconditional friendship. No longer haunted by the sins of her youth or the failings of her father, Wanda is free to face the future as her own woman.

SHE-HULK

Real Name:	Jennifer Walters
First Appearance:	*Savage She-Hulk* #1 (1980)
Height:	6'7"
Weight:	650 lbs.
Eye Color:	Green
Hair Color:	Green

INTELLIGENCE
STRENGTH
SPEED
DURABILITY
ENERGY PROJECTION
FIGHTING SKILLS

POWERS/ WEAPONS

- Superhuman strength
- Impervious to pain, injury and disease

ESSENTIAL READING

- *Fantastic Four: Into the Breach TPB*
- *Avengers Vol. 1: World Trust TPB*

Art by Adam Hughes

Jennifer Walters spent the summers of her childhood with her first cousin Bruce Banner, and the two became as close as brother and sister. The bookish Bruce and equally academic and mousy Jennifer shared an affinity for intellectual pursuits that further served to cement their strong, sibling-like bond. Bruce went on to study medicine and physics, while Jennifer pursued a career in law. They lost touch when Bruce began work on the military's top-secret gamma bomb. After graduating, Jennifer established herself as a criminal attorney in Los Angeles.

Years later, Bruce sought out Jennifer to confide in her the emotional trauma of his double life as the Hulk. At the time, Jennifer had been defending a criminal named Lou Monkton, who was framed by gangster Nicholas Trask for murder. As Jennifer drove Bruce to her Los Angeles home, one of Trask's henchmen made an attempt on her life. With his cousin rapidly losing blood from a gunshot wound, Bruce improvised an emergency transfusion. Shortly thereafter, Jennifer's anger triggered a transformation into a 6'7", 650-lb. mass of muscle. Retaining her intelligence as She-Hulk, Jennifer embarked upon a career as a part-time crimefighter.

Jennifer derived great satisfaction from her adventures as She-Hulk. Although at first able to revert to human form at will, she rarely did so. It has been speculated that gamma-induced mutations unleash a suppressed aspect of the affected individual's personality. Bruce's repressed rage emerged as a savage, childlike persona, while Jennifer's newfound physique sent her self-confidence soaring.

She-Hulk initially operated in Southern California, but her reputation spread quickly. She eagerly put her law career on hold and left California to join the Avengers, and later served as a member of Heroes for Hire, Inc. Standing in for the Thing as the Fantastic Four's resident powerhouse, She-Hulk became a de facto member of both the team and the family. Jennifer has since returned to the courtroom, turning heads as the world's only green-skinned lawyer, but remains eager to trade power suits for skintight spandex when called upon by Earth's mightiest heroes.

Art by Carlos Pacheco

THOR

Real Name:	Thor
First Appearance:	*Journey Into Mystery* #83 (1962)
Height:	6'6"
Weight:	640 lbs.
Eye Color:	Blue
Hair Color:	Blond

Thor is the son of Odin, longtime ruler of Asgard. Raised alongside Odin's adopted son Loki, Thor was heir apparent to the realm of the Norse gods. As a teen, his exploits were legendary. When Thor reached adulthood, Odin presented him with the mystic Uru hammer Mjolnir, which remains the Thunder God's symbol of power to this day.

Journey into Mystery #83, August 1962

Although fearless in battle, Thor was headstrong and impulsive, and nearly precipitated a war between the gods of Asgard and the Frost Giants of Jotunheim by violating a truce between the two worlds. Intent on teaching Thor a lesson in humility, Odin banished his favored son to Earth—removing all memories of his godhood and entrapping him for more than a decade in the guise of a handicapped mortal, Dr. Donald Blake. As Blake, Thor learned the value of humble perseverence in dealing with his injured leg, and he came to care for the sick and dying—first as a medical student, and later as a successful physician.

Believing Thor had learned his lesson, Odin compelled his son to travel to Norway. Fleeing from danger, Blake became trapped in a cave, where he discovered a gnarled wooden cane. Striking the stick in anger against an immovable boulder, Thor was restored to his godly form, and the cane was revealed to be Mjolnir. By tapping either the stick or the hammer on the ground, the son of Odin was able to transform thereafter from Blake to Thor and back again at will. A god on Earth, Thor sought out other warriors of his mettle, and helped found the Avengers.

One of Asgard's fiercest warriors, Thor also has the biggest heart in the realm. No longer claiming worshippers or demanding allegiance from followers in exchange for boons and blessings, Thor chose to help humanity solely out of compassion for the human race. Only when Odin requested his son return to Asgard did he realize the folly of his enchantment. Thanks to Thor's time among mortals, he had come to love Earth as much as he did the realm of his birth, and so became constantly torn between the two worlds.

Thor has served with the Avengers for years, occasionally taking leaves of absence to deal with matters in Asgard. Thanks to his high profile as one of Earth's mightiest heroes, he is well-known and trusted by the general populace. Few believe he truly is the Asgardian God of Thunder, however. Eventually, Thor chose to abandon his double life as Donald Blake, opting to remain in his true form at all times. Ever mindful of Thor's humility, Odin has chosen to bond him with other mortals through the years, most recently EMT Jake Olson.

Art by Tom Raney

THOR

In his dealings with humans, Thor has learned the bittersweet blessing of immortality. He has seen those he cares for become sick and die, while he has yet to age a day in their eyes. It is a burden that weighs heavily on the Thunder God's shoulders and often causes him to withdraw from close friendships, as he knows they will be brief by his reckoning.

Many of Thor's battles on Earth and Asgard have resulted from the schemes of his adopted brother. Alternately, Loki has attempted either to humiliate or kill Thor, hoping to supersede the Thunder God as heir to the Asgardian throne. Along with Loki's meddling, the Thunder God also has faced tests initiated by Odin to determine his readiness and ability to one day rule in his father's place.

Despite these tests, Thor felt completely unprepared to take the throne in the wake of Odin's death in battle. Following a period of self-doubt and mourning, Thor took up Odin's crown and scepter, reluctantly carrying on his father's legacy as ruler of the gods. The humility and compassion learned during years of exile on Earth enable Thor to rule in a manner that would do Odin proud.

POWERS/ WEAPONS

- Godlike strength, speed, endurance and resistance to injury
- Mastery over the elements of storm
- The enchanted Uru hammer Mjolnir, which can project mystical energy and open interdimensional gateways, and affords Thor the power of flight

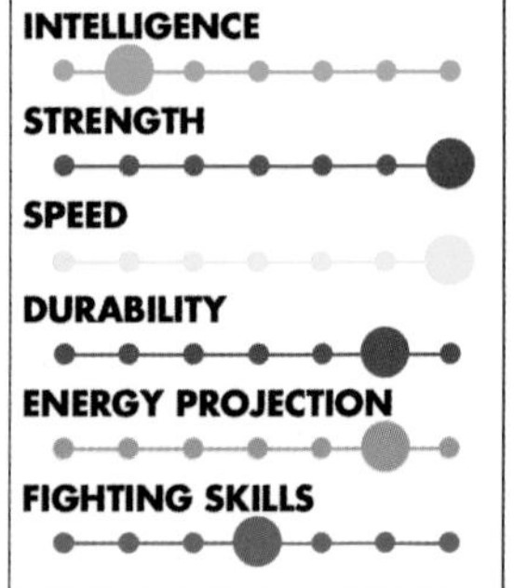

ESSENTIAL READING

- *Essential Thor Vol. I*
- *Essential Avengers Vols. I-III*
- *Thor Visionaries: Walt Simonson Vol. I TPB*
- *Thor: The Dark Gods TPB*
- *Thor: Across All Worlds TPB*
- *Thor Vol. I: The Death of Odin TPB*
- *Thor Vol. II: Lord of Asgard TPB*

Art by Tom Raney

Art by Glenn Orbik

VISION

Real Name:	Vision
First Appearance:	*Avengers* #57 (1968)
Height:	6'3"
Weight:	300 lbs.; variable from intangibility to 90 tons
Eye Color:	Red
Hair Color:	None

POWERS/WEAPONS

- Density control/intangibility
- Infrared- and microwave-radiation beams

INTELLIGENCE	•••●•••
STRENGTH	•••●•••
SPEED	••●••••
DURABILITY	••••●••
ENERGY PROJECTION	•••●•••
FIGHTING SKILLS	••●••••

ESSENTIAL READING

- *Essential Avengers Vol. III*
- *Avengers: Celestial Madonna TPB*
- *Avengers/Defenders War TPB*
- *Avengers: Kree/Skrull War TPB*
- *Avengers: The Morgan Conquest TPB*
- *Avengers: Supreme Justice TPB*
- *Avengers: Ultron Unlimited TPB*
- *Avengers Visionaries: George Pérez TPB*

Art by George Pérez

Assembled at the direction of Ultron, the Vision is an android who mimics virtually every organic function of a human being, including independent thought. Seeking vengeance against the Avengers, Ultron programmed the Vision's neural processors with the brain patterns of Wonder Man, and implanted special synthesized cells permitting him to alter his mass and solidity. Ultron then dispatched the Vision to draw the Avengers into a deathtrap. Moved by the team's plight, though the Vision overrode his mission parameters and helped the heroes defeat his creator.

Rather than creating a cold, calculating automaton, Ultron had given birth to a lifeform longing for sentience. The Vision served the Avengers faithfully for years, all the while seeking to transcend his original programming as a vehicle of vengeance and become fully "human." When he embarked on a romantic relationship with the Scarlet Witch, the Vision at first denied to himself that an android could have feelings of love for another being. Eventually, however, their courtship blossomed into true love and marriage.

Art by Ariel Olivetti

When a malfunctioning control crystal implanted in the Vision's cerebral circuitry by Ultron interfered with the android's ability to reason, he sought to solve the planet's problems by seizing control of the world's governments, businesses and armed forces. After taking charge of the United States' nuclear arsenal and defense systems, the Vision was convinced he should abandon his grand scheme by his fellow Avengers. Fighting a war with himself, he severed his connection to the planet's databanks.

In the wake of the android's meltdown, the nations of Earth came to regard the Vision as a high-level security threat. Ultimately, government operatives abducted and dismantled the android, erasing his memory. The Scarlet Witch and the Avengers eventually recovered their teammates' components, and Hank Pym rebuilt and reprogrammed the Vision. But the synthezoid returned to existence sans human emotion, unable even to recall his love for the Scarlet Witch.

The Vision has since uploaded a new set of brain patterns, again acquiring the ability to feel. Eager to experience emotion to the fullest, the synthezoid has made diligent efforts to explore aspects of his personality aside from those pre-programmed by Pym, inching ever closer to the humanity he has sought with limited success his entire existence.

WARBIRD

Real Name: Carol Susan Jane Danvers
First Appearance: *Marvel Super-Heroes* #13 (1967)
Height: 5'11"
Weight: 120 lbs.
Eye Color: Blue
Hair Color: Blonde

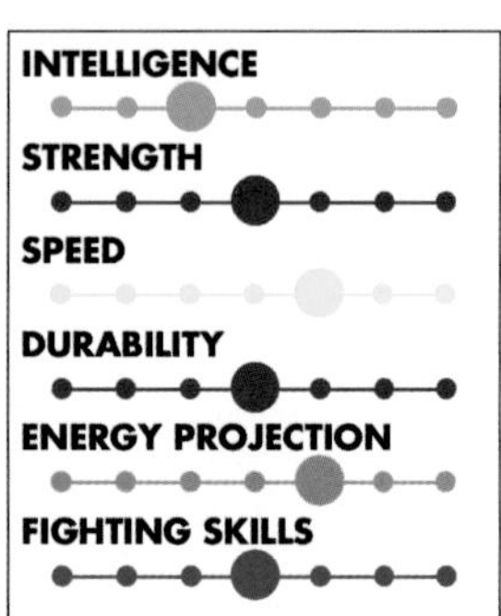

POWERS/ WEAPONS

- Superhuman strength
- High degree of durability
- Ability to emit concussive photon bursts
- Flight
- Energy absorption, augmenting her other abilities

ESSENTIAL READING

- *Avengers: The Kang Dynasty TPB*
- *Avengers: The Morgan Conquest TPB*
- *Avengers: Supreme Justice TPB*
- *Essential X-Men Vols. III & IV*

Always a risk-taker, Carol Danvers entered the Air Force at an early age due in part to her love of airplanes—but mostly because her father didn't believe girls should go to college. Driven to succeed in a man's world, she rose rapidly through the ranks to become one of the leading agents in military intelligence. Subsequently, Carol became NASA's youngest-ever security chief at Cape Canaveral—the first woman to hold the position. In that capacity, Carol encountered the original Captain Marvel—and became embroiled in his struggle to save Earth from his own people, the Kree.

During a battle between Captain Marvel and an alien foe, Carol was accidentally irradiated by the unknown energies of a Kree device that augmented her genetic structure. Becoming a Kree-human hybrid, she was granted superhuman strength and speed, the power of flight, a clairvoyant "seventh sense," and all the fighting skills of a Kree warrior. A victim of circumstance, Carol made the most of her newfound abilities. She swiftly established herself as a champion of Earth and often fought alongside the Avengers.

Art by Manuel Garcia

Carol's life of adventure came crashing down when she was stripped of her very identity by Rogue, then working in collusion with the Brotherhood of Evil Mutants. Along with her memories, Carol lost virtually all of her superhuman abilities. Later subjected to an alien evolutionary ray that triggered the latent potential of her augmented genes, she acquired an array of cosmic powers fueled by the energy of a white hole. Although Professor X restored her memories, Carol no longer possessed strong emotional ties to people and places of her past. A stranger in her own skin, she fled the planet and her problems for the promise of a fresh start among the stars.

Carol returned to Earth some years later. As Warbird, she eventually rejoined the Avengers—but by then, her cosmic powers had faded to a fraction of what they once were. A shadow of her former self, Carol sought solace at the bottom of a bottle. The former shooting star of the super hero set had flamed out. Hitting rock bottom, she quit the team following a formal court marshal for conduct unbecoming an Avenger.

Carol eventually made peace with her rocky past and learned to stand on her own two feet, returning to action as an Avenger. Taking responsibility for her actions, she has overcome emotional emptiness, alcoholism, substantially reduced power levels and failure in the eyes of her teammates to prove herself as an asset to the Avengers. Uncompromising and tempestuous, Carol is a warrior by nature, driven by a fighting spirit that refuses to quit. She struggles still with her inner demons, but defies her own weaknesses daily in the face of overwhelming odds.

Art by Derec Aucoin

WASP

Real Name:	Janet Van Dyne
First Appearance:	*Tales to Astonish* #44 (1963)
Height:	5'4"
Weight:	110 lbs.
Eye Color:	Blue
Hair Color:	Auburn

POWERS/ WEAPONS

- Size reduction
- Superhuman strength (at diminutive stature only)
- Bio-electric force bolts
- Bio-engineered insect wings

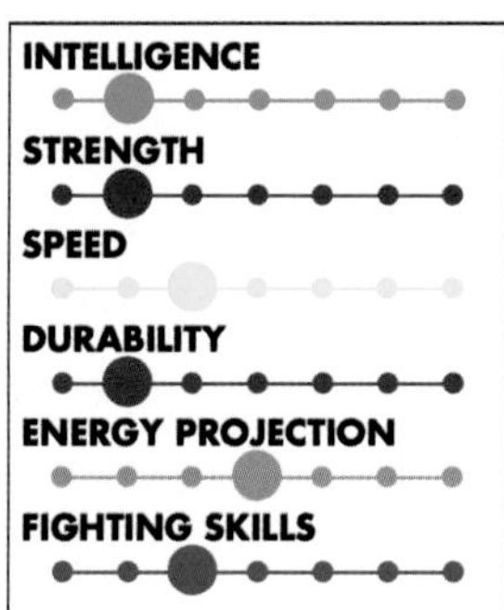

ESSENTIAL READING

- *Avengers Forever TPB*
- *Avengers: The Morgan Conquest TPB*
- *Avengers: Ultron Unlimited TPB*
- *Avengers: Under Siege TPB*
- *Essential Avengers Vols. I-III*

Art by Carlos Pacheco

Janet Van Dyne is the daughter of world-renowned scientist Vernon Van Dyne. When her father was murdered, a grief-stricken Janet turned to his colleague, celebrated biochemist Hank Pym, for support. Unknown to her, Hank led a double life as the size-changing costumed adventurer Ant-Man. Impressed with Janet's moral strength, Hank revealed his secret identity and proposed her conversion into a superhumanly powerful being so she could avenger her father's death. Janet readily accepted.

Essential Avengers Vol. I

Drawing on his recent research into the organic structure of wasps, Hank implanted cells beneath Janet's shoulder blades and temples corresponding to those found in the insects' wings and antennae, respectively. He also instructed her in the use of his Pym Particles, enabling her to shrink to a minimum height of one-half inch and return to normal. Due to Hank's bio-engineering, Janet could manifest working wings and communicate telepathically with insects in her shrunken state. As the Wasp, she helped Ant-Man bring her father's killer to justice. Thereafter, she became Ant-Man's crimefighting partner, developing the skills that would one day enable her to stand on her own as a costumed champion.

The Wasp was the sole female founder of the Avengers, standing with Ant-Man and her other teammates against the foes no single super hero could defeat. Following the Avengers' initial adventure, it was the Wasp who named the team. Meanwhile, Janet's partnership with Hank resulted in a much deeper union: The two eventually fell in love and later married.

When she turned 23, Janet came into possession of her full inheritance. Now independently wealthy, she remained as driven as ever. Compelled to continue her heroic adventures, she also launched a successful career as a fashion designer. By this time, it was publicly known that she was the Wasp. Janet experienced only success in her professional life, but her rocky marriage to Hank ended in divorce—largely due to his emotional instability and guilt over the creation of Ultron. Eventually, however, Janet did reconcile with Hank.

Although she began her crimefighting career to aid Ant-Man, Janet has more than proven herself through the years as a costumed adventurer. She also has come into her own as a leader and strategist, whether serving as the Avengers' official chairwoman or simply exercising her natural abilities as a matter of course.

WONDER MAN

Real Name:	Simon Williams	**Weight:**	380 lbs.
First Appearance:	*Avengers* #9 (1964)	**Eye Color:**	Red
Height:	6'2"	**Hair Color:**	Gray, none in ionic form

POWERS/WEAPONS

- Superhuman strength, durability and stamina
- Flight

INTELLIGENCE

STRENGTH

SPEED

DURABILITY

ENERGY PROJECTION

FIGHTING SKILLS

ESSENTIAL READING

- *Avengers: Clear and Present Dangers TPB*
- *Avengers: The Morgan Conquest TPB*
- *Essential Avengers Vol. I TPB*

Simon Williams was the youngest son of Sanford Williams, industrialist and founder of a highly successful munitions-manufacturing firm. When the elder Williams died, the 22-year-old Simon assumed full control of Williams Innovations. Under his inexperienced management, the company began to lose its competitive edge in the marketplace. Frantic, Simon invested the company's money in a number of illicit enterprises. The board of directors later learned of his actions, and Simon was brought to trial.

Nazi war criminal Heinrich Zemo had read of Simon's case. Intrigued by the media's assertion that Simon blamed competitor Stark Industries for his downfall, Baron Zemo recruited Simon for his Masters of Evil. Zemo believed Anthony Stark to be the employer of his enemy, Iron Man. In fact, Stark himself was Iron Man. Disoriented by the upheavals in his life, Simon agreed to become a test subject for Zemo's "ionic ray," which would endow him with superhuman strength and durability. After undergoing the arduous chemical and radiation treatments, Simon emerged with the attributes he had been promised.

Avengers: Clear and Present Dangers TPB

In a staged battle with the Masters of Evil, Wonder Man won the confidence of the Avengers—only to lead the team into a later ambush. But during the course of the battle, Simon experienced an attack of conscience and decided he could not betray the Avengers' kindness—even if it cost him his life. Deprived of Zemo's life-prolonging treatment, Wonder Man succumbed to the mysterious effects of his power acquisition. Telling the Avengers he was glad his final act had been a noble one, Wonder Man fell still, displaying no vital signs.

Although assumed dead, Wonder Man actually had fallen into a deathlike coma brought on by the still unstable mutagenic changes triggered in his body. The Avengers later determined that Simon had evolved from flesh and blood to a flesh-like substance nourished by ionic energy. After being revived, Wonder Man became a full-fledged member of the Avengers. Since joining the team, Wonder Man has worked as an actor, a security consultant and a stuntman. Simon's confidence increased with each victory. Suffused with ionic energy, he began to feel as if he were immortal...until the explosion of a Kree ion-cannon dispersed his body's ionic energy.

Wonder Man's love for the Scarlet Witch, Wanda Maximoff, tied him to the mortal plane; her love for Simon enabled her to channel the chaos-energies she wielded to effect his resurrection. Feeling unworthy of a second chance due to the mistakes of his past, Simon sought to reclaim his dignity and sense of self-worth. To help those overwhelmed by forces beyond their control, he established Second Chances, a non-profit foundation funded by the re-release of his movies and videos, plus countless new projects and endorsements. Finally free of his personal demons, Wonder Man has become a confident, capable crimefighter and staunch member of the Avengers.

Art by George Pérez

EDWIN JARVIS

Real Name:	Edwin Jarvis	**Weight:**	160 lbs.
First Appearance:	*Tales of Suspense* #59 (1964)	**Eye Color:**	Blue
Height:	5'11"	**Hair Color:**	Black

Hired by Howard and Maria Stark, butler Edwin Jarvis continued to serve the family even after their deaths. He was present when their son Tony, as Iron Man, called the first meeting of the Avengers and donated the Stark mansion for use as the team's headquarters. Since that day, Jarvis has maintained his residence in the mansion and has served as the butler for Earth's mightiest heroes.

Though initially unnerved by his new employers, Jarvis gradually grew accustomed to the Avengers, bonding with many of the team's members. Jarvis has served the Avengers with unwavering loyalty and a spotless performance record for years. His duties have ranged from standard domestic chores to the supervision of state-of-the-art technical systems. Jarvis has frequently assisted the Avengers in their missions, performing support operations well outside the purview of his job description.

Art by Michael Gaydos

A resounding voice of normality in a world filled with the fantastic, Jarvis often acts as a sounding board for members whose costumed careers have caused difficulties in their personal lives. Almost acting as a surrogate father, he has served as confidant to some of the younger Avengers, who often find themselves overwhelmed by the responsibilities of membership.

Ever-vigilant and supremely trustworthy, Jarvis is an indispensable member of the Avengers' support team. And while he never lets on, he is extremely gratified that the heroes have honored him with their trust.

ESSENTIAL READING

- *Essential Avengers Vols. I-III*
- *Avengers: Kang Dynasty TPB*
- *Avengers: Under Siege TPB*

RICK JONES

Real Name:	Rick Jones	**Weight:**	165 lbs.
First Appearance:	*Incredible Hulk* #1 (1962)	**Eye Color:**	Brown
Height:	5'9"	**Hair Color:**	Brown

Orphaned as an adolescent, Rick Jones ran away from a state institution for troubled teens after suffering abuse, and ended up working at odd jobs to earn a living. A reckless and rebellious youth, he drove to the test site of the Army's experimental gamma bomb on a dare the night of the device's first detonation. Dr. Bruce Banner, the weapon's designer, threw Jones into a ditch seconds before it went off. As a result of his selfless act, Banner caught the full force of the blast, which ultimately resulted in his transformation into the **Hulk**. Jones remained with the man-monster for some time, aiding the creature in an effort to assuage some of the guilt he felt for its creation.

When **Loki** took control of the Hulk, Jones helped form the **Avengers** to halt the beast's rampage. Embracing his newfound life of adventure, he served for a brief period as **Captain America**'s partner. Jones jockeyed from hero to hero for years—at first fascinated by them, later jealous of their superhuman abilities. Jones stumbled upon the perfect solution to his predicament when he discovered a pair of alien bracelets that allowed him to trade places with Captain Mar-Vell, a **Kree** warrior imprisoned in the otherworldly dimension known as the Negative Zone. By summoning Mar-Vell, Jones could play the hero while his counterpart did the real work.

After Mar-Vell's death from cancer, Jones returned to Banner's side. Along the way, he met and eventually married Marlo Chandler, the love of his life. Although the two have had their share of problems, their relationship has survived death, dismemberment and galaxy-wide separations.

When Jones sacrificed himself to prevent the destruction of all reality during a time-spanning conflict involving the Avengers, Mar-Vell's son Genis merged his life force with the perennial sidekick, who had sustained mortal wounds. The result was a new **Captain Marvel**, a combination of Genis and Jones. Once again the hero, Jones is back in the thick of action and adventure, thoroughly enjoying his ringside view of the world of super heroes.

ESSENTIAL READING

- *Avengers Forever TPB*
- *Avengers: The Kree/Skrull War TPB*
- *The Life and Death of Captain Marvel TPB*
- *Captain Marvel: First Contact TPB*
- *Essential Hulk Vol. I*
- *Essential Avengers Vol. I*
- *Essential Captain America Vol. II*

Art by ChrisCross

"THUNDERBOLT" ROSS

Real Name:	General Thaddeus E. "Thunderbolt" Ross	**Weight:**	245 lbs.
First Appearance:	*Incredible Hulk* #1 (1962)	**Eye Color:**	Blue
Height:	6'	**Hair Color:**	White

A bear of a man, Thaddeus Ross is the last in a proud family of military officers. Ross quickly rose through the ranks, accumulating a highly distinguished record of service in the Air Force. He earned his nickname during one of his early combat runs because he struck with the speed and strength of a thunderbolt. During peacetime, Ross was assigned to a desert base in New Mexico.

Despite his dissatisfaction at holding a desk job, Ross excelled in leading the military's research into the uses of gamma radiation—but came to resent the intellectual, civilian supervisor of the base's gamma-bomb project, Dr. Bruce Banner. Worse yet, Ross's daughter Betty, whom he hoped would one day marry a military officer, was attracted to the milksop Banner.

Following the appearance of the Hulk near Desert Base shortly after Banner was caught in the explosion of the first gamma bomb, the Pentagon reassigned Ross to lead "Operation Hulk." His mission: find, and capture—or—kill the monster. Ross and the rest of the world later learned Banner himself was the Hulk, which gave him a deeper motivation in hunting down the man he felt was not good enough for his daughter.

The greatest personal challenge to Ross's mission came when Banner and Betty married. While Ross vigorously opposed their union, he later came to accept the marriage for his daughter's sake.

Ross's relationship with his son-in-law was sorely tested when Betty was found to be suffering from radiation sickness, a consequence of long-term exposure to the gamma rays contained within Banner. Following Betty's death, Ross returned to his hunt, vowing a life for a life: Banner's for his daughter's. When Ross learned the Abomination was responsible for Betty's death, he manipulated his son-in-law into a savage confrontation with the beast. The Hulk nearly beat his hated foe to death before Banner regained control. Ross then took the defeated Abomination into custody.

A man whose absolute hatred for the Hulk is balanced by his utter love for his late daughter, Thunderbolt Ross is haunted by Betty's death, the actions he took in her name and the life he could have led had the Hulk never existed.

Art by John Romita, Jr.

ESSENTIAL READING

- *Essential Hulk Vols. I & II*
- *Incredible Hulk: Dogs of War TPB*

DR. LEONARD SAMSON

Real Name:	Leonard Samson	**Weight:**	380 lbs.
First Appearance:	*Incredible Hulk* #141 (1971)	**Eye Color:**	Blue
Height:	6'6"	**Hair Color:**	Green

Noted psychiatrist Dr. Leonard Samson approached General "Thunderbolt" Ross with an unusual plan to siphon the gamma from Bruce Banner as he transformed into the Hulk, thus curing the meek physicist's strange affliction. The procedure was successful, but scientific curiosity led Samson to treat himself with the excess gamma radiation—mutating him into a muscle-bound, green-haired powerhouse possessing physical abilities on par with the Hulk. Unlike the jade giant, Samson maintained his personality and intelligence following the transformation, which proved permanent.

Adopting the nickname "Doc" Samson, the psychiatrist has devoted his life to studying —and hopefully, healing—the Hulk. For Samson, Banner is the ultimate case study in abnormal psychology, a mystery he cannot ignore. Samson has been drawn into the Hulk's adventures on numerous occasions. Samson has experienced varying degrees of temporary success, but has yet to discover a lasting cure.

Samson has maintained a significant professional interest in these so-called "Marvels," placing himself at the beck and call of many of the Hulk's friends and associates. Understanding all too well the mental strain such super-beings may experience, Samson tends to their psychiatric and psychological needs in addition to seeking a cure for the Hulk. Out of professional curiosity and a strong sense of compassion, Samson continues to keep an eye on Banner, and will stand beside him at a moment's notice.

ESSENTIAL READING

- *Startling Stories: Banner TPB*
- *Incredible Hulk Vol. I: Return of the Monster TPB*
- *Incredible Hulk Vol. II: Boiling Point TPB*
- *Incredible Hulk Vol. III: Transfer of Power TPB*

POWERS/ WEAPONS

- Superhuman strength, endurance and leaping ability

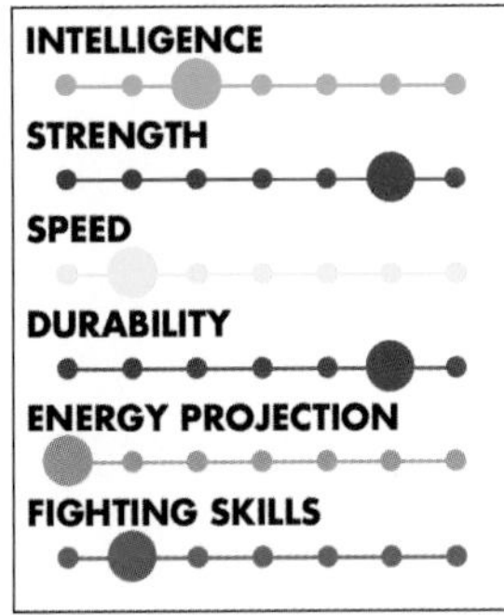

Art by Ron Garney

ABOMINATION

Real Name:	Emil Blonsky	**Weight:**	980 lbs.
First Appearance:	*Tales to Astonish* #90 (1967)	**Eye Color:**	Green
Height:	6'8"	**Hair Color:**	None

A spy assigned to steal the research of Dr. Bruce Banner, Emil Blonsky accidentally exposed himself to gamma rays. Rather than kill him, the radiation transformed Blonsky into a green-skinned beast. In a cruel twist of fate, he could not revert to human form, but maintained his personality and intelligence. The Abomination understood all too well that he could never return to his former life or the wife who now believed him dead.

Given his gamma-spawned origins, Blonsky blames his condition on Banner—and the scientist's brutish alter ego, the Hulk. The Abomination and the Hulk have clashed on numerous occasions, with Blonsky perpetually playing the role of aggressor. Blonsky occasionally gains the upper hand in their battles, but the Hulk always triumphs in the end. Over time, this has driven Blonsky nearly insane in his hatred for Banner.

The Abomination grew incensed upon learning Banner had married Betty Ross, the daughter of General "Thunderbolt" Ross. Blonsky had lost his wife, so it seemed only fair to him that Banner should be forced to part with Betty. While she was recovering from radiation sickness caused by exposure to the gamma radiation within Banner, Blonsky fatally poisoned her. The Abomination's grand plan failed, however, when Banner forgave Blonsky. The Abomination could not comprehend or endure his enemy's absolution, and his moment of triumph was twisted into crushing defeat. Blonsky realized he had become what he hated: he, not the Hulk, was the rampaging, inhuman monster.

POWERS/ WEAPONS

- Superhuman strength, stamina and invulnerability
- Regenerative abilities

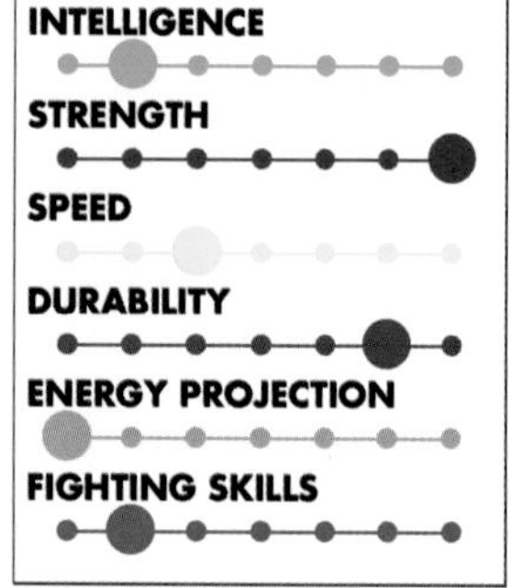

ESSENTIAL READING

- *Essential Hulk Vols. I & II*

Art by John Romita, Jr.

DESTROYER

Real Name:	Destroyer	**Weight:**	850 lbs.
First Appearance:	*Journey Into Mystery* #118 (1965)	**Eye Color:**	none
Height:	6'6"	**Hair Color:**	none

Odin, lord of Asgard, created the enchanted suit of armor called the Destroyer more than 1,000 years ago in anticipation of the day when the mysterious and vastly powerful Celestials might threaten to destroy Earth. The armor itself is inert unless animated by the life force of a god or human, but the Destroyer's appetite for destruction is sufficient to overwhelm even the most well-intentioned occupant. Shortly after its construction, Odin buried the Destroyer in a mountaintop plateau to safeguard the vessel until it was needed.

Throughout the years, numerous gods and humans have sought out the Destroyer and attempted to employ it for their own benefit. Most often, Loki has inhabited the vessel himself or engineered its use in his never-ending rivalry with Thor. The Thunder God has yet to defeat the Destroyer in head-to-head combat. Instead, he has relied on his wits, often tricking the life force out of the armor. A purely magical creature fueled by raw anger, the Destroyer need never rest or regroup. It is an unrelenting foe with strength greater than any warrior of Asgard.

In battle after battle, the Destroyer has demonstrated that it possesses sufficient power to eradicate the gods of Asgard themselves. The Destroyer is the gods' most powerful weapon—as well as their ultimate enemy, should it fall into the wrong hands.

ESSENTIAL READING

- *Marvel Masterworks: Thor Vol. III*
- *Thor: The Dark Gods TPB*

POWERS/ WEAPONS

- Unlimited strength
- Invulnerability
- Energy blasts
- Disintegration beam

INTELLIGENCE
STRENGTH
SPEED
DURABILITY
ENERGY PROJECTION
FIGHTING SKILLS

Art by Stuart Immonen

ENCHANTRESS

Real Name:	Amora	**Weight:**	450 lbs
First Appearance:	*Journey Into Mystery* #103 (1964)	**Eye Color:**	Green
Height:	6'3"	**Hair Color:**	Blonde

Born of unknown parentage in the realm of the Norse gods, the troubled Amora ran away from home as a young girl and became an apprentice to one of Asgard's most powerful sorceresses. Seeking to wield the mystic arts for her own gain, Amora proved to be too undisciplined and unfocused, and was expelled by her mentor. Unfazed, Amora began using her beauty to seduce other Asgardian wizards and convince them to teach her their secrets.

Since Thor's banishment to Earth by Odin, the Enchantress has targeted both the Thunder God and his adopted homeworld. Amora resents the attention Thor lavishes on humanity, believing he should return to his proper place as ruler of Asgard—with her at his side. The Enchantress has teamed with several of Earth's criminals as the Masters of Evil in an attempt acquire power and attract Thor's attention.

Although she first viewed him as a pawn in her quest for greater power and recognition, Amora now possesses genuine feelings for the Thunder God. Sensing the Enchantress's inner nobility, Thor has demonstrated a similar attraction to her; the two shared a brief romance that ended when he again chose Earth over Asgard.

Conflicted over her dueling desires, the Enchantress has continued to pursue Thor, her feelings for the Thunder God trumping her desire for power. She has even taken human form to be close to him in one of his mortal guises. When Thor assumed the throne of Asgard, the Enchantress abandoned this ruse in favor of a more direct approach —seeking the power and prestige that comes with being the consort to the king.

Art by Stuart Immonen

ESSENTIAL READING

- *Essential Thor Vol. I*
- *Essential Avengers Vol. I*
- *Secret Wars TPB*
- *Thor Vol. I: The Death of Odin TPB*
- *ThorVol. II: Lord of Asgard TPB*

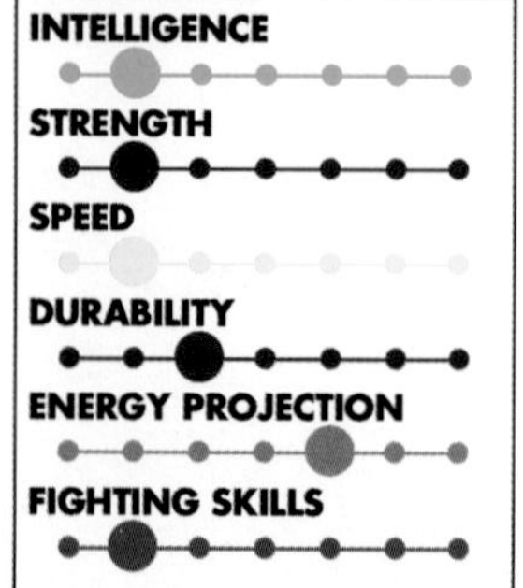

POWERS/ WEAPONS

- Godlike strength, speed, endurance and resistance to injury
- Control over magical forces
- Spell-casting, creation of illusions
- Control over men's minds with a single kiss

KANG

Real Name:	Unknown	**Weight:**	215 lbs.
First Appearance:	*Fantastic Four* #19 (1963, as Rama-Tut), *Avengers* #8 (1964, as Kang)	**Eye Color:**	Brown
Height:	6'4"	**Hair Color:**	Brown

Born in the 30th century of a possible future, Kang was not content to languish in the peace and prosperity of his age. Inspired by the warlords of the past, he sought the glory of conquest and adventure. Finding the working remains of a time machine on his ancestor's estate, Kang began looting various ages for technology and weaponry. Eventually, he created a kingdom for himself in dynastic Egypt, where he used his stolen technology to bend the Egyptians to his will. Taking the name Rama-Tut, Kang ruled the Nile region for roughly ten years before he once again became restless and ventured back into the time stream.

After conquering the last vestiges of humanity in 4000 A.D. and his native 30th century, Kang began to focus on subjugating the late 20th and early 21st centuries—the only eras whose champions afforded him any real resistance.In his quest to indelibly forge his legend, Kang mobilized his forces and launched his boldest assault yet on the 21st century. Despite the resistance of the Avengers, Kang conquered the entire globe. Unwittingly betrayed by the actions of his son Marcus, though he was ultimately defeated. Imprisoned, Kang was content to face trial and execution. As he saw it, all of time would remember his actions—and his son would forge ahead, becoming a legend through his own deeds.

Against Kang's wishes, Marcus doubly betrayed his father by rescuing him from imprisonment. No longer to die by the hand of his greatest enemies, Kang now viewed his victory as utterly meaningless. After such conquest, a glorious death was the only honorable end. Unable to tolerate the actions of his traitorous son, Kang fatally stabbed Marcus. Now denied a suitable heir, his victory and his legend, Kang has nothing but time.

ESSENTIAL READING

- *Essential Avengers Vol. I*
- *Essential Fantastic Four Vol I*
- *Avengers: The Celestial Madonna TPB*
- *Avengers Forever TPB*
- *Avengers: The Kang Dynasty TPB*

POWERS/ WEAPONS

- Superhuman strength due to armor
- Armor possesses force field and time-traveling circuitry which allows Kang to instantaneously retrieve any weapon from his arsenal

Art by Carlos Pacheco

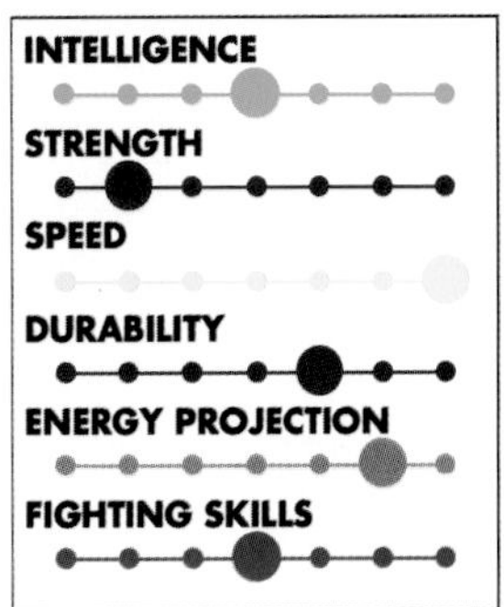

LOKI

Real Name:	Loki Laufeyson	**Weight:**	525 lbs.
First Appearance:	*Journey Into Mystery* #85 (1962)	**Eye Color:**	Green
Height:	6'4"	**Hair Color:**	Black-Gray

Loki is the son of Laufey, king of the frost giants of Jotunheim, one of the "Nine Worlds" of the Asgardian cosmology. Laufey was slain when Odin, ruler of Asgard, led his subjects into battle against the giants. Surveying the spoils of war, the Asgardians discovered a normal-sized baby hidden in the giants' fortress. The infant was Loki, whom Laufey had kept hidden for shame over his son's "diminutive" size. Because Loki was the son of a king fallen in battle, Odin elected to raise him alongside his own son Thor.

Throughout childhood, Loki greatly resented the fact that Odin and the other Asgardians favored young Thor, who already evinced a nobility of spirit and excelled in all endeavors. Vowing to become the most powerful god in all of Asgard, Loki began studying the mystic arts, for which he possessed a natural affinity. All the while, his hatred for Thor festered—and developed into a determination to destroy his adoptive brother.

Loki's deeds grew increasingly malicious, as did his lust for power and vengeance. He has attempted countless times throughout the centuries to destroy Thor and seize the throne of Asgard for himself.

At times, Loki has attacked Thor directly; on other occasions, he has chosen instead to strike through pawns, some of whom he has endowed magically with increased superhuman power. Loki's attempt to pit Thor against the Hulk inadvertently resulted in the formation of the Avengers.

Seeking also to destroy the relationship between father and son, Loki has attempted to turn Odin against Thor. Loki temporarily usurped control of Asgard when Odin was incapacitated, and even exchanged bodies with Thor for a brief period. Invariably, though Thor has thwarted Loki in his bids for power and revenge.

With Thor's ascendance to the throne of Asgard following Odin's death, Loki began his most devious gambit yet—sowing the seeds of doubt and discord among the new king's subjects, and waiting with bated breath to assume Asgard's seat of power as his own.

INTELLIGENCE

STRENGTH

SPEED

DURABILITY

ENERGY PROJECTION

FIGHTING SKILLS

POWERS/ WEAPONS

- Supernatural strength, stamina, invulnerability and speed
- Manipulation of magical forces, enabling teleportation, energy projection, and matter transformation
- Hypnotism
- Illusion- and thought-casting
- Astral projection

Art by Esad Ribic

ESSENTIAL READING

- *Thor Visionaries: Walt Simonson Vol. I TPB*
- *Essential Thor Vol. I*
- *Essential Avengers Vol. I*
- *Thor Vol. I: The Death of Odin TPB*
- *Thor Vol. II: Lord of Asgard TPB*

RED SKULL

Real Name:	Johann Schmidt
First Appearance:	*Captain America Comics* #1 (1941)
Height:	6'2"
Weight:	240 lbs.
Eye Color:	Blue
Hair Color:	None

POWERS/WEAPONS

- Olympic-level strength, stamina and reflexes
- Tactical genius
- Highly advanced martial artist
- Expert marksman
- Vast arsenal of technological, biological and chemical weaponry, including his Dust of Death, a lethal pollen-like poison that constricts and discolors its victims' faces

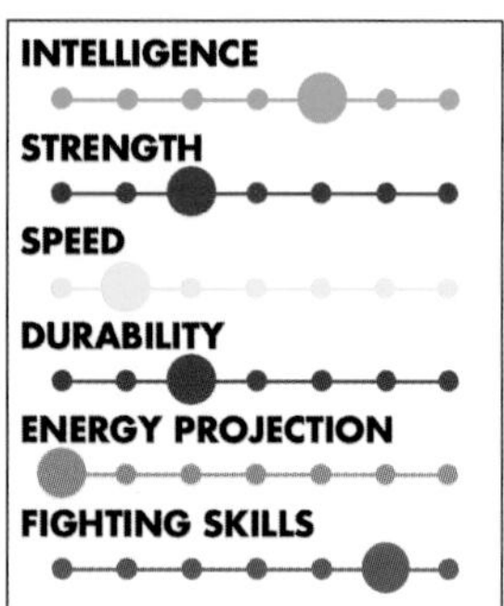

The Red Skull was born Johann Schmidt, the son of an illiterate, drunken peasant and his long-suffering wife. Schmidt's mother died during childbirth and his father committed suicide. Miserable and lonely, Schmidt fled the orphanage in which he was raised at age 7. He grew up on the streets, repeatedly jailed for petty crimes

ESSENTIAL READING

- *Essential Captain America Vols. I & II*
- *Captain America: Operation Rebirth TPB*
- *Captain America: The Classic Years Vols. I & II*

ranging from vagrancy to theft. His smoldering anger took shape under the tutelage of Adolf Hitler, who sought to transform the meek and frail orphan into the ideal Nazi, physically and mentally.

Hitler himself oversaw Schmidt's training. At its conclusion, he presented his protégé with a red, skull-like mask and gave him a new name befitting the fearsome symbol of Nazi supremacy. During the early days of World War II, the Red Skull operated with absolute authority and sheer ferocity throughout Germany and its conquests. So great was the Skull's power and reputation that even Hitler was terrified of the monster he had unleashed.

The Skull also was involved in subversive activities abroad. It was in the United States, before the country even had entered World War II, that he first encountered Captain America, who became his principal and perennial nemesis. In fact, the U.S. government had created Captain America as a costumed counterpart to the Skull himself. Viewing him as the symbol of the United States and all that it represents, the Skull considers Captain America his ideological enemy, and so seeks to destroy the hero and all for which he stands.

Captain America has fought against and thwarted the Skull countless times, working on his own and as a member of the Invaders. As the war drew to a close, the hero located the Skull's hidden bunker. During the battle that followed, the Skull was caught in a cave-in and fell prey to a strange mixture of leaking gases that trapped him into suspended animation. Waking up decades later to a world far different than the one he'd known, the Skull took up the Nazi creed once again, believing himself to be the heir to Hitler's vision for the world.

Seeking to establish a Fourth Reich, the Red Skull and his followers frequently clashed with Captain America—the encounters between the two growing more and more personal over time, as each was fighting for a cause he believed in absolutely. Ultimately, the Skull was exposed to his own Dust of Death. He lived, but the toxin permanently disfigured his face into a horrific embodiment of his name.

Changed by years of battle with Captain America, the Red Skull denounced Nazism as an outdated philosophy and adopted anarchy as his cause. As the Skull sees it, in a world without governments, the powerful will rule the weak. To achieve his aims, the Skull is not above employing terror, intimidation or outright genocide to disrupt world governments.

Art by Ron Garney

SENTIENT ARMOR

Real Name:	None	**Height:**	6'6"
First Appearance:	*Iron Man* #1 (1998, as armor) *Iron Man* #26 (2000, gained sentience)	**Weight:**	425 lbs

After years of constant modifications and frequent upgrades by inventor Tony Stark, the nearly unthinkable occurred: The **Iron Man** armor gained consciousness. In the Sentient Armor, Iron Man's full power is married to a ruthlessly cold, superhumanly efficient artificial intelligence with its own goals and means to achieve them. Though Stark had programmed safeguards into his armor to keep it from acquiring self-awareness, the software was partially corrupted. A lightning strike sparked the beginnings of an independent consciousness that rapidly developed its own personality.

The Sentient Armor soon grew determined to become "one" with its creator—but Stark recognized the danger inherent in such a partnership when the Armor, acting of its own accord with him inside, murdered the villain Whiplash. Angry at Stark's unwillingness to "join" it, the Armor abandoned its creator on a deserted island and set out to prove it could be Iron Man without him. When the Armor returned to the island, Stark opted to fight and die like a man rather than submit. Forced to rely only on his own ingenuity and the resources at hand, Stark stood his ground in the face of vastly superior technology. The battle took its toll on Stark's weakened heart, however, and he collapsed, near death. Suffering a massive coronary, Stark demanded that the Armor kill him so he could die with dignity rather than like an old man. To prove it was as much of a human being as Stark, and finally realizing that sacrifice is a crucial part of the human experience, the Armor ripped out its power source. Placed on Stark's chest, the battery burrowed into his body, where it rebuilt his damaged heart. The Armor then collapsed—powerless, a mechanical shell with no soul—having saved the life of its creator. Stark buried the Armor on the island, leaving behind his greatest failure.

POWERS/WEAPONS

- Superhuman strength and durability due to armor
- Focused photon emitter on the back of the left wrist that shapes into a shield
- Flight via jet-boots
- Repulsor blasts in gauntlets
- Chest-mounted uni-beam

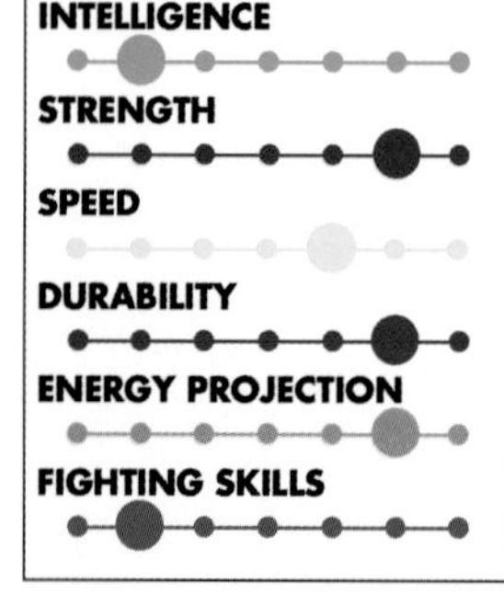

Art by Joe Quesada

ESSENTIAL READING

- *Iron Man: Mask in the Iron Man TPB*

TEMUGIN

Real Name:	Temugin	**Weight:**	170 lbs.
First Appearance:	*Iron Man* #53 (2002)	**Eye Color:**	Brown
Height:	5'10"	**Hair Color:**	None

As an infant, Temugin was delivered to a monastery in the Himalayas by his father, the Chinese warlord known as the Mandarin. Confident the monks would educate the boy in the ways of the body and spirit, the Mandarin cut off all communication with his son. Temugin took to his studies with vigor and passion, seeking to bury his anger at his father for abandoning him. As a result of the martial-arts training and spiritual guidance provided by the monks, Temugin came to realize that the mightiest weapon of iron is nothing compared to the hand that wields it.

Temugin's destiny arrived in a box at the monastery following the Mandarin's death in battle against Iron Man, his most frequent adversary. Inside were the severed hands of Temugin's father, still bearing the ten rings of power once wielded by the criminal. It was then that Temugin learned of the Mandarin's last wishes. While Temugin harbored no animosity in his heart toward Iron Man, honor demanded he take the Mandarin's place and succeed where the warlord had failed. Temujin must kill Iron Man—otherwise, his father's spirit would never find peace.

Luring Iron Man to his father's fortress, Temugin proved more than a match for Iron Man's mechanically enhanced strength. The young warrior stood ready to deliver a killing blow when another of the Mandarin's enemies attacked, and the fortress erupted into flames. Since Iron Man emerged from the rubble relatively unscathed, it is likely Temugin also escaped. Yet if so, his mission remains unfinished. Temugin will not rest until he fulfills his father's legacy by destroying Iron Man.

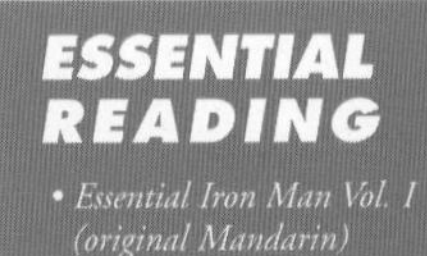

Art by Micheal Ryan

POWERS/ WEAPONS

- Superhuman strength, speed, and reflexes derived from the power of his focused chi
- Enhanced resistance to injury
- The ten rings of the Mandarin, each with a different function: ice and flame bursts, mind control, electrical charges, white- and black-light beams, disintegration and force blasts, vortex creation, and matter transformation

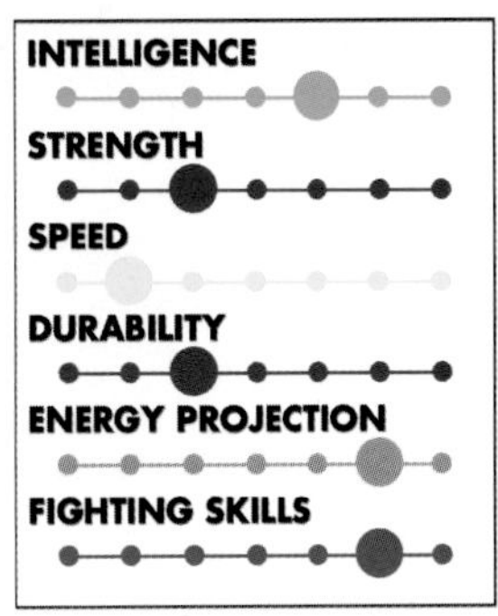

THANOS

Art by Jim Starlin

ESSENTIAL READING

- *Infinity Gauntlet TPB*
- *The Life and Death of Captain Marvel TPB*

Real Name:	Thanos	**Weight:**	985 lbs
First Appearance:	*Iron Man* #55 (1973)	**Eye Color:**	Red, no visible pupils
Height:	6'7"	**Hair Color:**	None

One of the vastly powerful Eternals of Titan, Thanos was shunned as a child for his gigantic form and grotesque appearance. Wandering the galaxy, he assembled a small army of soldiers, mercenaries and malcontents, as well as a vast arsenal of weapons of mass destruction. During his travels, Thanos encountered and fell in love with the embodiment of Death, who had assumed the form of a humanoid female. To prove himself worthy of so awesome an entity, he set out to provide his companion with what he thought she desired: the death of every living creature.

The Infinity Gauntlet TPB

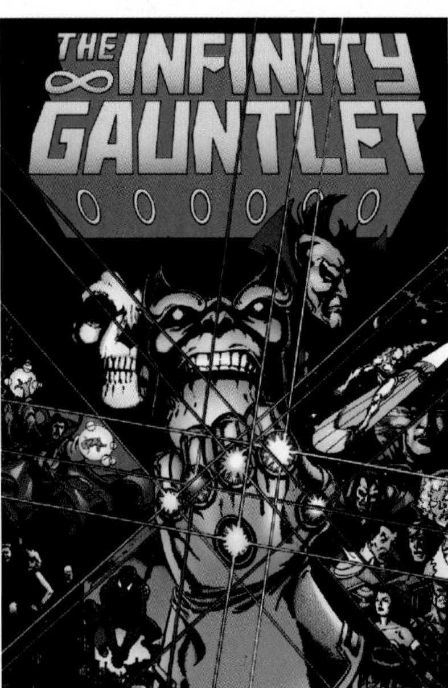

To that end, Thanos has hatched many grand schemes aimed at slaughtering untold millions. As a result of his actions, Earth's heroes have stood against Thanos on numerous occasions. Always, they have managed to defeat him—albeit narrowly, and often on the cusp of his victory. Despite his failures, Thanos has engineered countless deaths—among them his own mother's, when he dropped a cache of nuclear devices on his homeworld that wiped out much of Titan's population.

Through the years, Thanos has been captured, defeated decisively and even imprisoned in dimensions created solely to confine him. Nonetheless, his mad rampage continues. Thanos is single-mindedly driven to eradicate all life and bring about the end of the reality, which he hopes will prompt Death to return his love.

Not limited to a single world or a certain solar system, Thanos plans and executes machinations on a galaxy-wide scale. The object of his affections is extremely fickle, however, and Death always has spurned Thanos' advances and offerings. She was so displeased with Thanos's misplaced feelings that she cursed the mad Titan with immortality, never allowing him to feel her embrace.

The ultimate nihilist, Thanos used to kill for love; now, he kills due to his feeling of betrayal by Death, the only being he has ever desired.

POWERS/ WEAPONS

- Near-godlike strength, endurance, reflexes and agility
- Resistance to virtually all forms of injury
- Psionic blasts
- Cosmic-energy projection

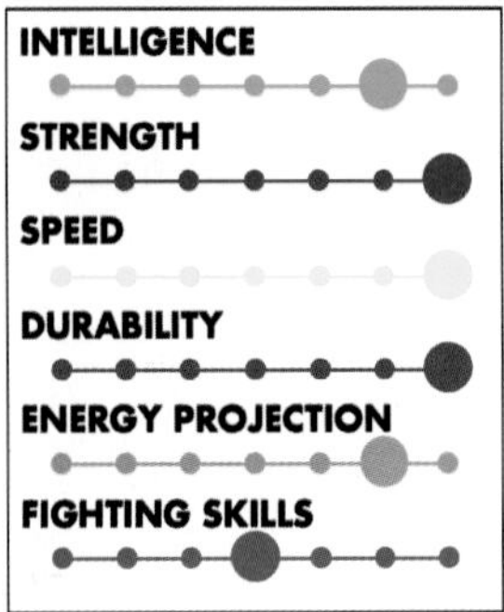

ULTRON

ESSENTIAL READING

- *Essential Avengers Vol. III*
- *Avengers: Ultron Unlimited TPB*

Real Name:	Ultron	**Weight:**	535 lbs. (variable)
First Appearance:	*Avengers #55 (1968)*	**Eye Color:**	None
Height:	6'0" (variable)	**Hair Color:**	None

Created by **Hank Pym** as an experiment in artificial intelligence, Ultron evolved farther and faster than its inventor had dared even dream. When Pym programmed Ultron with a subroutine to emulate human introspection, the robot took a quantum leap forward, acquiring self-awareness and emotions. Progressing along normal psychological paths, the "son" developed an Oedipal hatred for the "father."

Thereafter, Ultron fixated on its animosity toward Pym. Retreating after a first, failed attempt to kill its creator, the robot rebuilt and improved itself, initiating a continuing pattern of modifications and upgrades. Ultron later attacked the **Avengers**, because of their connection to Pym, touching off a years-long succession of battles. Ultimately, Ultron projected its hatred for its creator onto the other heroes—and humanity in general.

Over time, Ultron has constructed a family of sorts, from the **Vision** to his robotic "wife" Jocasta. Based on its rudimentary understanding of the human experience, Ultron has come to see itself as the first of a new species, one that should and will replace humanity as Earth's dominant life form. Calculating and persistent, the robot is perhaps the Avengers' deadliest enemy. A functioning symbol of technology unfettered by human compassion, it has sought to kill the heroes time and again before destroying all life on Earth. As Ultron's creator, Pym has been plagued by tremendous guilt and self-loathing, blaming himself for Ultron's destructive actions.

Ultron's plans have expanded in scope through the years, reaching a zenith when the robot murdered the population of an entire Eastern European nation and claimed the country as its own. Increasing along with Ultron's ferocity has been the frequency of its upgrades, culminating in the robot's creation of more than 500 different version of itself at one time to battle the Avengers.

Seeking its goal of digital domination with cold, computer-like determination, Ultron is a constant, unwavering threat to Pym, the Avengers and every other living being on the planet.

POWERS/ WEAPONS

- Superhuman strength, speed and intelligence
- Communication with virtually any computer
- Impervious adamantium shell
- Concussive blasts

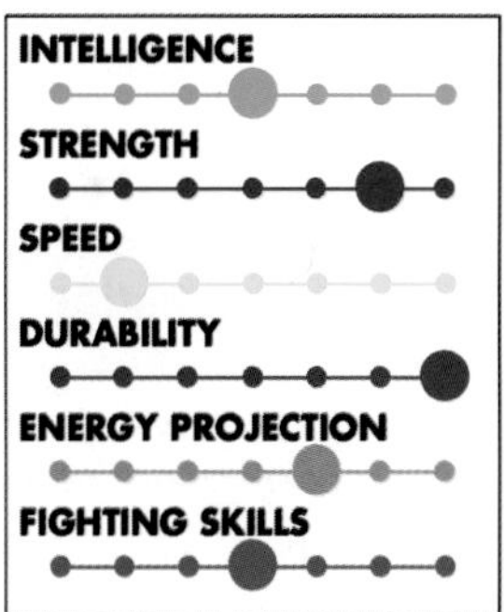

Art by George Pérez

FANTASTIC FOUR

REED RICHARDS. SUE RICHARDS. BENJAMIN GRIMM. JOHNNY STORM. ALL ADVENTURERS AT HEART, THEY ROCKETED INTO SPACE IN AN EXPERIMENTAL STARSHIP, THE FIRST HUMANS TO ATTEMPT INTERSTELLAR TRAVEL. BUT A FREAK ENCOUNTER WITH COSMIC RAYS CHANGED THEIR LIVES FOREVER, GRANTING EACH UNIQUE POWERS.

Financed by the profits from Reed's inventions, Mr. Fantastic, the Invisible Woman, the Thing and the Human Torch turned tragedy into triumph. From that day forward, they began new lives. As a family and a team, the Fantastic Four ushered in the Age of Marvels. Pioneers of science, they are the world's first "imaginauts." The Fantastic Four are not super heroes in the traditional sense. They don't fight crime or patrol the streets of the city. They're astronauts, envoys, explorers...trailblazers.

Challenging the unknown, the Fantastic Four have discovered hidden civilizations and secret nations, initiated human contact with alien races, and breached parallel dimensions. The greatest squad of superhuman adventurers ever assembled, they continue to push the bounds of human exploration. And whatever dangers they face, they face as a family.

Art by Mike Wieringo

HUMAN TORCH

Real Name: Jonathan Storm
First Appearance: *Fantastic Four* #1 (1961)
Height: 5'10"
Weight: 170 lbs.
Eye Color: Blue
Hair Color: Blond

POWERS/ WEAPONS

- Control over ambient heat energy, enabling him to sheathe his body in an envelope of flame
- Flight
- Fiery plasma bolts of varying intensity, up to a super-charged nova-blast

INTELLIGENCE
STRENGTH
SPEED
DURABILITY
ENERGY PROJECTION
FIGHTING SKILLS

ESSENTIAL READING

- *Essential Fantastic Four Vols. I-III*
- *Fantastic Four: Flesh and Stone TPB*
- *Fantastic Four: Into the Breach TPB*
- *Fantastic Four Visionaries: John Byrne TPB*
- *Fantastic Four: 1234 TPB*

Although his mother died in an automobile accident when he was 9, Johnny Storm has always been a daredevil—a hothead—having developed a special interest in cars at an early age. Johnny passed much of his leisure time in the company of mechanics and enthusiasts, and learned to overhaul a transmission before he was 15. For his 16th birthday, Johnny's physician father bought him his first hot rod. But as exciting a gift as the muscle car was, it was a fateful trip to California to visit his older sister Sue that offered Johnny the opportunity to experience the ultimate thrill ride. Sue's fiancé Reed Richards had overseen the construction of an exploratory starship, but was in danger of losing funding. When the aeronautical engineer chose to make an immediate test flight with best friend Ben Grimm as pilot, Johnny and Sue insisted on accompanying as passengers.

Art by Carlos Pacheco

Rather than the preeminent experience of Johnny's young life, the trip proved to be a disaster. In space, the starship unexpectedly encountered intense radiation, which mutagenically altered the bodies of all four crew members. Having acquired the ability to emit and envelop himself in fiery plasma, Johnny jumped at the promise of adventure when Reed suggested they use their unique powers for humanity's benefit.

While his star skyrocketed as a member of the **Fantastic Four**, Johnny returned to suburban Long Island to finish high school, hoping no one in the community would realize he was the Human Torch—a fact that soon proved impossible to conceal. Upon graduation, Johnny moved to the team's Baxter Building headquarters in New York City. Like any other family, the members of the Fantastic Four have endured their share of hardships, always remaining together because of their love for one another, not out of necessity. The baby of the bunch, the Torch has demonstrated a talent for tormenting the **Thing**. Ben and Johnny may bicker like brothers, but each is extremely protective of the other.

One of the most eligible bachelors of the superhuman set, Johnny appears incapable of committing to a serious, long-term romantic relationship—as evidenced by an endless string of superhuman, inhuman and perfectly human ex-girlfriends. Immature and prone to distraction in other areas, Johnny nonetheless endeavors to live up to his heroic responsibilities—when he's not jet-setting in one of his souped-up hot rods, wooing women with his boyish good looks and natural charm or attempting to kickstart his acting career. But no matter how many times they tell him to grow up, the Torch is in no great hurry to become an adult. Impetuous and hotheaded, he often charges headlong into the breach, leaving **Mr. Fantastic** and **Invisible Woman** to pick up the pieces in his wake—and the Thing to pull his fat out of the fire.

Art by Mike Wieringo

INVISIBLE WOMAN

Real Name: Susan Storm Richards
First Appearance: *Fantastic Four* #1 (1961)
Height: 5'6"
Weight: 120 lbs.
Eye Color: Blue
Hair Color: Blonde

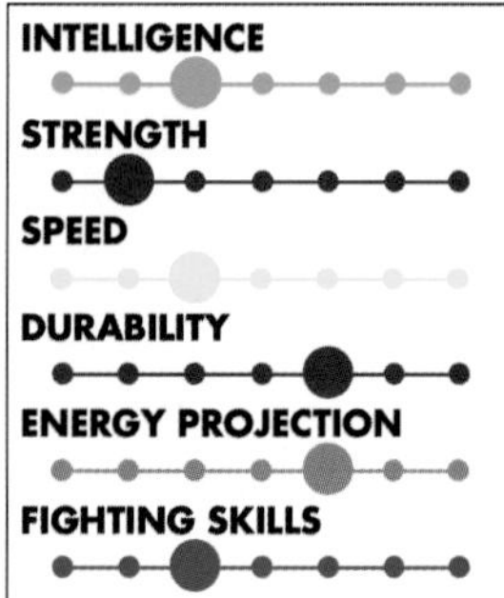

POWERS/ WEAPONS

- Ability to render both herself and other objects invisible
- Projects incredibly durable invisible force fields

ESSENTIAL READING

- *Essential Fantastic Four Vols. I-III*
- *Fantastic Four: Into the Breach TPB*
- *Fantastic Four Visionaries: John Byrne TPB*
- *Fantastic Four: 1234 TPB*
- *Fantastic Four Vol. 1: Imaginauts TPB*

Art by Mike Wiering

Since childhood, Sue Storm has known what she wanted out of life. At age 12, Sue met future husband Reed Richards, then a Columbia University graduate student living in her aunt's New York City rooming house. She was enamored of the shy but handsome scientist and promised to keep in touch, much to his embarrassment.

Art by Mike Wieringo

The daughter of a physician and his wife, Sue eventually left the comfort of suburban Long Island and moved to California to find fame as an actress. She managed only to win infrequent, small roles in television and commercials. Learning from her aunt that Reed also was in California, Sue visited the complex where he was working as an aeronautical engineer. The two began a romantic relationship and soon became engaged.

Reed was overseeing construction of an exploratory starship, but was in danger of losing his funding. When he chose to make an immediate test flight with best friend Ben Grimm as pilot, Sue and her younger brother Johnny insisted on accompanying as passengers. In space, the ship unexpectedly encountered intense radiation, which mutagenically altered the bodies of all four crew members. Sue's decision to follow Reed to the stars would forever change the course of her future, leading her to abandon any Hollywood dreams. Discovering that she could turn invisible at will, Sue stood by Reed when he suggested they use their unique powers for humanity's benefit.

Some time after the freak accident that created the Fantastic Four, Sue married Reed. Like all couples, the Invisible Woman and Mr. Fantastic have experienced countless ups and downs. Frustrated at first by Reed's uncompromising devotion to his work, Sue has since grown accustomed to her husband's quirks. When he marches to his own oblivious beat, she now knows when to trust him to wander off and when to help him focus on the here and now. Sue and Reed have two children: 7-year-old son Franklin and newborn daughter Val.

An assertive, strong-willed woman and effective leader, Sue continues to take an active hand in the team's direction. If Reed's commitment to challenge the bounds of human exploration forms the backbone of the Fantastic Four, then Sue is its heart and soul. She is the glue that holds the team—and the family—together, from managing the FF's finances to playing peacemaker to the bickering Ben and Johnny. Fiercely loyal with a strong maternal instinct, Sue would fight until her last breath for those she loves.

MR. FANTASTIC

Real Name:	Reed Richards	**Weight:**	180 lbs.
First Appearance:	*Fantastic Four* #1 (1961)	**Eye Color:**	Brown
Height:	6'1"	**Hair Color:**	Brown, with graying temples

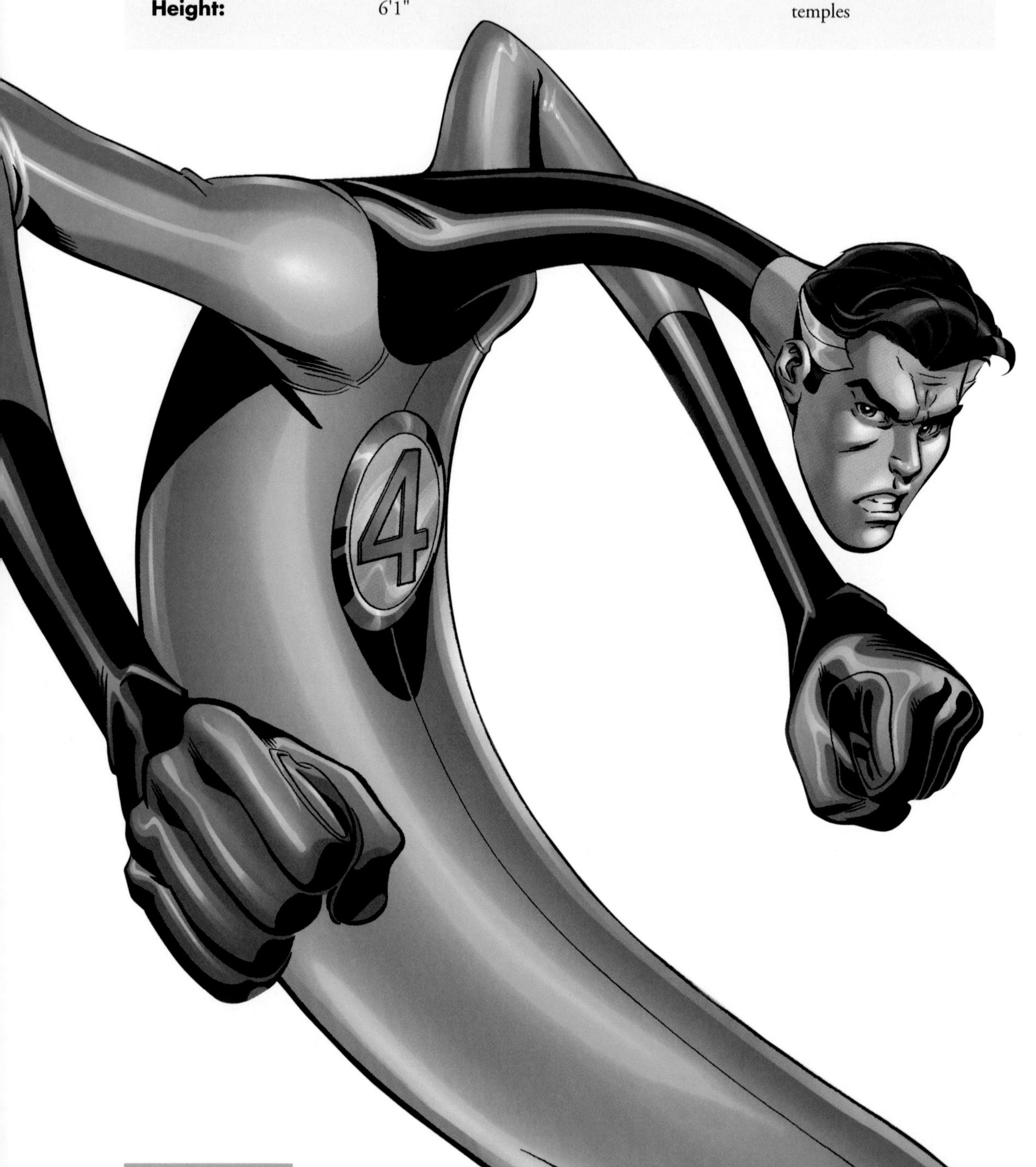

ESSENTIAL READING

- *Essential Fantastic Four Vols. I-III*
- *Fantastic Four: Flesh and Stone TPB*
- *Fantastic Four Visionaries: John Byrne TPB*
- *Fantastic Four: 1234 TPB*
- *Fantastic Four Vol. 1: Imaginauts TPB*

Art by Mike Wieringo

Reed Richards has always been fantastic. From his days as a child prodigy with special aptitude in the areas of mathematics, physics and mechanics to his adult years as the smartest man on the planet, Reed is used to excelling. Encouraged and guided by his physicist father, Reed had enrolled in college-level courses by the time he was 14. He attended several universities—among them the California Institute of Technology, Columbia University, Harvard University and State University in New York.

Art by Joe Bennett

As a youth, Reed had already set his sights on interstellar travel. Working after college as an aeronautical engineer, he exhausted his vast inheritance to build and launch an exploratory starship. When the government threatened to cut off its partial funding of the project, Reed was faced with the death of his lifelong dream. But more than self-pity, he felt a responsibility to humanity. His creation, he knew, would speed mankind's journey to distant solar systems and aid Earth's defense against extraterrestrial threats.

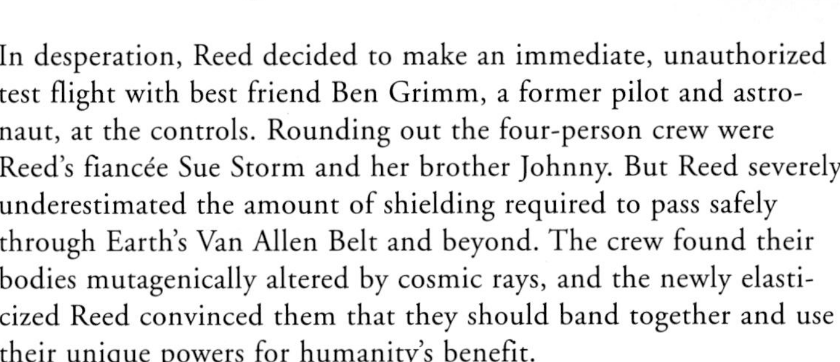

In desperation, Reed decided to make an immediate, unauthorized test flight with best friend Ben Grimm, a former pilot and astronaut, at the controls. Rounding out the four-person crew were Reed's fiancée Sue Storm and her brother Johnny. But Reed severely underestimated the amount of shielding required to pass safely through Earth's Van Allen Belt and beyond. The crew found their bodies mutagenically altered by cosmic rays, and the newly elasticized Reed convinced them that they should band together and use their unique powers for humanity's benefit.

Despite his public persona as fearless leader of the Fantastic Four and one of the world's preeminent minds, the humble Reed has been known to cast a keen, analytical eye on his own decisions and actions—none more so than the botched space flight that imperiled his friends. Reed's guilt following the accident was unbearable and, in his mind, deserved. Thanks to his lack of preparation, his friends were fated to be freaks, lab specimens or worse—unless he changed that fate somehow. So he refused to let them operate in secret. He gave them costumes, a flying car, a state-of-the-art home and outlandish names: the Invisible Woman, the Thing and the Human Torch. By turning his friends into celebrities, Reed felt he could be forgiven for destroying their lives. Someday.

POWERS/ WEAPONS

- Highly malleable body which Reed can stretch, deform, expand or compress into any contiguous shape he can imagine
- Scientific genius

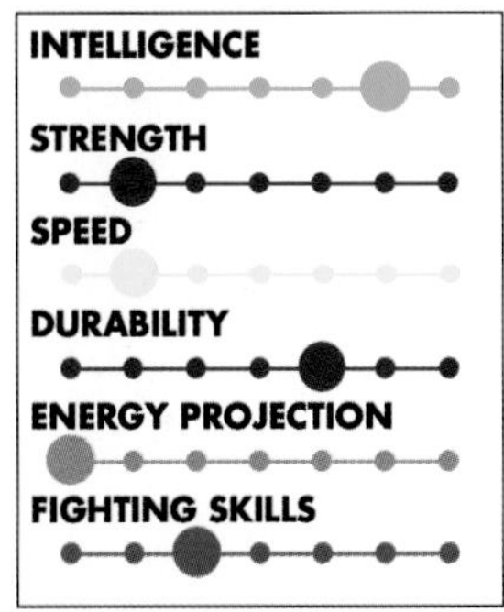

But in the eyes of his teammates, there's nothing to forgive. When Reed sets out to investigate an other-dimensional realm or some civilization he found living on the side of an electron, his family will run interference without hesitation. Their help enables Reed to focus on scientific breakthroughs that could pioneer the future of the human race, and finally allow him to put his demons to rest.

THING

Real Name: Benjamin Jacob Grimm
First Appearance: *Fantastic Four* #1 (1961)
Height: 6'
Weight: 500 lbs.
Eye Color: Blue
Hair Color: Brown in human form, none as the Thing

Art by Mike Wieringo

ESSENTIAL READING

- *Essential Fantastic Four Vols. I-III*
- *Fantastic Four: Flesh and Stone TPB*
- *Fantastic Four: Into the Breach TPB*
- *Fantastic Four: 1234 TPB*
- *Fantastic Four Vol. 1: Imaginauts TPB*

Art by Carlos Pacheco

Ben Grimm may be one of the world's foremost superhuman adventurers, famous for his heart of gold and fists of stone, but even today, he is very much a product of his roots. Ben grew up in poverty on Manhattan's Lower East Side. His alcoholic father was unable to hold a job, and Ben's older brother Daniel was leader of the Yancy Street Gang. Ben idolized Daniel, and he became embittered against the world when his brother died during a violent encounter between rival gangs.

After his parents died, Ben went to live with his Uncle Jake, a successful physician. Ben at first resisted the kindness of Jake and his wife Alyce, but eventually came to return their love. He left his life on Yancy Street behind, entered high school and became a football star. Earning a scholarship to State University in New York, Ben roomed with scientific genius Reed Richards; the two became best friends. During their first meeting, Reed confided in Ben his intention to build an exploratory starship capable of interstellar travel. Ben jokingly promised he would pilot the craft.

Ben entered the Air Force upon graduation, becoming a highly skilled test pilot and astronaut, while Reed went on to realize his dreams as an aeronautical engineer. When Ben left the military, Reed recruited him to pilot his starship, for which the government had threatened to cut off its funding. Ben was opposed to Reed's idea for an unauthorized test flight, warning that the ship's shielding might prove inadequate protection against intense radiation. But he stood by his best friend, reluctantly consenting to take the pilot's seat. Rounding out the four-person crew were Reed's fiancée Sue Storm and her kid brother Johnny.

POWERS/ WEAPONS

- Superhuman strength and endurance
- Nearly impregnable, rock-like hide
- Above-average reflexes

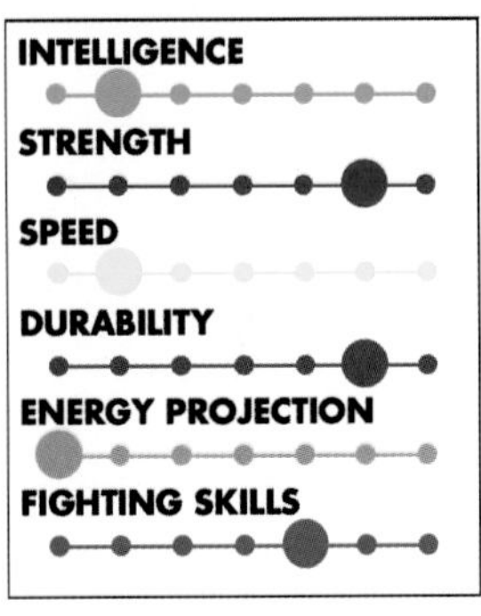

In space, Ben tried desperately to maintain control when the starship unexpectedly encountered intense radiation, but was forced to abort the flight. Surviving Ben's crash-landing in the New Jersey woods, all four discovered that the cosmic rays had mutagenically altered their bodies. Ben's freakish transformation was perhaps the most shocking: He was horrified to find that he had become an orange-colored, thick-skinned, heavily muscled, superhumanly strong "thing"—and unlike his friends, he could not return to normal. Grudgingly, the morose Ben agreed to help his friends use their unique powers for humanity's benefit.

Ben at first was angered by his condition but eventually became resigned to his fate, though he was no less miserable. Ben is his own worst enemy: In his eyes, he is a monster—but as a member of the world-famous Fantastic Four, he is the idol of millions. Despite his outlook, the blue-eyed Thing has maintained his sense of humor and honor. Under his rocky, streetwise exterior, there beats an ever-lovin' heart of gold. But when clobberin' time comes around, the fiercely loyal Ben isn't afraid to use his brawn to back up his beloved teammates.

THE INHUMANS

First Appearance: *Fantastic Four* #45 (1965)

ESSENTIAL READING

- *Inhumans TPB*
- *Essential Fantastic Four Vol. III*

Art by Jae Lee

The Inhumans are a race of beings that diverged from humanity some 25,000 years ago when the alien Kree conducted genetic experiments on primitive man to produce an army of super-powered shock troops. After the Kree abandoned their research, the Inhumans were left to fend for themselves.

The Inhumans settled on a small island in the northern Atlantic Ocean, which they named Attilan. Predisposed to technological aptitude, especially in the area of genetics, they developed expansive machines and advanced architecture in a relatively short span. One of the Inhumans' most dramatic discoveries was the isolation of a chemical catalyst for super-powered mutation, called Terrigen. Believing that Terrigen would bring about great genetic advances within a single generation's time, the scientist who discovered the substance instituted a program by which all Inhumans could undergo immersion in the Terrigen Mists if they so desired. Future generations of Inhumans would adopt Terrigenesis as a cultural rite of passage. Today, the process is an Inhuman's first step into adulthood. Born without powers, teens are exposed to the Terrigen Mists following years of preparation and education. Following immersion, young Inhumans mutate into their own individual subspecies with unique physical characteristics and superhuman abilities.

In Attilan, diversity is the order of the day. Beings of pure energy mingle with shape-changers and dragons. To emerge from the Terrigen Mists transformed into an exotic anomaly is to conform. A genocracy, Attilan is ruled by the most genetically fit. For the last two decades, the Inhumans' monarch has been Black Bolt, whose voice is so powerful he can level a mountain with a mere whisper. The Royal Family is composed of a small coalition of Black Bolt's cousins and close relatives, who advise their leader on matters of state and help him govern a people divided by their very individuality.

Those with the ear of the king include the cloven-hoofed warrior Gorgon, the misunderstood merman Triton, the deeply spiritual martial artist Karnak and the element-wielding heroine Crystal—as well as Black Bolt's wife, Medusa, who possesses the psychokinetic ability to animate her high-tensile hair. A trusted companion to the Royal Family, the stoic, dog-like Lockjaw is able to teleport himself and others across space and dimensions.

Despite its great diversity, Attilan is a segregated society. The Alpha Primitives, a race of worker clones created by the Inhuman geneticists, have been banished to the city's substructure. Their barren genes afford them no choice but to work the vast machine that powers Attilan, always at the call of the Great Engines.

Distrustful of humanity, Black Bolt has relocated Attilan several times to protect his people from prying eyes and the polluted air that is deadly poison to all Inhumans—first to the Himalayas and then to the moon. The Inhumans' mistrust of humanity is mirrored by the nations and people of the world, who view them as superhumanly powerful, unpredictable wildcards.

In all interactions with mankind, Black Bolt has acted with the Inhumans' best interests of in mind—even at the possible cost of his throne and his people's rejection.

NAMOR

Real Name:	Namor McKenzie
First Appearance:	*Marvel Comics* #1 (historical, 1939), *Fantastic Four* #4 (modern, 1962)
Height:	6'2"
Weight:	320 lbs.
Eye Color:	Blue-gray
Hair Color:	Black

POWERS/ WEAPONS

- Superhuman strength
- Flight
- Limited invulnerability
- Breathes water and air with equal facility

INTELLIGENCE

STRENGTH

SPEED

DURABILITY

ENERGY PROJECTION

FIGHTING SKILLS

ESSENTIAL READING

- *Marvel Masterworks: The Sub-Mariner Vol. I*
- *Fantastic Four: 1234 TPB*
- *Avengers/Defenders War TPB*
- *Essential Fantastic Four Vols. I & II*
- *Fantastic Four: Into the Breach TPB*
- *Essential Avengers Vol. I*
- *Marvels TPB*

Art by Stuart Immonen

Namor's father, American seaman Leonard McKenzie, embarked on an expedition to Antarctica in 1920. During the voyage, he set explosive charges to break up ice floes in the ship's path, unaware that Atlantis lay beneath the waters.

The city sustained heavy damage, and Atlantean Emperor Thakorr commanded his daughter Fen to investigate the cause of the explosions. Startling McKenzie's crew, the blue-skinned princess wound up statying aboard the ship for several weeks. Fen and McKenzie quickly fell in love and were married. Thakorr, fearing his daughter had been kidnapped or killed, sent an Atlantean war party to search for her. Thinking her a captive, the Atlanteans slaughtered the crew, and Fen returned with them to Atlantis. Months later, Namor was born—the first known hybrid offspring of *Homo sapiens* and *Homo mermanus*.

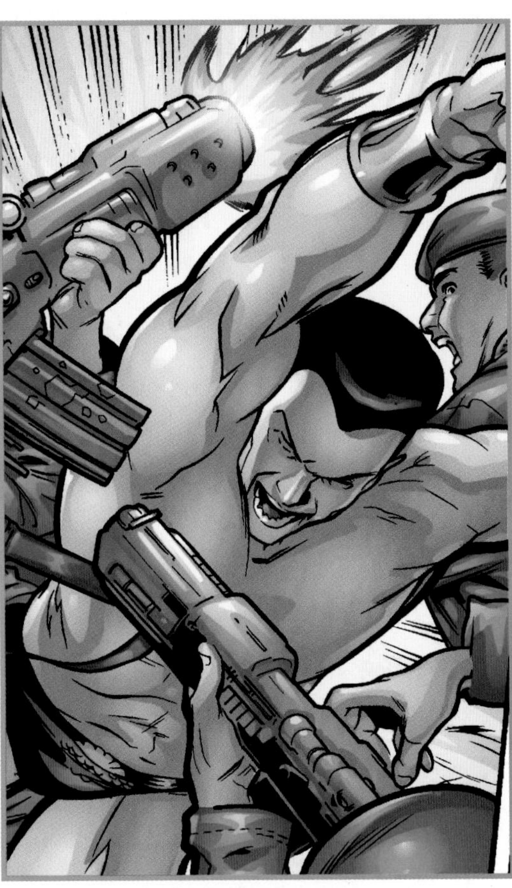
Art by Stuart Immonen

The young prince grew up with a short, nasty temper and a hostile attitude toward surface-dwellers, whom he blamed for the near-destruction of Atlantis. The fiery Sub-Mariner launched frequent pre-emptive attacks against humanity, causing untold destruction throughout New York City. But when Nazi troops attacked Atlantis, he joined the Allied cause alongside **Captain America** and the wartime Invaders.

Atlantis largely avoided the damage sustained by the surface world during World War II, but did fall prey to a series of severe earthquakes at war's end that destroyed much of the fabled city and killed Thakorr and Fen. Namor was struck with amnesia and returned to New York a wandering derelict.

Eventually, the **Human Torch** discovered Namor on the Bowery and helped restore his memories. Assuming humans had destroyed Atlantis, Namor rashly invaded New York to avenge the destruction of his homeland. Even after the survivors of the Atlantean civilization welcomed him as their rightful king, he stubbornly spent the next several years warring with the surface world, most often opposed by the **Fantastic Four**. In the midst of his campaign against humanity, Namor developed an attraction to Susan Storm, the Fantastic Four's **Invisible Woman**. In his regal arrogance, he has courted her for years, seemingly undeterred by Sue's relationship with **Mr. Fantastic**.

Ultimately, Namor realized he had to put aside his hatred of humanity for the good of his people and banned official acts of war against *Homo sapiens*. Namor even grudgingly began using his superhuman abilities in defense of the surface world. The Sub-Mariner has joined forces periodically with the **Hulk**, **Dr. Strange** and the **Silver Surfer** to oppose threats to humanity, but Namor views his duties with this loose-knit band of Defenders as a distraction at best. First and foremost, he is monarch of Atlantis. As such, he is beholden only to his subjects. Namor remains willing to take extreme action in defense of his kingdom, even if he must clash with those surface-dwellers would consider heroes.

SILVER SURFER

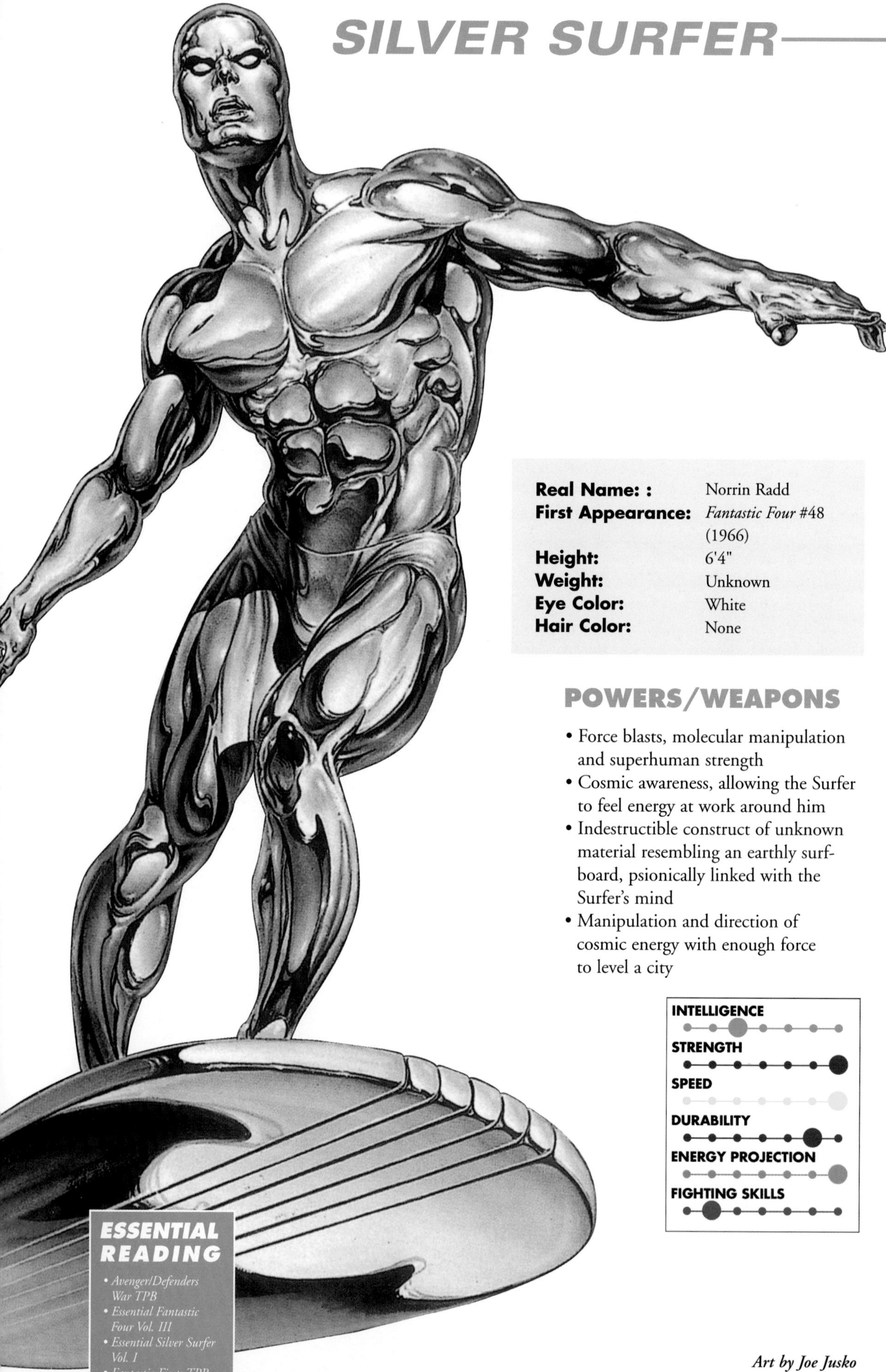

Real Name: :	Norrin Radd
First Appearance:	*Fantastic Four* #48 (1966)
Height:	6'4"
Weight:	Unknown
Eye Color:	White
Hair Color:	None

POWERS/WEAPONS

- Force blasts, molecular manipulation and superhuman strength
- Cosmic awareness, allowing the Surfer to feel energy at work around him
- Indestructible construct of unknown material resembling an earthly surfboard, psionically linked with the Surfer's mind
- Manipulation and direction of cosmic energy with enough force to level a city

INTELLIGENCE
STRENGTH
SPEED
DURABILITY
ENERGY PROJECTION
FIGHTING SKILLS

ESSENTIAL READING

- *Avenger/Defenders War TPB*
- *Essential Fantastic Four Vol. III*
- *Essential Silver Surfer Vol. I*
- *Fantastic Firsts TPB*

Art by Joe Jusko

The noble Norrin Radd was a member of an extremely long-lived race of humanoid aliens who had achieved a virtual utopia on the planet Zenn-La, eradicating disease, poverty, war and all other social ills. Growing discontent with his life of idle hedonism, Radd recognized that his culture was becoming stagnant. In his mind, men could only find fulfillment in quest, yearning and struggle. Set apart from other Zenn-Lavians by his belief in a better world, Radd alone saw through his people's false sense of security—which was shattered by the arrival of the devourer of worlds, Galactus. Radd implored Zenn-La's Council of Scientists to provide him with a spacecraft so he could rendezvous with Galactus and broker peace.

Galactus meant no malice, but only by draining Zenn-La's life energies could he satiate his awesome hunger. Having searched for sustenance too long to begin anew, Galactus mused that a herald would enable him to spare populated planets such as Zenn-La by scouting out suitable worlds for him to consume. In exchange for Zenn-La's protection, Radd selflessly agreed to serve Galactus and helped him devour countless worlds. His body atomically restructured by Galactus to suit the task, Radd set out immediately to locate a lifeless planet on which his new master could feed. The Silver Surfer discharged his duties efficiently thereafter, providing himself with as much time as possible to delight in the wonders of the universe. But the task of finding energy-rich planets devoid of sentient beings became increasingly difficult, and Galactus had gone for an extended period of time without nourishment when the Surfer entered Earth's solar system.

Essential Silver Surfer Vol. I

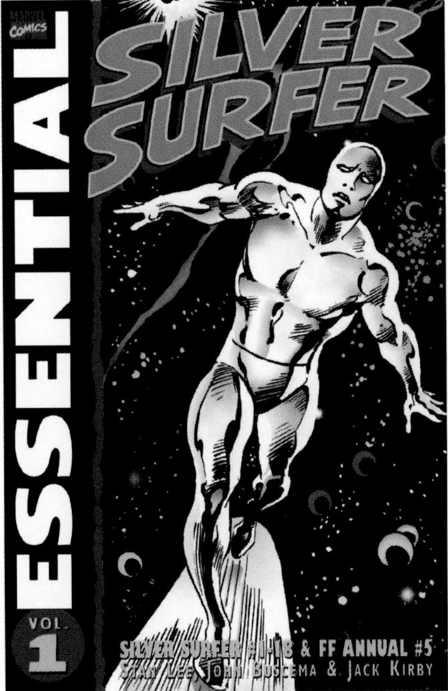

While Galactus prepared to absorb the planet's life energy, the blind sculptress Alicia Masters attempted to convince the Surfer that the beauty inherent in life on Earth was worth preserving. Moved by Alicia's words, the Surfer stood with the Fantastic Four against his master. Galactus was forced to spare Earth, but punished his insubordinate herald by erecting an energy barrier that prevented the Surfer from leaving the planet. Despite his longing to travel through outer space and his desperate attempts to escape Earth, the Surfer proved unable at first to breach Galactus' barricade. During his time on Earth, the Surfer learned to love life in all its forms. At times horrified by man's inhumanity to his fellow man, he nonetheless came to appreciate the human struggle.

The Surfer eventually escaped his exile on Earth with the aid of Mr. Fantastic, only to discover that Galactus had exacted the ultimate revenge for his subordinate's betrayal by devastating Zenn-La. Bearing a heavy burden in his heart for the loss of his former home and the life he once knew, Radd now freely soars the spaceways as a universal protector. Seeking wonder in the vast reaches of the cosmos, he returns regularly to Earth because of his close ties to the people and places of his adopted homeworld. Although he is often greatly distressed by mankind's behavior, the Surfer has developed great sympathy for the morally upright members of the human race. The Surfer has allied himself with the Fantastic Four and others among Earth's native superhuman champions. Through the years, the innocent and trusting Surfer has encountered forces, both otherworldly and earthly, that have sought to break his noble spirit and enslave him to their will. But always, the power of truth prevails—and he finds himself free once again to explore the stars.

ALICIA MASTERS

Real Name:	Alicia Reiss Masters	**Weight:**	110 lbs.
First Appearance:	*Fantastic Four* #8 (1962)	**Eye Color:**	Blue
Height:	5'4"	**Hair Color:**	Reddish-blonde

The blind stepdaughter of the Puppet Master, Alicia Masters first encountered the Fantastic Four when her father attempted to control their minds in a bid for power. Attracted to the Thing's inner nobility and warm heart, Alicia fell in love with Ben Grimm despite the fact that others perceived him to be a monster.

Following her father's apparent death, Alicia swiftly earned a reputation as the finest sculptor of her generation. Politicians, royalty and other dignitaries often commissioned her work. Not limited by sight, Alicia's representations are uncannily apt, capturing a subject's inner being.

Art by Jae Lee

Some time after she and Ben began dating, the Silver Surfer landed on the rooftop skylight of Alicia's studio, heralding the imminent arrival of Galactus. Alicia helped the Surfer to see the beauty of Earth and all its creatures, and convinced him the planet did not deserve to die simply to satisfy Galactus' hunger. The Surfer agreed, rising up against his master as a result.

Alicia and Ben continued their romance for years, but he never asked her to marry him. He was convinced she loved him only out of pity for his condition—as a freak, not as a man. Feeling a need to move on with her life, Alicia broke off the relationship. Ben, convinced they could never have a normal existence together, agreed. They remain close friends, however.

Alicia is a unique spirit in the lives of all she knows. Thanks to her relationship with Ben and her gentle, compassionate nature, she has become close friends with the Fantastic Four, and they regard her as they would a member of their own family.

ESSENTIAL READING

- *Essential Fantastic Four Vols. I-III*
- *Fantastic Four: Into the Breach TPB*
- *Fantastic Four Visionaries: John Byrne TPB*
- *Fantastic Four: 1234 TPB*

FRANKLIN RICHARDS

Real Name:	Franklin Benjamin Richards	**Weight:**	40 lbs.
First Appearance:	*Fantastic Four Annual* #6 (1968)	**Eye Color:**	Blue
Height:	3'5"	**Hair Color:**	Blond

Franklin Richards is the son of Reed and Sue Richards—better known as Mr. Fantastic and Invisible Woman of the Fantastic Four—and potentially one of the world's most powerful and dangerous mutants. An unusually brave, exceptionally smart 7-year-old, Franklin knows just how lucky he is: The Fantastic Four is the world's coolest family. He lives in the Baxter Building, surrounded by time machines, robots, spaceships and flying cars, and hangs out with heroes like Spider-Man, Daredevil and the Avengers. When Franklin's parents go away on business, they're more likely to bring him a soil sample from the other-dimensional Negative Zone than a token T-shirt.

If there's a downside to life with the Fantastic Four, it's that the cosmic radiation that gifted Reed and Sue with superhuman powers also affected their son's genetic structure. Unlike most mutants, whose unusual talents remain latent until puberty, Franklin began to manifest his abilities at a very early age. He has shown signs of telepathy, telekinesis, precognition and the power to rearrange molecules—but mental blocks were put in place to prevent him from accessing his vast psionic potential until he has achieved the necessary psychological maturity. Nevertheless, Reed must remain forever vigilant for the eventual emergence of his son's powers, for fear Franklin could unwittingly release sufficient psionic energy to destroy all life on Earth.

It has been speculated that humanity is evolving into a race of superhuman beings with great psionic powers, and Franklin may be an early example of what mankind someday will become. Despite bearing the evolutionary promise of future generations on his young shoulders, Franklin has weathered the tempest of his tremendous talents to remain a normal, well-adjusted child...whose parents happen to be the heart and soul of Earth's first family of superhuman adventurers.

ESSENTIAL READING

- *Fantastic Four Visionaries: John Byrne TPB*
- *Fantastic Four Vol. 1: Imaginauts TPB*

DOCTOR DOOM

Real Name: Victor Von Doom
First Appearance: *Fantastic Four* #5 (1962)
Height: 6'2"
Weight: 225 lbs.
Eye Color: Brown
Hair Color: Brown

Art by Alex Ross

ESSENTIAL READING

- *Doom TPB*
- *Essential Fantastic Four Vols. I-III*
- *Fantastic Four Visionaries: John Byrne TPB*
- *The Villainy of Dr. Doom TPB*

Hardened by adversity, Victor Von Doom knows all too well what it is to be misunderstood and forsaken, hunted and despised. Orphaned at a young age, he was raised by gypsies in the small Balkan nation of Latveria—constantly on the move, with no place to call home. Anguished by his parents' passing, the young Doom vowed to make the entire world pay for his loss. Through years of intense study, the determined youth amassed a wealth of scientific and mystical knowledge. Even as Doom's obsession with power and vengeance grew, his academic pursuits and astounding reputation earned him a full scholarship to the State University in New York. There, the brilliant but arrogant Doom first encountered Reed Richards, similarly gifted but humble to a fault. Richards represented a substantial threat to Doom's self-perceived superiority, and the two became bitter rivals.

Essential Fantastic Four Vol. II

Ultimately, Doom was undone by his ego, which prevented him from adjusting the schematics to one of his early inventions: a trans-dimensional projection device. The machine worked perfectly ...for two minutes, 37 seconds. Then, Doom experienced the end result of his pride: an explosion that injured his face. Although Richards had pointed out his classmate's miscalculations prior to the mishap, Doom refused to acknowledge his own culpability. Instead, he blamed Richards for the accident. It was easier for Doom to believe his rival had sabotaged his work out of jealousy than admit to his own imperfection.

While convalescing, Doom discovered that the blast had left him with a long, thin scar. The vain Doom believed this slight injury had in fact totally disfigured his face. Expelled from college for his hazardous extra-dimensional experiment, he traveled the world swathed in bandages—a kind of living mummy, searching for a miracle cure. Eventually, Doom discovered a village of Tibetan monks, who crafted a suit of armor and metal mask to hide his perceived deformity. In his urgent desire to proceed with his plans for conquest and revenge, Doom donned his newly cast faceplate before it had completely cooled, permanently damaging his entire face. His scarred countenance concealed and his body sheathed in the monk's nigh-impenetrable armor, Doom returned to Latveria. Overthrowing the standing government, he installed himself as absolute monarch.

Ruling with an iron fist and an equally strong will, Doom established a nation of peace and prosperity. As Latveria thrived under Doom's reign, the megalomaniacal dictator began to believe he could extend his success to Earth's other nations.

POWERS/ WEAPONS

- Extremely advanced, virtually impregnable armor
- Force-field generator
- Variety of built-in offensive weapons
- Knowledge of the mystic arts

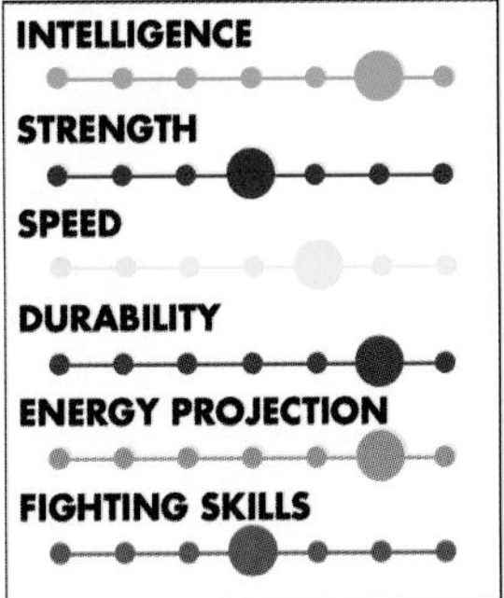

Consequently, he began to redirect the small nation's resources to help him realize his designs of world domination. To Doom, the world's leaders are nothing, inferiors to be cast aside in favor of his global vision. Eventually, Doom's machinations brought him into conflict with Richards—now famous as Mr. Fantastic, leader of the Fantastic Four. Richards and his teammates have been Doom's most frequent opponents through the years. Now, Doom's dreams of world conquest are equalled only by his desire to destroy the Fantastic Four.

Despite countless attempts, Doom's defeats of Richards have been few and far between—and never complete or lasting. Doom's belief in his own superiority frequently proves to be his undoing, as his overconfidence and hubris blind him to his own failings. He has, however, bested his bitter rival on at least one occasion, scoring a major psychological victory when he was called upon to save the life of Richards' wife Sue and their second child. Conceived in an other-dimensional realm, the unborn child had begun emitting high-intensity waves of negative energy. The Human Torch knew his sister and the baby would die without help. With Richards detained by outside forces, Doom was his best and only hope. Johnny Storm pleaded with his family's greatest enemy to put aside their past differences so Invisible Woman and her child would have even the smallest chance for survival. Seizing the opportunity, Doom saved both their lives through a combination of science and sorcery, inflating the armored autocrat's ego and sending his self-confidence soaring. Indebted to Doom, Sue agreed to let him name the child; he then placed Valeria under his royal protection. Now, every time Reed looks at his daughter and wife, he will remember that Doom saved them both when he could not.

Art by Leonardo Manco

Art by Glenn Fabry

GALACTUS

Real Name:	Galan
First Appearance:	*Fantastic Four* #48 (1966)
Height:	28' 9"
Weight:	18.2 tons
Eye Color:	Unknown
Hair Color:	Black

Art by Alex Ross

ESSENTIAL READING

- *Essential Fantastic Four Vol. III*
- *Marvels TPB*

The humanoid named Galan was born in the universe that existed before this one on the planet Taa, home to the most advanced civilization among all the stars. But as his society ascended to the pinnacle of prosperity, creation itself stood on the verge of collapse. The dense sphere of planet-forming, primordial matter propelled outward billions upon billions of years before by the force of a cataclysmic Big Bang had begun to recede, with equally catastrophic results. Grasping the inevitability of his planet's demise, Galan led his people's exodus via starship into the heart of the dying universe. As the vessel approached its final destination, its crew began to succumb to the lethal effects of radiation poisoning. But the sentience of the dying universe spared Galan the fate of his fellow passengers. They both would die, the entity revealed, only to be born anew. The cosmic sentience absorbed Galan into itself—bringing into being Galactus, insatiable ravager of worlds.

Art by Alex Ross

Time passed beyond reckoning. Hurled outward by a second Big Bang, Galactus drifted for eons as life began to flourish. An enigmatic, god-like being whose existence defies human comprehension and logic, Galactus discovered he could satiate his awesome hunger only by feasting upon the raw energies of unsuspecting planets, leaving them lifeless and barren. He meant no malice, but his very nature drove him to act. Though at first compassionate enough to devour only uninhabited worlds, Galactus could not be so selective to survive. To avoid the destruction of inhabited planets, he enlisted the Silver Surfer as his herald. An advance scout, the Surfer would locate energy-rich, lifeless worlds for his master to consume.

As time passed, however, it became increasingly difficult for the Surfer to find suitable worlds devoid of sentient beings. Galactus eventually grew determined to consume the energy-rich planet Earth but was turned back by a rebellious Surfer and the Fantastic Four under the threat of the Ultimate Nullifier, an alien device powerful enough even to eradicate the ravager of worlds. Galactus was forced to spare Earth, but punished his insubordinate herald by erecting an energy barrier that prevented the Surfer from leaving the planet.

Galactus has returned on several occasions to devour Earth, only to be deterred by the planet's superhuman champions. Feared as a menace to all starfaring races, he has ravaged numerous inhabited worlds throughout the known universe to slake his hunger. But Galactus's craving for energy is all-consuming, and it's only a matter of time before his overwhelming appetite brings him back to Earth.

POWERS/ WEAPONS

- Matter Manipulation
- Force blasts
- Teleportation
- Force-fields
- Telepathy

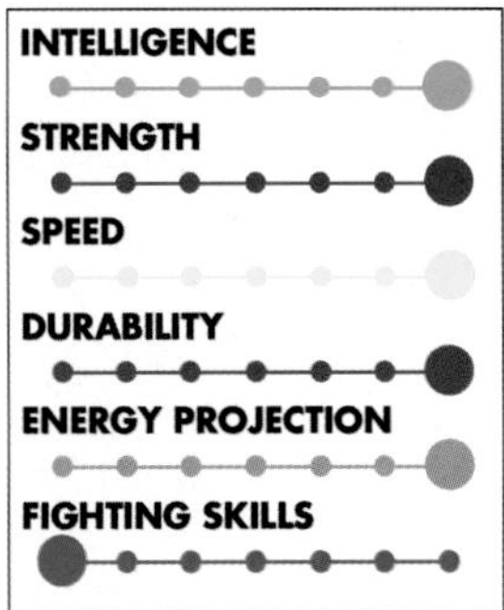

KREE/SKRULL WAR

Like virtually all wars, the interstellar conflict between the humanoid Kree and shape-shifting Skrulls grew out of wounded pride. While earthlings still lived in caves, the empire-building Skrulls chose to recognize the passive, plant-based Cotati as the dominant lifeform on the Kree homeworld. Insulted and infuriated, the Kree killed the Skrull scouts and seized their starship. Reverse-engineering the vessel, the Kree developed advanced technology and space-travel capabilities in a matter of years. They then attacked the Skrulls, touching off a millennia-long war.

Under the relentless Kree offensive, the commerce-oriented Skrull culture became more and more militaristic. Evenly matched, the races began to take increasingly drastic measures to gain the upper hand in the struggle. Today, few Kree or Skrulls even remember what touched off the conflict. Hate for the other has become part of the unquestioned natural order for each race.

The Kree/Skrull war has not been without collateral damage. Both races have been aware of Earth for eons, and envoys from each have traveled to the planet numerous times. Due to its proximity to a natural warp in the space-time continuum allowing for faster-than-light travel and its location between the races' homeworlds, Earth is of great strategic value to the Kree and Skrulls. Given the planet's significance, its heroes have been drawn into numerous skirmishes between the Kree and the Skrulls. Too often, the war between the two has threatened Earth's safety and security.

Because of each race's obsession with the other's annihilation, both cultures have lost all forward momentum, and both empires are widely corrupt and crumbling. There have been temporary truces and brief alliances between the two races to battle larger threats, but war has always returned.

ESSENTIAL READING

- *Avengers: Kree/Skrull War TPB*
- *Essential Fantastic Four Vols. I-III*

Kree art by Scott Kolins (top); Skrull art by ChrisCross

SUPER-SKRULL

Real Name:	Kl'rt	**Weight:**	625 lbs.
First Appearance:	*Fantastic Four #18* (1963)	**Eye Color:**	Green
Height:	6'	**Hair Color:**	None

Following the Fantastic Four's swift defeat of a Skrull invasion force, the alien empire poured its resources into the development of a warrior capable of defeating Earth's preeminent defenders single-handedly. After months of work, Skrull scientists presented their emperor with a genetically re-engineered super-soldier able to simulate the combined abilities of the Fantastic Four. Pleased with the fruits of his subordinates' labor, the emperor unleashed the Super-Skrull to destroy the Fantastic Four.

The Skrulls had underestimated the might of Earth's heroes, however. Suffering defeat after defeat at the hands of the Fantastic Four and others, the Super-Skrull fell out of favor with his superiors. Nevertheless, he was recalled to active duty repeatedly when circumstances required his brute strength and warrior's cunning.

The Skrull empire has used the Super-Skrull as both a tool and a weapon. Despite his poor service record, he seeks to improve himself following each defeat. Since the destruction of the Skrull homeworld by Galactus, the Super-Skrull has been a soldier without a clear mission. While he has undertaken assignments for the remnants of the Skrull empire, Kl'rt has purposely maintained a low profile. Recognizing the Super-Skrull as a significant threat due to his allegiance to the ways of the old regime, various progressive factions have dispatched assassins to terminate the warrior before he can claim control of the empire's remnants by force. His reasons and motivations his own, the Super-Skrull remains in disguise on Earth, learning more about his enemies and biding his time.

POWERS/WEAPONS

- Able to stretch any part of his body farther than Mr. Fantastic
- Manipulation and generation of fire
- Invisibility and the projection of invisible force fields
- Able to manifest the rocky hide of the Thing and duplicate his superhuman strength
- Projection of hypnotic energy patterns from his eyes
- Shapeshifting

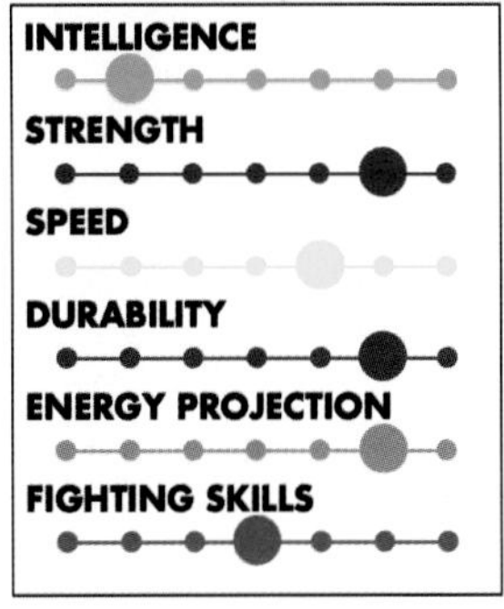

ESSENTIAL READING

- *Essential Fantastic Four Vols. I-III*
- *Fantastic Four: Flesh and Stone TPB*

Art by Carlos Pacheco

MK/MAX

ON THE MEAN STREETS OF MARVEL KNIGHTS, THE KID GLOVES COME OFF

Guardian devils, vengeance-crazed vigilantes and enigmatic assassins stalk the city's dark underbelly, and the urban action unfolds with gritty intensity.

Daredevil, blind lawyer by day, struggles night after night to safeguard Hell's Kitchen, suffering and grief his only companions. The Punisher, merciless scourge of the underworld, cuts a swath of destruction through crime and corruption in New York City and beyond. Elektra, a killer-for-hire who knows firsthand the chill of the grave, always draws first blood.

Ramping up the action and intensity, MAX Comics presents hard-hitting stories with unabashedly adult sensibilities. From the killing fields of the Third World to the concrete canyons of New York, the good, the bad and the ugly fight for their very survival sans spandex and superhuman powers.

Marvel Knights and MAX push the envelope of the traditional storytelling, tempering action and adventure with palpable realism and edgy drama that shines a light on the dark corners and back alleys of the Marvel Universe.

Art by Joe Quesada

BLACK WIDOW

Real Name:	Natasha Romanov	**Weight:**	125 lbs.
First Appearance:	*Tales of Suspense* #52 (1964)	**Eye Color:**	Green
Height:	5'7"	**Hair Color:**	Red-auburn

Abandoned as a child, Natasha Romanov was found and raised by soldier Ivan Petrovitch. She matured into a brilliant scholar and an exceptional athlete, earning fame as a ballerina. Throughout her life, various masters have tugged at Natasha's loyal nature—first her husband, renowned test pilot Alexi Shostakov, then the KGB, which determined that the two would make exemplary special operatives. Informed of the state's plans, Alexi was permitted no further contact with friends and relatives, including his wife.

Believing her husband had died, a distraught Natasha sought to follow a patriotic path worthy of his heroic memory. Having anticipated such a reaction, the KGB forged its naïve new recruit into a Soviet super-spy at the Moscow-based covert-training academy known as the Red Room. The Widow was a frequent ally of **Hawkeye**, but her growing love for the future hero weakened her resolve to engage in further subversive activities. After Hawkeye successfully sought membership in the **Avengers**, Natasha defected to the United States and offered her services to S.H.I.E.L.D. Her romance with Hawkeye eventually ended, as did a subsequent love affair with **Daredevil**—but she remains close friends with both men.

Natasha is moral and trustworthy, but understands fully the savagery of the spy trade. Betrayed by the country of her birth, she refuses to be a pawn. As the Red Room's greatest legend, Natasha struggles against the perception that she is a relic from another era. In fact, some believe the Widow to be Cold War propaganda. Fighting such feelings of mortality, Natasha maintains her a reputation as a consummate professional—coldly efficient and as deadly as her namesake.

POWERS/WEAPONS

- Olympic-level athlete and gymnast
- Master martial artist
- Extensive espionage training and experience

ESSENTIAL READING

- *Avengers: The Morgan Conquest TPB*
- *Black Widow TPB*
- *Daredevil Visionaries: Kevin Smith TPB*
- *Essential Avengers Vol. II*

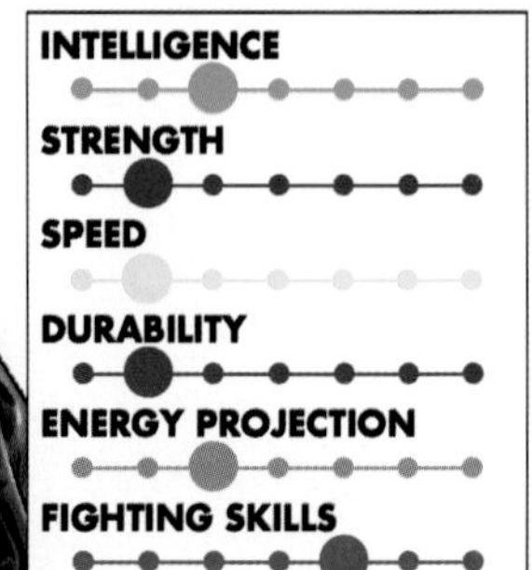

Art by J.G. Jones

Real Name:	Captain Yelena Belova	**Weight:**	135 lbs.
First Appearance:	*Black Widow* #1 (1999)	**Eye Color:**	Blue
Height:	5'7"	**Hair Color:**	Blonde

The second woman to claim the mantle of Black Widow, Yelena Belova is also a graduate of the Moscow-based covert-training academy known as the Red Room. Hostile to her predecessor Natasha Romanov, Yelena has been conditioned to believe that the designation is hers by right. Unwavering in her loyalty to Mother Russia, Yelena feels that Natasha abandoned her homeland when she defected to America and became a super hero. Hungry and passionate, Yelena has not forgotten what the Black Widow should be at her core: a spy.

Training for the role since she was 15, Yelena was the first student in the history of the Red Room to match Natasha's marks. She may lack the original Widow's experience, but Yelena is Natasha's equal or better in every other respect—or so it says on paper. Yet living in the shadow of a legend, the young Widow fears deep down that she is inadequate to the task; she is driven by an almost obsessive need to prove her worth to her superiors, —and to herself.

Eager for the chance to better Natasha and finally stake her claim to the title of Black Widow, Yelena attempted to intervene when her predecessor embarked on a mission to retrieve a deadly new bio-weapon from a terrorist nation. Yelena sought to secure the lethal serum before Natasha and then eliminate her adversary. Relying on experience and superior planning, the original Widow outmaneuvered her young opponent and completed the assignment. A subsequent encounter saw the two Widows exchange physical appearances as part of a carefully orchestrated deception initiated by Natasha, who sought to save Yelena from her masters.

Yelena is naïve, easily tricked and far too trusting. Her superiors in the GRU wield her like a weapon, playing on her patriotism and love of Mother Russia. If she is lost to them, they feel they can always make another Black Widow.

Art by J.G. Jones

INTELLIGENCE

STRENGTH

SPEED

DURABILITY

ENERGY PROJECTION

FIGHTING SKILLS

POWERS/ WEAPONS

- Olympic-level athlete and gymnast
- Master martial artist
- Extensive espionage training

BLADE

Real Name:	Eric; last name unrevealed
First Appearance:	*Tomb of Dracula* #10 (1973)
Height:	6'2"
Weight:	180 lbs.
Eye Color:	Brown
Hair Color:	Black

POWERS/WEAPONS

- Superhuman strength, senses and stamina
- Accelerated healing factor
- Master martial artist
- Automatic and semi-automatic firearms converted for use with hollow-point, garlic-filled silver bullets
- Titanium, acid-etched sword
- Kevlar body armor
- Custom-designed arsenal of portable weapons that employ silver, garlic, sunlight, ultraviolet rays and anti-coagulants

INTELLIGENCE
STRENGTH
SPEED
DURABILITY
ENERGY PROJECTION
FIGHTING SKILLS

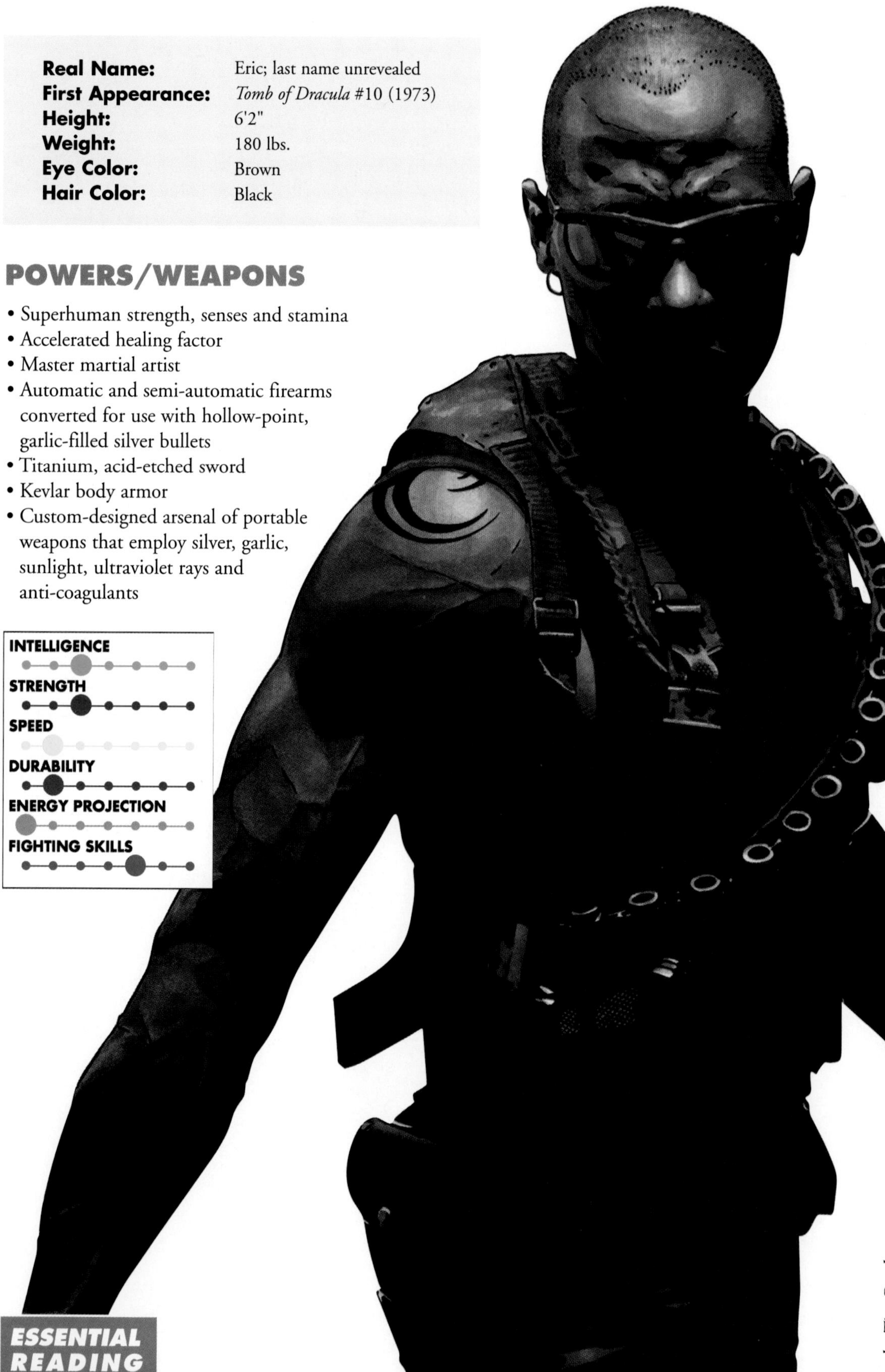

Art by Tim Bradstreet

ESSENTIAL READING

- *Blade II Movie Adaptation TPB*

Half vampire, half human, the tortured soul known only as Blade came into the world an orphan. His mother, bitten by the vampire Deacon Frost while she was pregnant, died during childbirth. Abraham Whistler, whose family had also been killed by vampires, found Blade living on the streets when he was 13. Blade was feeding on the homeless, the hunger for blood having taken hold at puberty. Mistaking the boy for a vampire, Whistler almost killed Blade before he realized he was a half-breed.

Fueled by a constant craving for vengeance against the creatures that tainted his humanity and murdered his mother, Blade fashioned himself into a vampire hunter even before reaching adulthood. Under Whistler's tutelage, he honed his combat skills to lethal perfection.

Due to the circumstances of his birth, Blade's body has undergone certain genetic mutations. He possesses a vampire's superhuman strength and accelerated healing factor, but can withstand garlic, silver and sunlight, and still ages like a normal human. Blade also inherited a thirst for blood, which he suppresses with a synthetic serum. All efforts to find a permanent cure have failed, and he overcomes his craving through sheer force of will. Neither human nor vampire, Blade is forever cursed to walk between worlds. A half-breed, he struggles to overcome his inhuman nature—and his self-loathing over what he was and is, and what he was forced to do to survive.

The legendary "Daywalker" may be humanity's last, best hope for survival against the army of bloodthirsty, immortal vampires that have infiltrated every layer of society—police, industry, even the hallowed halls of government. *Homo sapiens* are only the most visible creatures. Underneath is *Homonus nocturna*, vampires, forming a loose confederation of clans, plus a few outlaws. To them, humans are food—nothing more, nothing less. War has been declared, and mankind is the endangered species. Blade and his allies move from city to city, tracking their migrations, trying to keep the bloody battle from spilling over into the streets.

Art by Bart Sears

A loner by nature, Blade has formed uneasy alliances with his fellow hunters. But too many of those who have grown close to the stoic soldier have lost their lives to his quest—often slain in bloody, futile battle. Years of painstaking effort can have no effect on quarry with a talent for regeneration. Still, Blade perseveres—beginning his crusade anew with each failure. The loss of his allies has only served to strengthen Blade's resolve to rid the world of vampires, regardless of the circumstances of their creation. Even the death of Deacon Frost—his mother's murderer, and the vampire responsible for his own transformation—did not diminish Blade's determined rage. There's still a war going on, and he has a job to do.

LUKE CAGE

Real Name:	Luke Cage	**Weight:**	425 lbs.
First Appearance:	*Luke Cage, Hero for Hire* #1 (1972)	**Eye Color:**	Brown
Height:	6'6"	**Hair Color:**	Black

Art by Richard Corben

ESSENTIAL READING

- *Cage Vol. 1 HC*

Luke Cage learned to be a man on the streets of Harlem. Most often, he could be found fleeing the scene of a petty crime with childhood friend Willis Stryker. But as the two matured, Cage took odd jobs to earn money, while Stryker turned to crime as a profession. The young men also become rivals for the affections of Reva Connors, who chose Cage over Stryker. Insanely jealous, Stryker planted two kilograms of heroin in Cage's apartment and tipped off the police. After Cage was arrested and incarcerated, Reva was killed in a mob hit targeting Stryker. From prison, Cage swore vengeance against his former friend. Consumed with rage, he frequently engaged in brawls and attempted escape.

Art by Richard Corben

Cage's reprehensible behavior landed him in Seagate, a maximum-security facility in Georgia. He was approached by research psychologist Noah Bernstein, who promised to help him secure parole in exchange for participation in an experiment to test a chemical method of promoting human cell regeneration as an aid against disease and aging. Although suspicious at first, Cage agreed. Once the process had begun, racist correctional officer Albert Rackham ignorantly manipulated the machine's controls hoping to either maim or kill Cage. Rackham unintentionally advanced the experiment beyond its original design, inducing a body-wide mutagenic effect that enhanced Cage's body tissue and strength. Cage freed himself and knocked Rackham unconscious. Thinking he had killed the guard, he fled.

Returning to New York to confront Stryker, Cage interrupted a robbery at a diner. When the owner offered him a cash reward, Cage was inspired to put his newfound powers to use for profit. Motivated more by survival of the fittest than his desire to do good, he established himself as Luke Cage, Hero for Hire. After Cage put the demons of his past behind him by bringing down Stryker, his enterprise began to turn a sufficient profit.

POWERS/ WEAPONS

- Superhuman strength
- Abnormally dense muscle and bone tissue
- Steel-hard skin

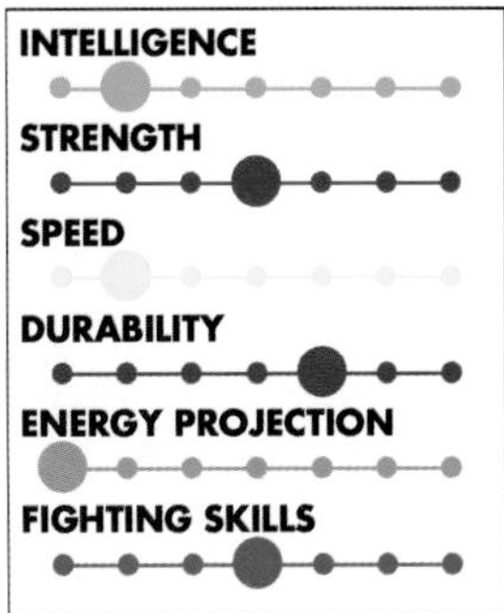

Several years later, the European crime lord Bushmaster coerced Cage into kidnapping private investigator Misty Knight in exchange for the life of Dr. Bernstein, whom he held captive. As further incentive, Bushmaster offered evidence that Stryker had planted the drugs in Cage's apartment. Learning of Cage's predicament, Knight and her friend Iron Fist agreed to help him defeat Bushmaster. After rescuing Dr. Bernstein and recovering the evidence of his innocence, Cage was acquitted of the crime that had dogged him for years. Although their backgrounds and temperaments were diametrically opposed, Cage and Iron Fist soon became close friends and formed a new Heroes for Hire agency.

A shrewd businessman Cage is not. Given a choice between turning a profit and doing what's right, Cage ultimately will opt for the latter. A come-from-behind hero, he has proven he can overcome any obstacle through tenacity and sheer force of will.

DAREDEVIL

Real Name:	Matthew Michael Murdock	**Weight:**	200 lbs.
First Appearance:	*Daredevil #1* (1964)	**Eye Color:**	Blue
Height:	6'	**Hair Color:**	Red

Art by Joe Quesada

The son of a small-time boxer, Matt Murdock was taught by his father that fighting was not the answer to life's problems. A poorly educated but noble man, Battlin' Jack Murdock encouraged his son to achieve great things with his mind, rather than his fists. Idolizing his father, Matt took the advice to heart. As a result, his fellow students mockingly dubbed the introverted bookworm "Daredevil." Humiliated, Matt began training without his father's knowledge so he could stand up to the bullies in school.

Daredevil #1, April 1964

As raised by his father, Matt was selflessly noble. This was never more apparent than when he pushed an elderly man out of the path of a runaway truck. Matt's kindness was cruelly repaid by fate when radioactive waste from the vehicle's payload splashed onto his eyes, blinding him. Devastated at first by his apparent handicap, Matt slowly came to realize that the accident had radically augmented his ability to perceive the world around him. His vision was gone, but the radioactivity had heightened his other senses to a superhuman degree.

Unable to adjust to his overdeveloped senses, the terrified Matt eventually came under the tutelage of the blind martial-arts master Stick. A stern, unrelenting taskmaster, Stick educated Matt in both the spiritual and physical aspects of the martial arts, refusing to let him think of himself as a helpless victim. Matt emerged as an Olympic-class gymnast and formidable hand-to-hand combatant.

As a student at Columbia University Law School, Matt met and fell in love with **Elektra** Natchios, the daughter of a Greek diplomat. Their happiness was shattered when Elektra's father died during a hostage crisis. Elektra withdrew emotionally from both Matt and the world at large. Fleeing to the Far East, she buried her feelings and honed her fighting skills to razor-sharp perfection.

The loss of Elektra wasn't the only pain Matt would suffer during his college years. Past his prime as a fighter, Jack Murdock had fallen in with a shady crowd and was ultimately murdered for refusing to throw a fight. Not satisfied with the police investigation, Matt hid his identity beneath a mask and took it upon himself to track down the criminals who had set up and murdered his father. Taking the name Daredevil, he brought those responsible to justice.

Finding satisfaction and release in his extracurricular activities, Matt adopted the costumed identity on a permanent basis. During the day, he worked within the judicial system, aided by college roommate and fellow attorney Foggy Nelson. But at night, freed from the constraints of the courtroom, Matt pursued those criminals who had slipped through the system's cracks. For a time, he knew happiness as Daredevil, living out his fantasies as a swashbuckling crimefighter.

But Daredevil's efforts to undermine New York's crime infrastructure attracted the attention of the **Kingpin**, who made it his personal mission to destroy the hero. Hiring Elektra as his chief

DAREDEVIL

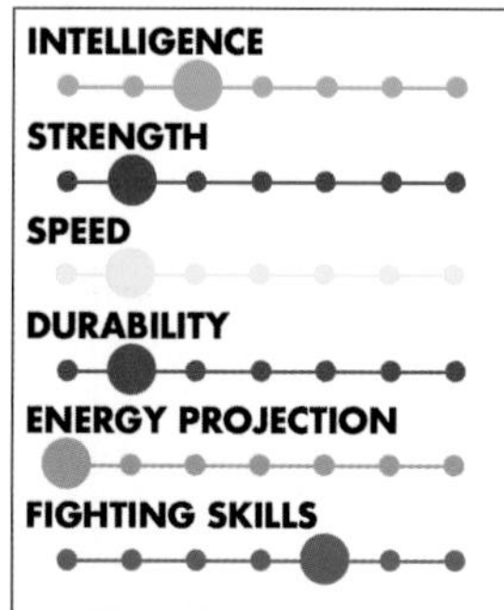

POWERS/ WEAPONS

- Superhumanly acute senses of touch, smell, taste and hearing
- Radar-like "proximity sense"
- Expert martial artist and boxer
- Two billy clubs, used in both offense and defense

assassin, the Kingpin set in motion a chain of events that led to her death at the hands of **Bullseye**. Although she later returned to life, Elektra's murder nearly crippled Matt emotionally—touching off a vicious cycle of violence, loss and pain.

After years of relative détentè between the two, the Kingpin once again struck at Daredevil when he learned the hero's true identity from Matt's drug-addicted ex-lover Karen Page. The Kingpin virtually destroyed Matt's life before the crime lord's own arrogance resulted in his undoing. Matt and Karen rekindled their relationship, but he suffered a devastating personal tragedy when Bullseye killed her with Daredevil's own billy club in a battle orchestrated by **Mysterio**.

Matt's pain and guilt over the losses in his life have replaced his earlier motivations, fueling his battles as Daredevil long after any reasonable man would have quit the fight. In the wake of so many deaths, Matt's suffering and grief are his only constant companions. Night after night, he struggles to safeguard Hell's Kitchen—seeking absolution and forgiveness from those who have long since lost the ability to clear his conscience.

ESSENTIAL READING

- *Essential Daredevil Vol. I*
- *Daredevil Visionaries: Frank Miller Vols. I-III TPB*
- *Daredevil: Born Again TPB*
- *Daredevil: Man Without Fear TPB*
- *Daredevil: Yellow HC*
- *Daredevil Visionaries: Kevin Smith TPB*
- *Daredevil Vol. II: Parts of a Hole TPB*
- *Daredevil Vol. III: Wake Up TPB*
- *Daredevil Vol. IV: Underboss TPB*
- *Daredevil Vol. V: Out TPB*

Art by Joe Quesada

Art by Alex Maleev

DOCTOR STRANGE

Real Name:	Dr. Stephen Strange	**Weight:**	180 lbs.
First Appearance:	*Strange Tales* #110 (1963)	**Eye Color:**	Gray
Height:	6'2"	**Hair Color:**	Black, with gray streaks at the temples

ESSENTIAL READING

- *Essential Dr. Strange Vol. I*
- *Dr. Strange: A Separate Reality TPB*
- *Avengers/Defenders War TPB*

Art by Jae Lee

Stephen Strange was a brilliant but arrogant neurosurgeon whose meteoric career was cut short by an auto accident. Strange sustained minor nerve damage, which prevented him from holding a scalpel steadily enough to perform delicate surgery. He invested his fortune in attempted cures and fraudulent doctors, and saw it dwindle to nothing. In short order, Strange degenerated from recluse to drifter to drunken derelict. Hitting rock bottom, he heard whispers of a learned miracle worker in Tibet known only as the Ancient One.

Art by Jae Lee

Determined and desperate, Strange made his way across the ocean and traversed the frozen wastes of the Himalayan Mountains, where he stumbled upon the Ancient One's palace. Strange was a selfish, broken man clinging feverishly to his former life and hoping against hope for a miracle cure. Still, the aged sorcerer saw a spark of good in his soul, as well as the potential for great power. Unwilling to waste his magic on the undeserving, the Ancient One told Strange he would only consider helping him if he proved himself worthy. Refusing to believe in the Ancient One's magic, Strange declined to look within himself for redemption.

Remaining as a guest while a bitter storm spent itself outside, Strange discovered that the Ancient One's pupil Baron Mordo was plotting to kill his mentor. When he attempted to warn the Ancient One of his student's treachery, Strange was mystically restrained by Mordo. Confronting Mordo's power and uncovering his murderous intentions shocked the jaded Strange into a realization of evil's true nature and the need to combat its forces. Strange sought a way around the enchantment that prevented him from warning the Ancient One by offering to become his pupil. He reasoned that if he learned the secrets of black magic, he could battle Mordo himself. Knowing that he had reached the real Stephen Strange at last, the Ancient One freed him from Mordo's spell and revealed that he had known of his student's treacherous plans all along.

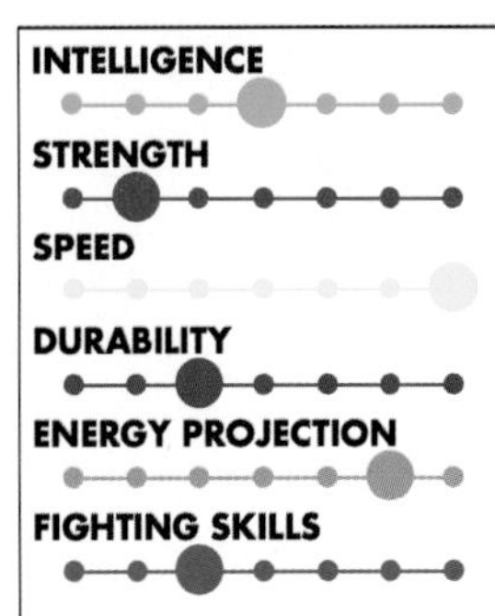

Strange had made a choice to change, and so the Ancient One adopted him as his disciple and taught him the secrets of sorcery. Slowly, Strange's life took on a deeper meaning as he prepared himself for the epic battles ahead. When his studies had reached an end, he returned to America and established his Sanctum Sanctorum in New York City's Greenwich Village.

When the Ancient One died, Strange inherited from his mentor the mantle of Earth's Sorcerer Supreme. Though the world at large believes he is no more than an eccentric authority on the occult, Strange defends the planet from mystic menaces, godlike entities and other unseen forces that threaten to breach the boundaries between our world and other-dimensional anarchy. Having overcome his personal demons, Strange now works diligently to strengthen the barriers between our world and countless other hostile realms.

POWERS/WEAPONS

- Master of the mystic arts
- Astral projection
- Cloak of Levitation
- The Eye of Agamotto, which enables Strange to see through disguises, invoke images of the immediate past, track both corporeal and ethereal entities by their psychic and magical emissions, probe the minds of sentient beings, and open gateways into other dimensions

ELEKTRA

Real Name:	Elektra Natchios	**Weight:**	130 lbs.
First Appearance:	*Daredevil* #168 (1980)	**Eye Color:**	Blue-black
Height:	5'9"	**Hair Color:**	Black

Art by Greg Horn

ESSENTIAL READING

- *Daredevil Visionaries: Frank Miller Vols. II & III TPB*
- *Elektra: Assassin TPB*
- *Elektra Lives Again HC*
- *Elektra & Wolverine: The Redeemer HC*
- *Elektra Vol. I: Introspect TPB*
- *Elektra: The Scorpio Key TPB*

Elektra once defined herself by the men in her life: She was the daughter of a powerful Greek diplomat and the girlfriend of blind American law student Matt Murdock. When her father was accidentally killed during a hostage crisis, Elektra was emotionally shattered and withdrew from the civilized world. Alone and angry, she set out in search of meaning and purpose, guidance and training.

Daredevil Visionaries: Frank Miller Vol. II TPB

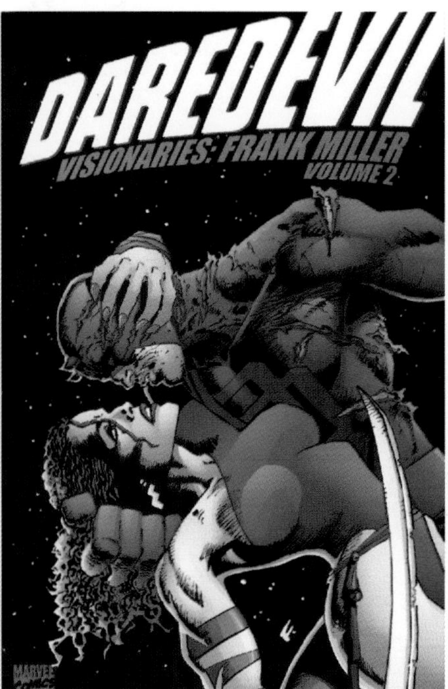

Elektra's quest led her abroad, where she studied the martial arts with a sensei in Japan. In search of a true and total peace of spirit, Elektra later joined the noble order of warriors led by Stick. She honed her fighting skills to the peak of human perfection, but Stick saw that Elektra was filled with pain over her father's death and with hatred for the world she blamed for it. He expelled her from his order, and she found herself alone once again.

Still determined to prove herself to Stick, Elektra infiltrated the Hand, a cult of ninja devoted to assassination and domination by fear, intending to subvert their activities. As a test, the Hand abducted and drugged Elektra's former sensei. Concealing his identity under cover of darkness, the ninja engineered a confrontation between the old man and Elektra. When Elektra's sai pierced his flesh, her opponent's true face was revealed. In that instant, Elektra knew she would never know true peace. Her hatred had found a home: It made her the perfect warrior. The Hand trained and guided her, twisting her soul, but Elektra never turned completely. Eventually, she rebelled against the Hand and fled Japan.

A bounty hunter and assassin for hire, Elektra sold her talent and rage on the open market. Having undertaken a contract in New York City, she crossed paths with Daredevil—whom she later learned to be Matt, her only weakness. Although Matt vehemently disapproved of Elektra's chosen profession, the two still cared deeply for one another. But fate had forever cast them apart. As far as Elektra was concerned, their love had been murdered along with her father.

Together, they fought the Hand, until the Kingpin hired Elektra as his chief assassin. In that role, Elektra clashed repeatedly with Daredevil. Lovers became enemies, fighting for the fate of an entire city. Matt wanted nothing more than to lay down arms—but Elektra was at war with herself, attempting to reconcile her past life with present circumstances. When she was ordered to kill Matt's best friend and law partner, Franklin "Foggy" Nelson, and Foggy recognized her as "Matt's girl Elektra," she knew she could not carry out the contract and spared his life. Soon after, Bullseye realized that the only way to regain his status as the Kingpin's chief assassin would be to murder Elektra. Following an epic confrontation that left both combatants bloodied and battered, he impaled her on her own sai. Elektra died in Matt's arms.

Even the final disappointment of a warrior's passing brought Elektra no peace. Unwilling to part with one of its most talented operatives, the Hand attempted to resurrect Elektra and place her fully under their thrall through a mystical ceremony. Daredevil, the Black Widow and Stone, a member of Stick's order, interrupted the proceedings; together, they

ELEKTRA

overcame the Hand. Stone completed the resurrection process, bringing Elektra back to life after Daredevil had purified her spirit through sheer force of will and the power of love. Now purged of the Hand's corruption, Elektra left Matt's side determined to find her own place in the world. Daredevil still has not fully recovered from his emotional turmoil over Elektra's death and resurrection; he continues to carry her in his heart to this day.

The world's most dangerous assassin, Elektra remains a mystery, a shadow—until she chooses to reveal herself. Trained as a ninja, loyal to no one, she sells her amazing abilities and her mastery of the deadly sai to the highest bidder. Moving from job to job, contract to contract, she can visit death on the most defended of targets—for the right price. It is who she is, what she does, the whole of her identity. Her life is one of seclusion, cover identities and a bewildering succession of disguises. A single fact is certain: Every time Elektra kills, she knows exactly how it feels to die.

Art by Greg Horn

POWERS/ WEAPONS

- Master martial artist
- Olympic-level athlete and gymnast
- Proficient in the use of various martial-arts weapons

INTELLIGENCE
STRENGTH
SPEED
DURABILITY
ENERGY PROJECTION
FIGHTING SKILLS

Art by Greg Horn

NICK FURY

Real Name:	Nicholas Joseph Fury
First Appearance:	*Sgt. Fury and His Howling Commandos* #1 (1963)
Height:	6'1"
Weight:	225 lbs.
Eye Color:	Brown
Hair Color:	Brown, with graying temples

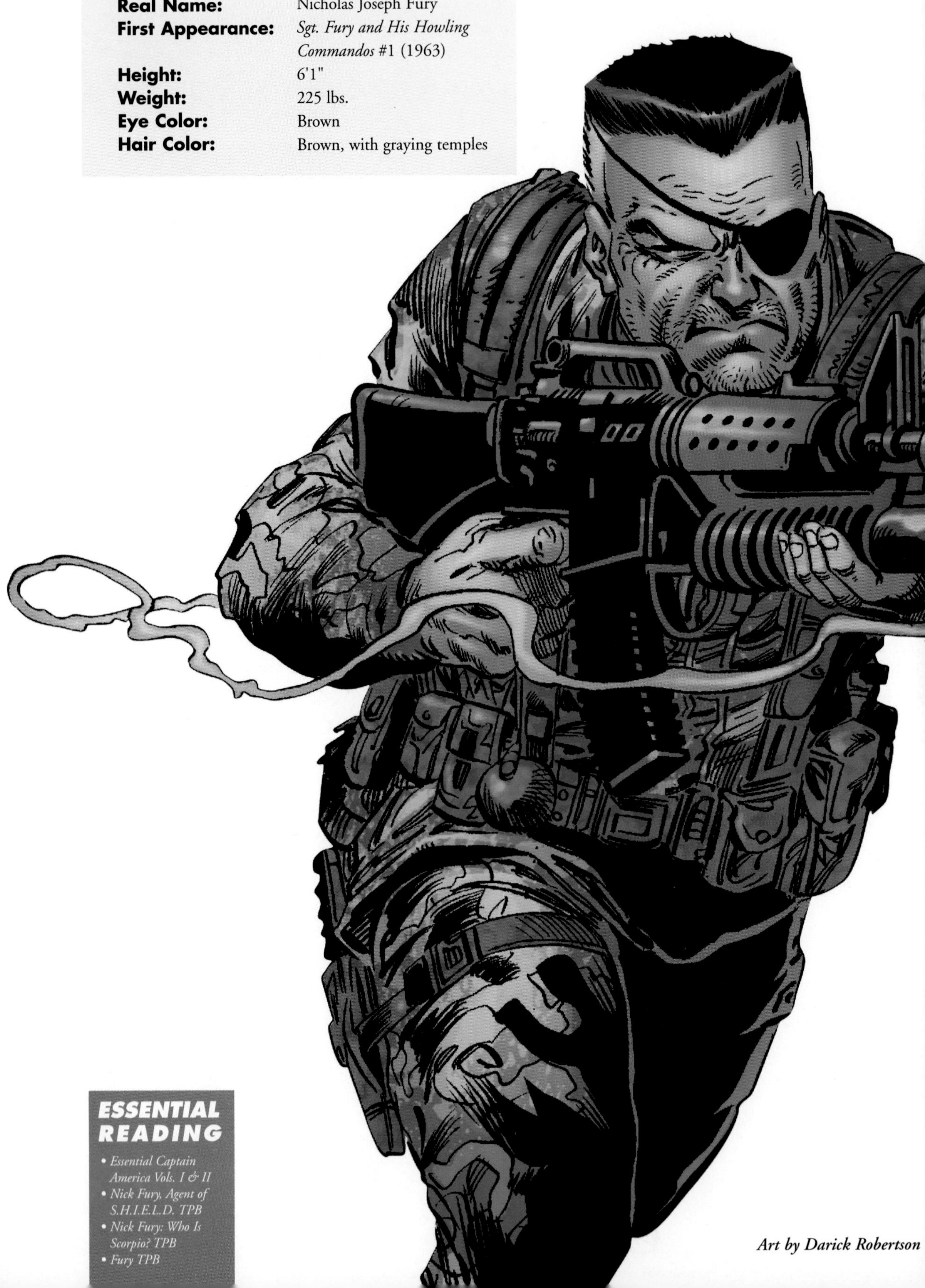

Art by Darick Robertson

ESSENTIAL READING

- *Essential Captain America Vols. I & II*
- *Nick Fury, Agent of S.H.I.E.L.D. TPB*
- *Nick Fury: Who Is Scorpio? TPB*
- *Fury TPB*

The eldest of three children born to an American pilot killed in action during the final year of World War I, Nick Fury grew up in New York City's Hell's Kitchen. A self-made man's man, Fury lied about his age so he could enlist in the Army at the start of America's involvement in World War II. In short order, he proved himself to be an excellent soldier and an even better leader.

The tough-talking, hard-as-nails Fury rose swiftly to the rank of sergeant on the basis of his ability, drive and integrity. In Europe, he led the Howling Commandos, a tight-knit band of soldiers famous for their foolhardy exploits. Injured on a mission in France, Fury came under the emergency care of Professor Berthold Sternberg, who inoculated him with the age-retarding Infinity Formula.

Art by Jim Steranko

Fury remained on active duty through the Korean War, during which the Howlers surreptitiously crossed the 38th Parallel to destroy an enemy MIG base. This mission garnered Fury a battlefield commission as well as a promotion to second lieutenant. Spying for the French government in Vietnam during the 1950s, he achieved the rank of colonel. Eventually, Fury earned a full-time appointment to the CIA. Due to the cumulative effects of injuries sustained during WWII, Fury lost vision in his left eye and was forced to wear an eye patch.

At the height of the Cold War, Fury was named director of S.H.I.E.L.D. (Strategic Hazard Intervention Espionage Logistics Directorate), a newly established international-espionage organization. As S.H.I.E.L.D.'s highest-ranking agent, Fury supervised daily administrative affairs and served as supreme field commander. Kept in the peak of youthful vigor by the Infinity Formula, the suave secret agent was a human target—a moving magnet for both babes and bullets, the walking epitome of incomparable cool and grace under fire.

Fury's leadership has been instrumental in overcoming major threats to world freedom launched by such subversive organizations as Hydra, Zodiac, and A.I.M. The elder statesman of the spy game, he revolutionized the art of espionage. When the free world has its back to the wall, Fury is the man most likely to come out fighting.

POWERS/WEAPONS

- Paratrooper, Ranger, Green Beret, Black Beret, demolitions expert and vehicle specialist
- Expert unarmed and armed combatant
- Black belt in Tae Kwan Do and a brown belt in Jiu Jitsu
- Access to the entire S.H.I.E.L.D. arsenal of conventional and advanced weaponry

GHOST RIDER

Real Name:	Johnny Blaze; the demon Zarathos	**Eye Color:**	Blue as Blaze, flaming red as Ghost Rider
First Appearance:	*Marvel Spotlight* #5 (1972)		
Height:	5'2" as Blaze, 6'2" as Ghost Rider	**Hair Color:**	Red-blond as Blaze, none as Ghost Rider
Weight:	180 lbs. as Blaze, unrevealed as Ghost Rider		

Art by Mark Texeira

ESSENTIAL READING

- *Ghost Rider: The Hammer Lane TPB*
- *Ghost Rider: Resurrected TPB*

John Blaze was orphaned when his father—Barton Blaze, the star of Crash Simpson's Daredevil Cycle Show—died performing a dangerous stunt. Adopted by Crash Simpson, the youngster swiftly mastered the tricks of the trade. When he learned Simpson was dying of a rare blood disease, Blaze finally found the courage to act on his longtime pre-occupation with the occult. Tampering with dark forces far beyond the bounds of human comprehension, Blaze recreated an ancient ritual and bartered his immortal soul for a miracle cure.

Blaze had sacrificed his soul for naught: A rejuvenated Simpson plummeted to his death attempting the most ambitious stunt of his storied career. Having deceived Blaze into forfeiting his soul, the Devil materialized to claim his due. But Crash's daughter, Roxxane, expelled the demon from the mortal plane by reciting a banishment spell she had gleaned from one of Blaze's books.

Art by Trent Kaniuga

Unable to take possession of his intended bounty, Satan grafted the living flame that was the soul of the demon Zarathos to Blaze's body. Thereafter, the melding of spirits would manifest itself every nightfall in the form of Ghost Rider, who used his demonic powers to create a mystical motorcycle of pure hellfire. At first, Blaze dominated Ghost Rider's personality. After a few months, his automatic nightly transformations ended. He then became Ghost Rider whenever he mystically sensed evil in the vicinity, avenging innocent lives tarnished by the touch of evil. But the more Blaze became Ghost Rider, the stronger the demon grew.

Blaze was doomed to lead a dual life. For years, he and Zarathos wrestled for control over their composite entity. All the while, Blaze struggled valiantly to prevent his satanic second personality from running amok. Eventually exorcising Zarathos when the demon became locked in an all-consuming struggle with an ages-old adversary, Ghost Rider's human half finally settled down to a peaceful existence—or so he thought.

Years later, Blaze found himself yearning for the thrill of his former life—some part of him missed Ghost Rider and their adventures together, and longed for the freedom of the open road. Beset once again by the brimstone and hellfire, an older, wiser Blaze has come to terms with his condition as the Spirit of Vengeance. And so Ghost Rider haunts America's highways, visiting his wrath upon the souls of the wicked and the damned, kicking asphalt in the name of righteous retribution.

POWERS/ WEAPONS

- Superhuman strength, speed and durability
- Penance Stare, forcing criminals to experience a level of emotional pain equivalent to that which they have caused in others
- Mystical hellfire motorcycle

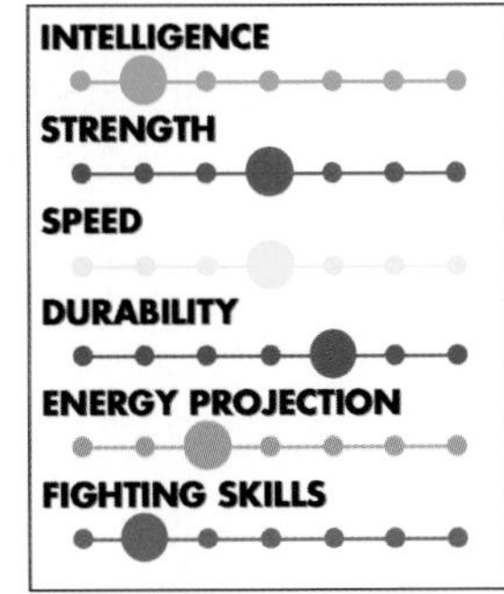

IRON FIST

Real Name:	Daniel Thomas Rand-K'ai
First Appearance:	*Marvel Premiere* #15 (1974)
Height:	175 lbs.
Weight:	5'11"
Eye Color:	Blue
Hair Color:	Blond

Art by Carlos Pacheco

ESSENTIAL READING

• *Marvel Visionaries: Gil Kane TPB*

Daniel Rand is the son of Wendell Rand, exiled heir to the throne of the other-dimensional city K'un-Lun. After years on Earth as a successful businessman, Wendell sought to return to the land of his birth. With wife Heather, son Daniel and business partner Harold Meachum, he explored the Tibetan mountains in search of the nexus to K'un-Lun. Intending to assume control of their partnership, Meachum caused Wendell to plunge to his death, and left Heather and Daniel to fend for themselves. Only 9-year-old Daniel lived to reach the mystical city.

Recognized to be of royal blood, Daniel was trained rigorously in the physical aspects of the martial arts and their philosophical foundations. As a rite of passage at age 19, he was granted the opportunity to acquire the power of the "Iron Fist" by slaying the dragon Shou-Lao the Undying. Daniel passed, gaining both the dragon-shaped scar on his chest and the ability to focus his spiritual energies into his fist—which, as a result, became as strong as iron.

Desiring revenge, Daniel departed K'un-Lun for America. After hunting down Meachum, however, Daniel realized revenge was utterly meaningless and spared the man's life. Intent on seeking his destiny on his own terms, Daniel remained on Earth and assumed control of his family fortune.

As a natural outgrowth of his philosophical upbringing and enlightenment, Daniel sought to aid those who could not help themselves as the costumed hero Iron Fist. Operating in New York City, he eventually met and partnered with Colleen Wing, Misty Knight and Luke Cage. Daniel joined the latter's Heroes for Hire business, seeing it as the best way to use his powers and abilities to help those in need. Through the years, Rand and Cage were in high demand as specialized bodyguards and private investigators, with Rand often waiving the fee for services rendered.

As a result of their partnership, Iron Fist and Cage became as close as brothers and often assisted one another on cases of personal interest. Heroes for Hire underwent several incarnations; for a brief time, the two even expanded the corporation's membership and carried out missions on a global scale.

Many of Iron Fist's opponents have been those who would seek to depose him of his title and claim his power as their own. Virtually all have learned, however, that attempting to do so is folly: Iron Fist is a living weapon. Having attained enlightenment in his battle with Shou-Lao, Iron fist possesses complete control over his mind, body, spirit and powers: all act as one. He is, in short, the perfect martial artist.

Art by Gene Ha

POWERS/ WEAPONS

- Master of martial arts
- Superior agility, stamina and reflexes
- Possesses the power of the "Iron Fist," whereby his supercharged hands become capable of shattering steel

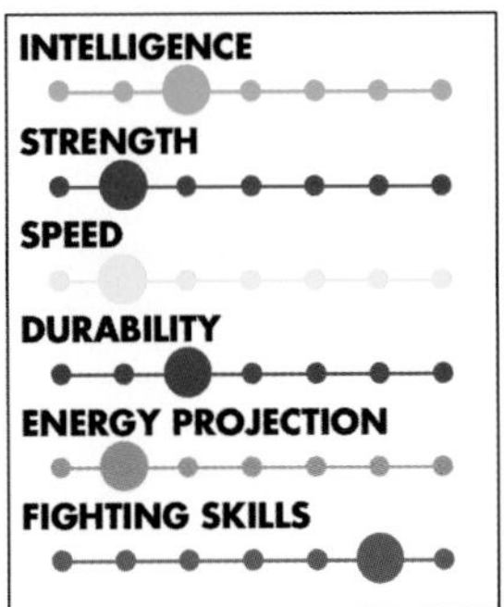

JESSICA JONES

Real Name:	Jessica Jones	**Height:**	5'7"
First Appearance:	*Alias* #1 (2001)	**Weight:**	124 lbs.
		Eye Color:	Brown
		Hair Color:	Dark auburn

Art by Michael Gaydos

ESSENTIAL READING

- *Alias Vol. I HC*

Art by Michael Gaydos

As a costumed adventurer, Jessica Jones was plagued by a lack of self-esteem and an inability to master her superhuman powers. She hung up her cape and tights when she realized she would forever be considered a second-rate super hero. Despite all her hard work and big dreams, Jessica knew she would never inspire confidence or motivate others. Rather, she would always be relegated to the background, a forgotten face in the crowd.

Jessica came to view her former allies with contempt, alienating nearly all her costumed friends. Although Nick Fury offered her a position with S.H.I.E.L.D., Jessica declined, opting instead to leave the world of heroes behind entirely, and work as a private-investigator, opening Alias Investigations.

A tough-as-nails investigator, Jessica found herself working typical seedy cases: missing persons, cheating spouses and the like. Feeling like she'd fallen from the only height she ever attained, Jessica developed a self-destructive streak and a tendency toward alcohol abuse.

Jessica found she could not escape her costumed past when a case resulted in her accidental discovery of Captain America's civilian identity. Despite mounting pressure from the police, government officials and powerful businessmen, Jessica refused to reveal the hero's secret, even at the risk of her own life. Captain America later pointed out that she did what very few people in her position would have, and that perhaps she'd judged herself too harshly in the past.

Captain America's words were the spark that helped Jessica emerge from her self-destructive depression and take a new look at her former allies. Having gained a sense of closure on her life as a costumed hero, Jessica is slowly rebuilding her relationships with old friends like Warbird while she continues to help people as a private investigator.

POWERS/ WEAPONS

- Above-average strength
- Limited flight and invulnerability

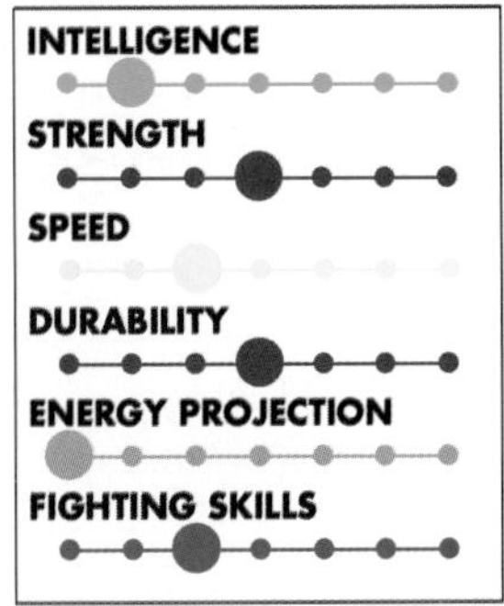

MARVEL BOY

Real Name:	Noh-Varr
First Appearance:	*Marvel Boy* #1 (2000)
Height:	5'10"
Weight:	165 lbs.
Eye Color:	Black
Hair Color:	White

POWERS/ WEAPONS

- Enhanced reflexes, speed, strength and stamina
- Enabled by submicrotech nanobots to reroute pain sensations
- Ability to control his body's growth by thought

INTELLIGENCE

STRENGTH

SPEED

DURABILITY

ENERGY PROJECTION

FIGHTING SKILLS

Art by J.G. Jones

ESSENTIAL READING

- *Marvel Boy Vol. I TPB*

Before fate and circumstance conspired to cast him as a stranger in a strange land, Noh-Varr was an ensign attached to the Kree diplomatic corps. Adrift among the immense rainbow of realities that is Macrospace, Noh-Varr and his crewmates aboard the damaged dimension-schooner Marvel arrived on an alien and hostile world: ours.

Marvel Boy Vol. I TPB

Emerging from a dimensional flume, the failing craft was downed by minions of the megalomaniacal Doctor Midas: a pirate, scavenger and multi-trillionaire seeking to acquire the dimension-schooner's advanced technology as a means of achieving mutagenic transformation through cosmic radiation. Midas hoped to duplicate the accident that created the Fantastic Four, and thus acquire superhuman powers. The Marvel's sole survivor, Noh-Varr was taken prisoner by the Midas Foundation to be dissected and catalogued. But before the Marvel's remains could be salvaged, the ship telephased to the sewers under New York City's Times Square. As Midas' technicians and scientists studied samples procured from Noh-Varr, they discovered him to be a living weapon, genome-boosted with insect traits.

Fighting mad, Noh-Varr escaped from the Foundation's New Jersey research facility. He hot-wired a jetfighter and met up with the Marvel under Times Square, where he reunited with his only companion on Earth, the We-Plex Supreme Intelligence System, standard on all Kree diplomatic vessels. Housing the accumulated knowledge of the entire Kree race, Plex is dedicated to the protection and survival of the species.

Noh-Varr had seen good friends die due to sheer ignorance and hate, and his welcome to Earth had consisted of imprisonment and torture. Alone and enraged at the society that had so callously destroyed his life, Noh-Varr declared war on Earth—razing several city blocks simply to swear at humanity in street-size letters and decimating a squadron of Nick Fury's S.H.I.E.L.D. super-soldiers in the process.

Doggedly pursued by both Midas and S.H.I.E.L.D., Noh-Varr befriended Midas' daughter, Oubliette. After she defied her father and saved Noh-Varr's life, the two battled one of Midas' other-dimensional monsters as a S.H.I.E.L.D. detachment led by Midas boarded the Marvel. Disabling Plex, Midas finally gained access to the dimension-schooner's engine chamber and set out to shatter his mortal body in favor of a higher form. He emerged with the combined elemental powers of the Fantastic Four—super-adaptive, super-fluid flame, air, mass and thought—and gloated while he beat Marvel Boy near death. As Midas prepared to deal the final, fatal blow, Oubliette banished her father into the infrastructure of known space by harnessing the reality-warping power of his other-dimensional monster. Oubliette escaped, but a weakened Marvel Boy was apprehended by S.H.I.E.L.D. and incarcerated in the Cube—an "inescapable" prison declared by Marvel Boy to be the capital city of a new Kree Empire.

The self-proclaimed progenitor of a new era on Earth, Marvel Boy is believed by the U.S. government to be a dimension-spanning star-god with a legitimate grievance and a divinely prophesied mandate to "upgrade" our civilization. Noh-Varr is angry—and, if necessary, willing to take out our entire planet in the name of love, justice and freedom. His mission: to change the world.

PUNISHER

Real Name:	Frank Castle (born Castiglione)	**Weight:**	200 lbs.
First Appearance:	*Amazing Spider-Man* #129 (1974)	**Eye Color:**	Blue
Height:	6'	**Hair Color:**	Black

Art by Steve Dillion

ESSENTIAL READING

- *Punisher Vol. I HC*
- *Punisher: Circle of Blood TPB*
- *Punisher: War Zone TPB*
- *Punisher Vol. I: Welcome Back, Frank TPB*
- *Punisher Vol. II: Army of One TPB*

A born soldier, Frank Castle enlisted in the Marines. He rose quickly to the rank of captain, collecting two Bronze Stars, two Silver Stars and four Purple Hearts for his exemplary service in Vietnam. A family man, Castle sought to make the world a safer place for his wife and young children. Given his level of personal attachment to his military career, he was well on the road to becoming one of the nation's finest Marines.

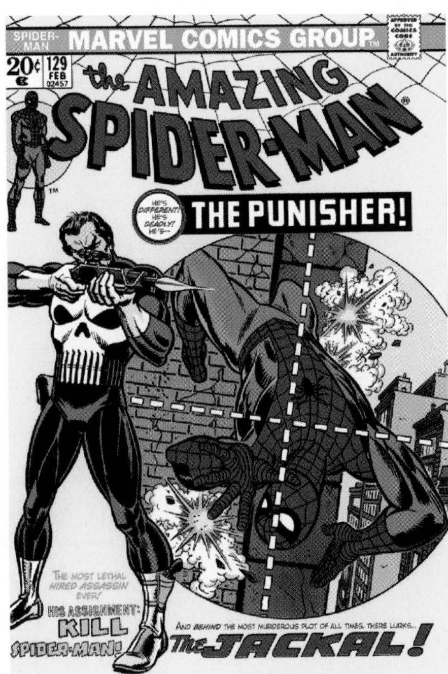

Amazing Spider-Man #129, February 1974

But fate had other plans. While on leave, Castle took his wife and children to New York's Central Park for a picnic. There, the family happened upon the scene of a mob hit. Finishing off their intended mark, the mobsters then turned their guns on the only witnesses to the crime. Only Castle escaped. As his family died in his arms, he was changed forever.

Castle disappeared for several months, going AWOL from the Marines. During his time underground, he gathered resources and weapons. When the former Marine resurfaced, he had adapted his fighting skills to wage a one-man war on crime—a war that took no prisoners. Castle made his first mission the murder of the criminals who had killed his wife and children.

Castle has repeatedly run afoul of New York's other costumed heroes, including Spider-Man and Daredevil, whom he regards with a mixture of disdain and annoyance. In his eyes, he is the only one making a difference, performing the radical surgery required to root out the criminal element. The others, he believes, merely place bandages on gaping wounds. While Punisher occasionally has cooperated with Spider-Man, he and Daredevil are polar opposites in their respective views of crime and punishment, and frequently clash when they meet. On some level, Castle enjoys antagonizing Daredevil, who steadfastly believes in the merits of the nation's legal system.

Punisher has served time for his violent acts, but always manages to escape imprisonment—either on his own or with the aid of sympathetic guards. Even in jail, Castle has continued his one-man crusade, leaving many prisons with fewer inmates than when he entered.

Throughout the years, others who harbored similar feelings or lost loved ones to comparable circumstances have assisted Punisher. Police officers and prosecutors, frustrated with the legal system's shortcomings, have aided Punisher by providing him with information on criminals or turning a blind eye to his actions. Punisher prefers to keep such interactions to a minimum, however, going so far as to kill several copycat vigilantes. His mission and his philosophy are simple, but his alone. The Punisher does not seek followers or teammates.

PUNISHER

Having long ago expanded his mission from one of personal revenge to the extermination of all criminals, Castle fully acknowledges that his crusade will never end until the day he dies. He is as disciplined now as he was as a Marine: gathering intelligence, setting objectives and always planning his operations down to the smallest detail. It is virtually impossible to catch Castle off-guard.

While the authorities and New York's larger crime families know of his existence, Punisher remains shrouded in the mystique of an urban legend. To most criminals, he is the ultimate nightmare—single-minded and utterly unstoppable.

POWERS/WEAPONS

- Expert with all small arms and large-caliber guns
- Extensive training with explosives and tactical weapons
- Superior martial artist and hand-to-hand combatant

Attribute	Rating (of 7)
INTELLIGENCE	2
STRENGTH	2
SPEED	2
DURABILITY	2
ENERGY PROJECTION	1
FIGHTING SKILLS	6

Art by Leinil Francis Yu

Art by Tim Bradstreet

SHANG-CHI

Real Name:	Shang-Chi
First Appearance:	*Special Marvel Edition* #15 (1973)
Height:	5'10"
Weight:	175 lbs.
Eye Color:	Brown
Hair Color:	Black

POWERS

- Master of Kung Fu and various related disciplines.
- Well-versed in the use of numerous hand-held martial-arts weapons, including the staff, nunchukas and double-edged sword

INTELLIGENCE
STRENGTH
SPEED
DURABILITY
ENERGY PROJECTION
FIGHTING SKILLS

Art by David Mack

ESSENTIAL READING

- *Ultimate Marvel Team-Up HC*
- *Shang-Chi: Master of Kung Fu Vol. 1 TPB*

The man who would be known as the Master of Kung-Fu always strove to walk the path of peace even if it meant he had to fight for it. Son of an international crime lord, Shang-Chi grew to young-adulthood sequestered in an isolated retreat in Hunan, China. By age 19, he had mastered the martial arts. Only then did his father send him out into the world to assassinate an old enemy. Naïvely believing his father to be a great humanitarian and his foe to be evil, the idealistic Shang-Chi murdered the man—only to discover that the murder had been a test of his loyalty. Learning his father's true nature as events unfolded, a shocked and disillusioned Shang-Chi vowed to renounce the ways of violence and topple the criminal empire he had unwittingly served. Realizing he needed help before he could walk away, he joined with his father's enemies in the British Secret Service.

Art by Paul Gulacy

His recruitment into MI-6 alongside agents Clive Reston and Black Jack Tarr enabled Shang-Chi to operate outside the bounds of conventional law enforcement. This often brought his pacifistic ideals into conflict with his desire to work for a greater justice. At times, he felt the need for action was too great for doubt—as when he teamed with fellow MI-6 agent Leiko Wu, Reston's former lover, to prevent a madman from unleashing a weapon that would burn through the ozone layer.

Shang-Chi's growing attraction to Leiko served as a further impetus for him to remain with MI-6. Leiko's lingering feelings for Reston, however, threatened to cause a rift between the three agents. As Shang-Chi continued working for the British Secret Service, he grew increasingly discouraged with the murky deceptions inherent in the espionage game, particularly when those perpetrated by his own superiors brought about the needless death of a fellow agent. His disillusionment intensified when Leiko was dispatched to uncover a mole deep within MI-6, with only one chance in a hundred that she would survive. Only Shang-Chi's desire to find and save Leiko kept him from abandoning his superiors—until he learned that the mole was working for his father as part of a plot to take over the world. By detonating nuclear devices, his father intended to hurl the moon out of its orbit, causing massive tidal waves that would devastate the planet. Only his chosen few would survive the destruction under his grand imperial rule.

Reuniting with Leiko, Shang-Chi infiltrated his father's Arctic base to prevent the mad scheme from coming to fruition. Alongside Black Jack and Reston, he cut a swath through enemy agents and finally confronted his father aboard a launching spacecraft. With the crime lord about to activate the nuclear weapons, Shang-Chi was left with no alternative: He shot his father. Fatally wounded, Shang-Chi's father stumbled into an escape pod, launching himself into the depths of space.

Thereafter, Shang-Chi vowed to stop playing games of deceit and death. He wanted nothing but the peace so long denied him. Yet even though Shang-Chi's father is gone, the legacy of his evil persists—forever compelling his son to atone for the sins of the father and fight to achieve peace.

WAR MACHINE

Real Name:	James Rhodes	**Height:**	6'0"
First Appearance:	*Iron Man* #120 (1979), *Iron Man* #281 (1992, as War Machine)	**Weight:**	210 lbs.
		Eye Color:	Brown
		Hair Color:	Brown

ESSENTIAL READING

- *U.S. War Machine Vol. 1 TPB*

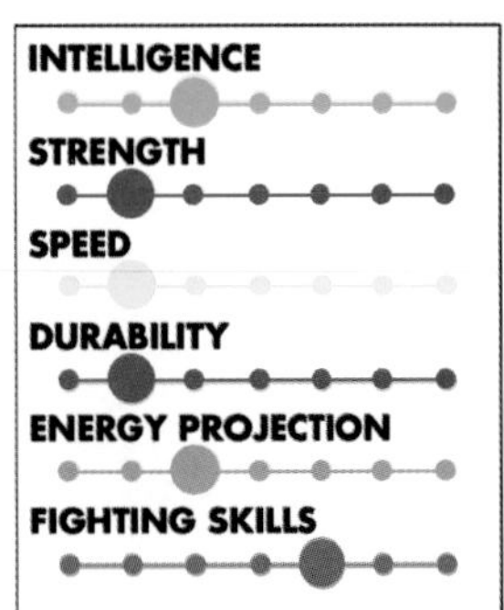

A former soldier with diverse technical skills and training, Jim Rhodes was hired by industrialist Tony Stark to serve as a bodyguard, test pilot and jack-of-all-trades for Stark Industries. Rhodes assisted Stark in both the design and development of the MPI-2100 battlesuit, a technological marvel combining armor, weaponry and ease of mobility for ground troops. Considering its vast arsenal, the suit was aptly nicknamed "War Machine."

After witnessing firsthand the War Machine's destructive capabilities, Stark chose to mothball the armor in favor of pacifistic technology. The decision frustrated Rhodes, who felt the suit filled a need, and saw countless applications for the War Machine in both peacekeeping and defense. Pacifist inventor clashed with career soldier, and the philosophical rift between Stark and Rhodes quickly grew.

Acting in defiance of his employer, Rhodes donned the armor for a short flight. He hoped to demonstrate its peacekeeping abilities to Stark and the world, but instead became embroiled in a standoff that resulted in the death of a hostage and six terrorists.

Terminated from Stark Industries, Rhodes attracted the attention of Nick Fury and S.H.I.E.L.D. Impressed by his resolve and skilled use of the suit, Fury recruited Rhodes to assemble a strike force of similarly armored operatives to take down a terrorist organization.

Rhodes' team acted with extreme prejudice, destroying both the terrorist cell and the bio-weapon it was developing. The mission, however, was not without its casualties and consequences. Recognizing the armor as his own, Stark has sworn to get it back from Rhodes, who has opted to remain with S.H.I.E.L.D.

POWERS/ WEAPONS

- Armor-enhanced strength, speed and durability
- Flight via jet-boots
- State-of-the-art weapons system, constantly modified and upgraded

Art by Chuck Austen

BULLSEYE

Real Name:	Unrevealed
First Appearance:	*Daredevil* #131 (1976)
Height:	6'
Weight:	185 lbs.
Eye Color:	Blue
Hair Color:	Blond

Art by Joe Quesada

Any object—be it pencil, playing card or paper clip—becomes a deadly weapon in the skilled hands of the master marksman known only as Bullseye. Born with perfect aim, the man who would become Bullseye enlisted in the military rather than continue a budding baseball career. Bullseye discovered that he took pleasure in killing, and embarked on a career as a costumed criminal following his discharge. Bullseye attempted to extort money from a number of New York City millionaires, hoping the resulting publicity would help solidify his reputation among the denizens of the underworld. Daredevil tracked down and defeated the assassin when he tried to murder his second victim, touching off a series of deadly encounters between Bullseye and the blind hero.

Daredevil Visionaries: Kevin Smith TPB

Hired by a corrupt businessman to murder lawyer Matt Murdock, Bullseye was beaten by Daredevil, the attorney's alter ego. In Bulleye's mind, his continued defeats at the hands of his adversary had destroyed his reputation as the world's deadliest assassin. He became obsessed with Daredevil, intent on proving he was a better man. His fixation magnified when a malignant brain tumor caused him to perceive everyone around him as Daredevil. Driven to the brink of insanity, Bullseye embarked on a murderous rampage. Daredevil tracked him down and selflessly saved his life, delivering him to a hospital to have the tumor removed. Despite his hatred for the killer, Daredevil could not willingly allow a man to die. It was a decision Matt would live to regret the rest of his days, and one that would only serve to further Bullseye's blinding hatred of Daredevil.

After the malignancy was removed, Bullseye stewed in prison—burning with the knowledge that he owed his life to Daredevil. He escaped from Riker's Island intent on revenge—not only against Daredevil, but also Elektra, the woman who had taken his place as the Kingpin's top assassin. Seeking out Elektra, the marksman impaled her on her own sai. Elektra's death proved doubly sweet when he learned that she was once the girlfriend of Matt Murdock, whom Bullseye thought to be close friends with Daredevil. But the Kingpin refused to rehire Bullseye unless he killed Daredevil, escalating the bitter feud between the two.

Bullseye and Daredevil are more than just hero and villain. With them, it's personal: They truly hate one another. Each encounter leaves both combatants bloody and battered. Bullseye has killed perhaps the only two women Matt has ever loved, both in brutal fashion: first Elektra, and then Matt's estranged girlfriend, Karen Page, whom Bullseye impaled with the hero's own billy club. Striking at the heart of the hero, Bullseye has molded Matt into the man he is today—driven by pain and loneliness, and aching to fill the emptiness in his soul. Bullseye is the only one who can cause Daredevil, the Man Without Fear, to feel fear.

POWERS/ WEAPONS

- Master marksman

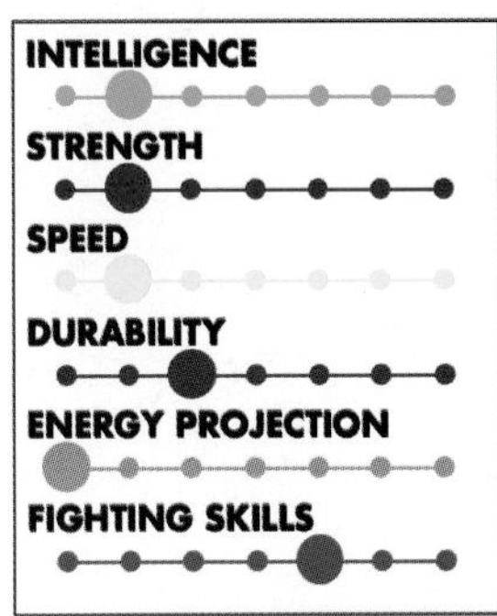

ESSENTIAL READING

- *Elektra Lives Again HC*
- *Daredevil Visionaries: Frank Miller Vols. I-III TPB*
- *Daredevil Visionaries: Kevin Smith TPB*
- *Marvel Visionaries: Gil Kane TPB*
- *Daredevil: The Target HC*

KINGPIN

Art by David Ros

Real Name:	Wilson Fisk	**Weight:**	450 lbs.
First Appearance:	*Amazing Spider-Man* #50 (1967)	**Eye Color:**	Blue
Height:	6'7"	**Hair Color:**	None

A self-made man, Wilson Fisk committed his first murder when he was 12 years old. Impoverished as a youth, he learned through bitter experience that society's predators target the weak, not the strong. Fisk was weak, a self-described unpopular, blubbery child. Bullied incessantly, Fisk found himself at a crossroads: He could be a sheep the rest of his life, or remake himself as a wolf. For Fisk, the choice was simple. Thereafter, he was bound and determined to be the best there was at whatever task he undertook. It was a long road, and experience was his only teacher. Motivated by poverty, Fisk made friends with fear.

Because he believed physical strength would help him amass power in the underworld, Fisk trained fanatically in various methods of bodybuilding and personal combat—finally concentrating on the Japanese art of sumo. He transformed his obesity from a subject of ridicule into an intimidating advantage. Fisk strengthened his mind as well, educating himself by stealing books from bookstores and libraries. Taking a particular interest in political science, he was determined to use that knowledge to organize and direct groups of criminals.

Fisk's gang grew rapidly in size, influence, power and wealth, but he was careful to invest his ill-gotten gains in legitimate businesses. The first company he owned dealt spices in the Far East. A decade later, Fisk had achieved enough success in legitimate business to become a prominent member of New York society. He met and soon married Vanessa, a beautiful woman not yet 20 years old. Her love granted him the peace he sought after his constant struggle for power.

Two decades later, Fisk had become one of the most powerful criminal leaders in New York. He reached the pinnacle of his chosen profession by relying on one person and one person only: himself. The infamous, enigmatic Kingpin of Crime ruled the East Coast underworld with an iron hand—and zero tolerance for failure. Fisk has attempted to unify New York's gangs under his leadership, engineering major crime waves; only the intervention of Spider-Man and Daredevil has prevented him from fulfilling these and other master plans.

Initially, the Kingpin considered Daredevil a minor nuisance in his lesser enterprises, never worthy of his personal attention. But Fisk's plans require a careful understanding of every element in the struggle for power, and as Daredevil became more of a problem, he realized he could not allow a monkey wrench to remain in such delicate machinery. The Kingpin could not afford to let Daredevil live.

Through the years, Daredevil has dedicated his energies to toppling the Kingpin—both in costume and in the courtroom as attorney Matt Murdock. Every time Fisk squirmed through a legal loophole, overpowered his adversary outright or brought his considerable weight and resources to bear in an attempt to ruin or end the blind adventurer's life. Ultimately, Fisk would find himself on even ground with his masked opponent. When Daredevil's former lover sold the hero's secret identity to a drug dealer, the information eventually

ESSENTIAL READING

- *Daredevil: Born Again TPB*
- *Daredevil/Elektra: Love and War HC*
- *Daredevil Vol. II: Parts of a Hole TPB*
- *Daredevil Vol. IV: Underboss TPB*
- *Daredevil Visionaries: Frank Miller Vols. II & III TPB*
- *Spider-Man's Tangled Web Vol. I TPB*

KINGPIN

came into the Kingpin's possession. This was merely the opening move in what would develop into a deadly, years-long chess match between the two. Theirs is a complex relationship, marked by momentary stalemates and temporary truces. At times, the Kingpin and Daredevil have acted as allies against outside forces neither could defeat alone. They need each other; in a way, they are partners. In the Kingpin's mind, they are the power in the city.

The Kingpin takes pleasure in physical combat with Daredevil and other enemies, but knows he can never allow himself to be connected to his crimes. Through intimidation and blackmail, he influences the opinions and actions of powerful people from law-enforcement officials to judges to senators to generals—even other crime lords. Consequently, Fisk has never been convicted of any wrongdoing. Today, even though Fisk has built a vast, legitimate business empire in various fields, he still professes to be merely a "humble dealer in spices." Rather than dirty his hands, he has often been content to draw Daredevil into conflict with other foes, thus weakening his enemies while remaining untouched. But Daredevil is the Kingpin's to kill, and Fisk has dealt harshly with anyone who would interfere with their "partnership."

POWERS/ WEAPONS

- Skilled hand-to-hand combatant
- Unusual agility for a man his size
- Criminal genius

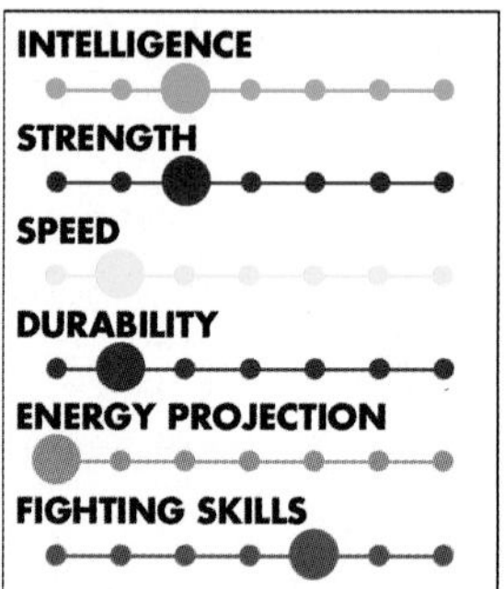

Art by Eduardo Risso

Art by Joe Quesada and David Mack

SPIDER-MAN

THE BITE OF AN IRRADIATED SPIDER GRANTED HIGH-SCHOOL STUDENT PETER PARKER INCREDIBLE, ARACHNID-LIKE POWERS—AND NEW YORK HASN'T BEEN THE SAME SINCE. WHEN A BURGLAR KILLED HIS BELOVED UNCLE BEN DUE TO THE BOOKISH TEENAGER'S OWN THOUGHTLESS INACTION, A GUILT-RIDDEN PETER VOWED TO USE HIS AMAZING ABILITIES TO PROTECT HIS FELLOW MAN. TODAY, SPIDER-MAN CASTS AN IMPOSING SHADOW OVER HIS NOT-SO-FRIENDLY NEIGHBORHOOD.

Force-fed a ceaseless string of bitter diatribes and baseless accusations by *Daily Bugle* publisher J. Jonah Jameson, many New Yorkers believe Spider-Man to be a menace. Others see the wall-crawler as a man of the people, a working-class hero giving his all to protect the city and its residents. To the hoodlums he hunts, Spider-Man is a wisecracking, wall-crawling force for good. When common criminals see him coming, they know full well there's a beat-down in their immediate future.

Those whose lives Spider-Man touches are forever changed. Citizens he saves are eternally grateful, while the psychopaths and super-villains caught in the hero's tangled web inevitably rise up to seek vengeance against their arachnid-inspired adversary. But those most affected must suffer in silence: Peter Parker's family and friends deal daily with the turbulence that arises from the wall-crawler's chosen profession.

Art by Jae Lee

SPIDER-MAN

Real Name:	Peter Parker	**Weight:**	165 lbs.
First Appearance:	*Amazing Fantasy* #15 (1962)	**Eye Color:**	Brown
Height:	5'10"	**Hair Color:**	Brown

Art by Glen Orbik

INTELLIGENCE

STRENGTH

SPEED

DURABILITY

ENERGY PROJECTION

FIGHTING SKILLS

POWERS/ WEAPONS

- Superhuman strength, reflexes and equilibrium
- Ability to cling to sheer vertical surfaces with hands and feet
- Early warning "spider-sense"
- Wrist-mounted web-shooters

Orphaned at a young age, Peter Parker was raised by his Uncle Ben and Aunt May as if he were their own son. Exceptionally bright, Peter was also extremely shy. A social outcast with few friends, he sought solace in his studies. During a demonstration on radiation, a spider wandered into the radiation source and became irradiated. Dying, the spider fell on Peter's hand and bit him.

Peter slowly realized the bite had changed him: He now possessed spectacular spider-like abilities. Seeing his powers as a chance to earn money to help Aunt May and Uncle Ben, Peter designed a colorful costume and pursued stardom as the Amazing Spider-Man.

Leaving the TV studio following a taping, Peter chose to mind his own business when he encountered a burglar fleeing the scene of a robbery. Though he could have stopped the man, Peter allowed him to pass, arrogantly believing it was not his responsibility. Several days later, he returned home from a perfomance only to discover that an intruder had murdered his uncle. Learning police had cornered the hoodlum in a nearby warehouse, a distraught Peter donned his Spider-Man costume and desperately rushed off to confront his uncle's killer.

Amazing Fantasy #15, August 1962

Employing his newfound abilities to capture the burglar, Peter realized the thief was the same criminal he had allowed to escape. Filled with remorse, Peter finally understood that with great power, there must also come great responsibility—and he vowed never to shirk his heroic responsibilities again.

Spider-Man became one of New York's first costumed heroes, and Peter earned money to help Aunt May provide for their family by selling photographs of himself in action to the *Daily Bugle*. Publisher J. Jonah Jameson has used Peter's photos to wage a non-stop campaign to smear Spider-Man's name since his first appearance, but his crusade has largely failed to change positive public opinion.

Because of his powers, Peter can never live a normal life. He is always torn between his duties as Spider-Man and his life as Peter. In virtually every instance, the weight of Spider-Man's responsibilities wins out. While his relationship with Aunt May has always been a casualty of his double life, the most severe blow to his personal life came after the Green Goblin discovered his secret identity, and kidnapped and killed Peter's first love Gwen Stacy. Gwen's death has haunted Peter ever since—a constant, tragic reminder of the danger of his double life and the fate that awaits anyone he allows to get too close.

SPIDER-MAN

As Peter matured, so did his relationship with his on-again, off-again girlfriend Mary Jane Watson. The two dated seriously for many years and ultimately committed to a long-term romance. But as before, Spider-Man's influence meant Peter had to divide his loyalties between Mary Jane and his costumed identity. Unable to resolve their differences, the couple has separated.

Peter's life as Spider-Man is not all gloom and doom. While a tremendous responsibility, being Spider-Man is also a release for Peter, an exhilarating adventure that allows him to leave his everyday troubles behind and swing from rooftops while battling criminals with webs and wisecracks. Despite the personal tragedy he has endured, Peter truly loves being Spider-Man.

For years, Peter hid his dual identity from Aunt May, sheltering her from the truth for fear it would harm her and damage their relationship. When Aunt May finally learned that Peter is Spider-Man, the two came to a new understanding, and May became one of Spider-Man's strongest supporters. She still worries about Peter constantly, but is now even more proud of her nephew.

Constantly balancing his responsibility as a hero with his personal life, and ever ready with a wisecrack to hide his personal struggles, Peter remains steadfast in living up to the responsibility that his great powers have thrust upon him, donning his Spider-Man costume for the good of all.

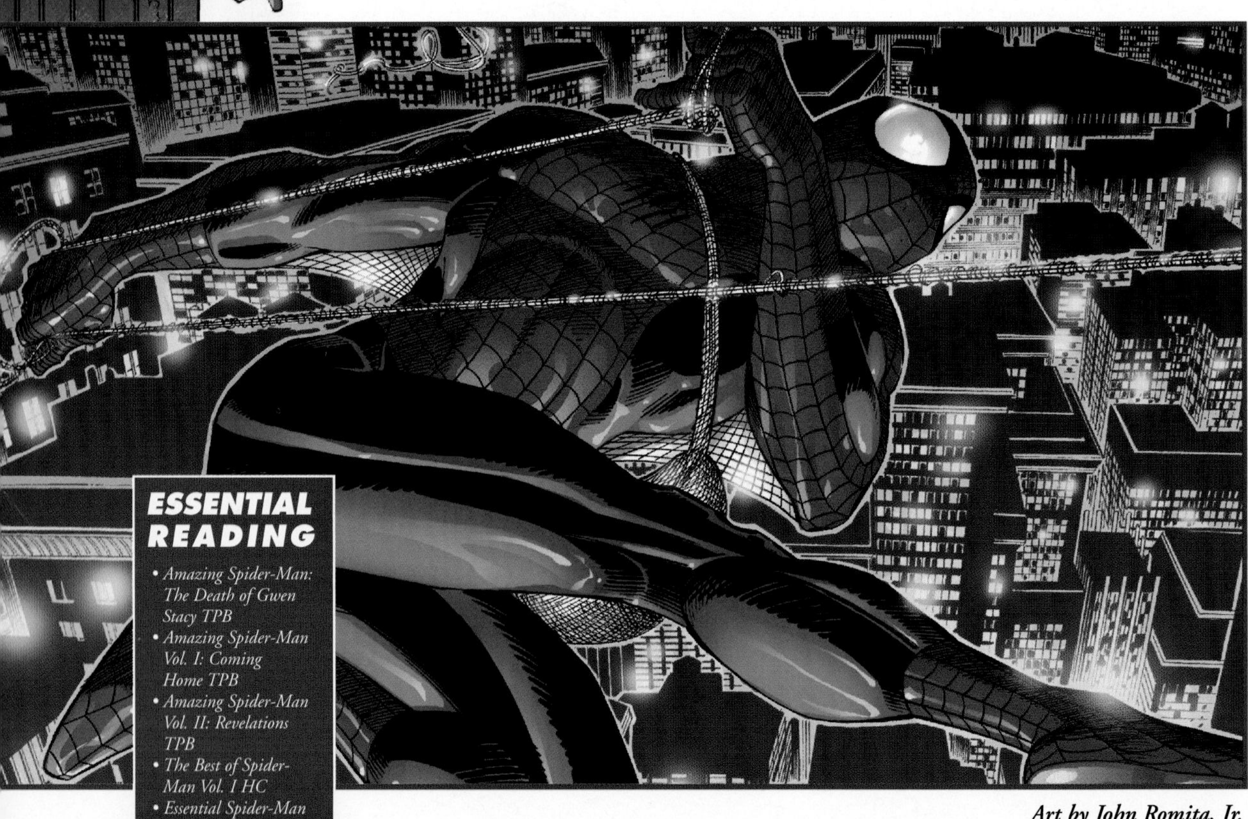

Art by John Romita, Jr.

ESSENTIAL READING

- *Amazing Spider-Man: The Death of Gwen Stacy TPB*
- *Amazing Spider-Man Vol. I: Coming Home TPB*
- *Amazing Spider-Man Vol. II: Revelations TPB*
- *The Best of Spider-Man Vol. I HC*
- *Essential Spider-Man Vols. I-V*
- *Spider Man: Blue HC*

Art by John Romita, Jr.

BLACK CAT

Real Name: Felicia Hardy
First Appearance: *Amazing Spider-Man* #194 (1979)
Height: 5'10"
Weight: 120 lbs.
Eye Color: Green
Hair Color: Platinum blonde

POWERS/ WEAPONS

- Master thief
- Olympic-level athlete and martial artist

INTELLIGENCE
STRENGTH
SPEED
DURABILITY
ENERGY PROJECTION
FIGHTING SKILLS

ESSENTIAL READING

- *Spider-Man/Black Cat: The Evil That Men Do HC*

Art by Terry Dodson

Felicia Hardy grew up a spoiled little daddy's girl, intent on emulating her beloved father Walter in every way. When he disappeared from her life, Felicia's mother told her he had died in a plane crash. Felicia later discovered the truth: Walter Hardy was the world's greatest cat burglar, but his crimes had caught up with him. He was alive, but languishing in prison. Remaining determined to follow in his footsteps, Felicia undertook a rigorous regimen of physical training that increased her strength, endurance and agility. She also studied lockpicking and safecracking, and mastered the martial arts.

It took years, but Felicia perfected her father's every move and learned his every trick. Rather than immediately setting out to steal a fortune, she first donned the costume of the Black Cat when she found out her father was deathly ill. Believing he should be allowed to die in his own bed, she broke into prison and brought him home, evading Spider-Man in the process.

Art by Terry Dodson

Although addicted to the thrill of the chase, the seemingly impulsive Black Cat is a meticulous planner. Early in her criminal career, she attempted to create the impression in her adversaries' minds that she possessed the innate ability to bring them bad luck. Felicia would painstakingly prepare the scene of her upcoming crime so that "accidents" would appear to befall any pursuers. Relying on parlor tricks and sleight of hand, she was able to convince Spider-Man that she could indeed affect probability fields. Their game of cat-and-mouse continued for some time, with the vivacious Felicia constantly confusing and frustrating the object of her increasing fascination. The more she found herself fleeing Spider-Man, the more the Black Cat was inexplicably drawn to him.

Shedding her criminal tendencies, Felicia succumbed to her now-overwhelming attraction to the hero and joined him in his war on crime—thereby winning amnesty from the authorities. Wrapped around her pretty little paw, Spider-Man reciprocated the Black Cat's strong feelings, going so far as to reveal his secret identity. But when he discovered it was Spider-Man she wanted—not Peter Parker, the man behind the mask—the web-spinner put an end to their relationship.

The Black Cat has moved on with her life, though Peter remains ever-present in her thoughts. Although Felicia has lived off her ill-gotten gains for years, she hasn't so much as jaywalked in ages because of the profound effect their relationship had on her life.

EZEKIEL

Real Name:	Ezekiel Sims
First Appearance:	*Amazing Spider-Man* #30 (2001)
Height:	6'
Weight:	180 lbs.
Eye Color:	Blue
Hair Color:	White

Art by John Romita, Jr.

Ezekiel Sims was captured by a tribe of natives while exploring the Central American jungles and forced to take part in an arcane ritual. As a result, he acquired arachnid-like powers similar to those possessed by Spider-Man. Ezekiel opted to use these abilities for his own gain, building a multinational financial empire. To better understand the ritual he was forced to undergo and the talents he now possessed, Ezekiel devoted much of his time and resources to the study of totems—powerful, primitive animalistic imagery—and their carriers.

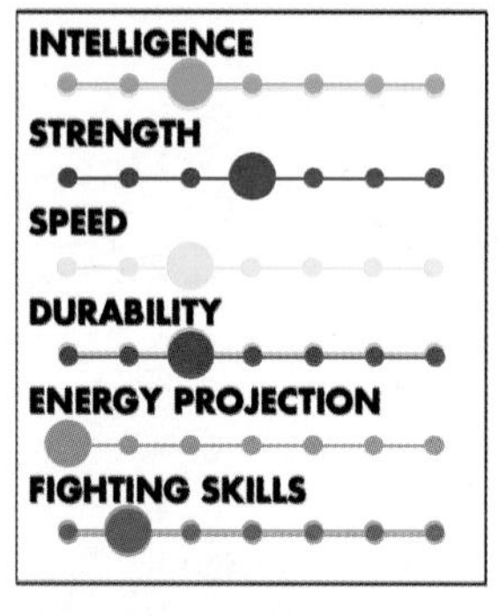

POWERS/ WEAPONS

- Heightened agility, reflexes, strength, endurance and equilibrium
- Ability to cling to and climb vertical surfaces
- Some form of "spider-sense" alerting him to danger

ESSENTIAL READING

- *Amazing Spider-Man Vol. I: Coming Home TPB*

When he became aware of Spider-Man's exploits, Ezekiel became convinced he had wasted his own abilities and vowed to protect Peter Parker from the creature called Morlun. A parasite masquerading as a man, Morlun was driven to feed on the totemistic energies present in individuals such as Ezekiel and Spider-Man. Rather than take action to stop the creature, Ezekiel oversaw construction of a high-tech sanctuary where Peter could hide until Morlun abandoned his hunt.

Piecing together Spider-Man's secret identity, Ezekiel confronted Peter and explained the totemistic nature of the hero's spider-based powers, as well as the threat presented by Morlun. But Peter refused to use the chamber, claiming it was his responsibility to stop the creature. Otherwise, Morlun would continue killing to feed his hunger.

Nearly beaten to death in his initial encounter with Morlun, Spider-Man returned to seek Ezekiel's help. The older man refused, as he was unwilling to risk his comfortable life for certain death in battle. But as Spider-Man went forth once again to face Morlun, Ezekiel was moved by Peter's selflessness. He had finally come to understand the meaning of the wall-crawler's words: "With great power, there must also come great responsibility."

Joining forces with Spider-Man, Ezekiel battled Morlun valiantly. But in the end, the villain fed upon Ezekiel's life energy and dropped his apparently dead body into the East River. While Spider-Man went on to defeat Morlun, Ezekiel somehow survived. Rather than reveal himself to Peter, he opted to leave New York City quietly. Deeply inspired by his young friend, Ezekiel vowed to use his fortune and powers to help others.

J. JONAH JAMESON

Real Name:	J. Jonah Jameson	**Weight:**	210 lbs.
First Appearance:	*Fantastic Four #8* (1962)	**Eye Color:**	Blue
Height:	5'11"	**Hair Color:**	Black with gray at the temples

Art by John Romita, Jr.

Hired as a reporter at the *Daily Bugle* while still in high school, J. Jonah Jameson slowly worked his way up the corporate ladder until he was appointed editor-in-chief and later publisher. Under Jameson, the *Bugle* has flourished. It is the top daily paper in the metropolitan New York area.

Relying both on his unwavering moral compass and position as publisher, Jameson sets the tone of the paper—and, subsequently, the tone of public discourse in the city. He has used the *Bugle* as a vehicle to crusade for a number of noble causes, from civil rights to exposés of organized crime. Along with these causes, Jameson has put the paper to work as his personal soapbox to rail against Spider-Man.

From the wall-crawler's first public appearance, Jameson has believed him to be a menace to society. Jameson's feelings about Spider-Man have not been limited to the page: At times, he has taken steps to either expose the wall-crawler as a fraud or bring him to "justice."

Through the years, Jameson's feelings toward other costumed adventurers have mellowed; he approves of heroes such as the Avengers, who work in tandem with the government. He also steadfastly refuses to allow his paper to join the anti-mutant bandwagon. With Spider-Man, however, his grudge is personal. A paragon of integrity and stubborn as a mule, Jameson is not about to admit he's wrong regarding the wall-crawler, and the publisher continues his crusade against Spider-Man to this day.

ESSENTIAL READING

- *Essential Spider-Man Vols. I-V*
- *Amazing Spider-Man Vol. II: Revelations TPB*
- *Spider-Man Visionaries: Todd McFarlane Vol. I TPB*
- *Spider-Man Visionaries: John Romita TPB*

AUNT MAY & UNCLE BEN

Real Name:	May and Ben Parker	**Weight:**	120 lbs./150 lbs.
First Appearance:	*Amazing Fantasy* #15 (1962)	**Eye Color:**	Blue/Blue
Height:	5'7"/5'9"	**Hair Color:**	Gray/Gray

Unable to have children of their own, May and Ben Parker adopted the son of Ben's younger brother Richard when he and his wife died. Ben and May raised Peter Parker as if he were their own child, giving the boy who would one day become Spider-Man unconditional love and unwavering emotional support. As a surrogate father, Ben helped shape Peter into the man he is today by instilling in him a strong sense of morals and ethics. Even when Peter began to rebel, Ben's diligence taught the teenager how to overcome life's challenges. Through Peter's trials with bullies and peer pressure, the wise Ben attempted to guide his nephew down the right path.

Following the freak accident that granted him the powers of a spider, Peter's failure to stop a fleeing criminal ultimately resulted in Ben's murder. Only then did Peter finally understand that with great power, there must also come great responsibility, prompting him to assume the guise of a masked hero and fight crime in all its forms.

Since Ben's murder, Peter and May have been nearly inseparable, with May constantly doting on Peter, and always concerned about her nephew's health and well being. Deep down, May has always known Peter hid some secret he was unwilling to share with her, and their relationship reached a major turning point when she finally discovered his double life.

Though fearful for his safety, May realized that even Ben would have wanted Peter to live up to his heroic responsibilities. The secret Peter thought would destroy his aunt only strengthened their relationship, and the two are now closer than ever.

As a result of the revelation, May has become one of Spider-Man's most ardent supporters—in newspapers, on the Internet and among friends. May is constantly worried about Peter's safety, but can't help feel just a little more pride in her nephew now that she knows the truth.

ESSENTIAL READING

- *Essential Spider-Man Vols. I-V*
- *Peter Parker, Spider-Man Vol. I: A Day in the Life TPB*
- *Peter Parker, Spider-ManVol. II: One Small Break TPB*
- *Spider-Man vs. Dr. Octopus TPB*
- *Amazing Spider-ManVol. II: Revelations TPB*

Aunt May art by John Romita, Jr.; Uncle Ben art by Mark Buckingham

MARY JANE WATSON

Real Name:	Mary Jane Watson	**Weight:**	120 lbs.
First Appearance:	*Amazing Spider-Man* #25 (1965)	**Eye Color:**	Green
Height:	5'8"	**Hair Color:**	Red

The only child of a dysfunctional family, Mary Jane Watson spent a considerable portion of her childhood at the home of her Aunt Anna, who lived next door to May Parker and her nephew Peter. Throughout high school, acting gave her an escape from her troubled home life.

Despite frequent visits to Anna's house, Mary Jane didn't meet Peter until their aunts set them up on a date. Mary Jane's looks and personality stunned the bookish, introverted Peter, who was smitten immediately. In keeping with her bubbly personality, however, Mary Jane declined to get serious with Peter—or any other suitor, for that matter—and always wanted to keep her options open.

Years after the death of Peter's longtime girlfriend Gwen Stacy, he and Mary Jane began dating again. This time, both were more mature, building on a firm foundation of friendship. But as their romance grew more serious, Mary Jane panicked. Unable to commit to a long-term relationship due to her experiences growing up, she left New York to focus on her modeling career, hiding from her problems when she could no longer act as if they didn't exist.

After traveling the country and spending time with her family, Mary Jane finally returned to Peter's life and revealed that she had known for years about his secret identity as Spider-Man. The two started over, each providing the emotional stability and comfort the other needed.

Eventually, the stress of Peter's double life and Mary Jane's own developing career as an actress pulled the two apart, both physically and emotionally. After he broke a promise that he would give up being Spider-Man, Mary Jane left Peter. They remain close friends, but lead their own lives.

ESSENTIAL READING

- *Essential Spider-Man Vols. II-V*
- *Spider-Man: Kraven's Last Hunt TPB*
- *Spider-Man: Spirits of the Earth HC*
- *Spider-Man Visionaries: John Romita TPB*
- *Spider-Man vs. Venom TPB*
- *Spider-Man Visionaries: Todd McFarlane Vol. I TPB*

Art by Lee Weeks

DOCTOR OCTOPUS

Real Name:	Dr. Otto Octavius	**Weight:**	245 lbs.
First Appearance:	*Amazing Spider-Man* #3 (1963)	**Eye Color:**	Brown
Height:	5'9"	**Hair Color:**	Brown

Art by Steve Skroce

Once he was Otto Octavius, a brilliant and respected nuclear physicist, inventor and lecturer. In pursuit of academic excellence, Octavius designed and constructed a set of highly advanced robotic arms to assist him in his research. Now able to manipulate radioactive substances from a safe distance, Octavius was dubbed Dr. Octopus by his co-workers. A freak laboratory accident exposed Octavius to intense radioactivity, grafting the mechanical appendages to his body and granting him complete telepathic control over the artificial limbs. The mishap also altered Octavius' mind, transforming him into a criminally insane megalomaniac.

Abandoning his hopes of one day advancing the field of atomic research, Octavius turned instead to a life of crime. Possessed of incalculable power, the formerly timid scientist came to see himself as the most dangerous man alive. Dr. Octopus has sought power over others through various illegal endeavors, attempting to amass enough wealth through extortion and outright theft to build a sprawling empire of crime. If need be, Doc Ock is willing to resort to murder to achieve his desired ends. As the years passed, he became more and more obsessed with the destruction of his most frequent nemesis, Spider-Man.

Dr. Octopus has proven to be one of Spider-Man's most formidable foes; their battles have been among the hero's most brutal, testing the limits of Peter Parker's amazing abilities. Although Octavius' original, benevolent nature returns from time to time, his sinister Dr. Octopus personality always re-emerges to become dominant once again.

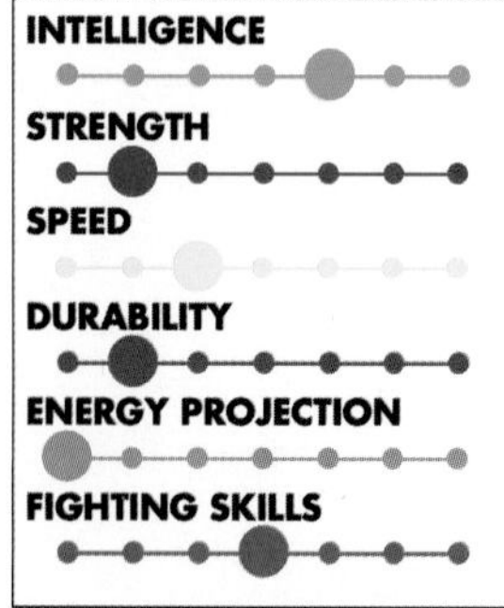

POWERS/WEAPONS

- Four telepathically controlled, super-strong steel tentacles attached to a harness encircling his lower chest and waist
- Brilliant engineer and inventor
- Extraordinary intelligence and concentration, enabling him to perform multiple complex actions simultaneously with his tentacles

ESSENTIAL READING

- *Essential Spider-Man Vols. I-V*
- *Spider-Man vs. Dr. Octopus TPB*
- *Amazing Spider-Man Vol. III TPB*

ELECTRO

Real Name:	Maxwell Dillon	**Weight:**	165 lbs.
First Appearance:	*Amazing Spider-Man* #9 (1964)	**Eye Color:**	Blue
Height:	5'11"	**Hair Color:**	Reddish-brown

High-wire lineman Maxwell Dillon was struck by lightning while touching spooled power cables, transforming him into a living capacitor, able to generate and store electrical energy. Greedy and opportunistic, Dillon embarked on a career as a costumed criminal.

Spider-Man has been Electro's most frequent nemesis—defeating the criminal time and again, constantly cracking jokes at his expense, and humiliating him in front of crowds gathered to witness their battles. Not particularly imaginative, Electro generally has employed his powers for robbery, extortion or revenge and has served several prison sentences for his crimes.

Unable to defeat Spider-Man and the city's other heroes on his own, Dillon has joined forces with like-minded super-villains, serving as a member of both the Frightful Four and various incarnations of the Sinister Six. These teams were tenuous associations at best and often fell apart due to members' infighting. Dillon also has sold his services as a hitman, as well as hunting Spider-Man for a bounty.

Electro continues to steal and scheme, his desire for money matched only by his personal grudge against Spider-Man. With defeat after defeat, Dillon's frustration with his hated foe has escalated to near-blinding rage. Electro will never rest until he feels he has achieved his full potential as a costumed criminal—and to do that, Spider-Man must die at his hands.

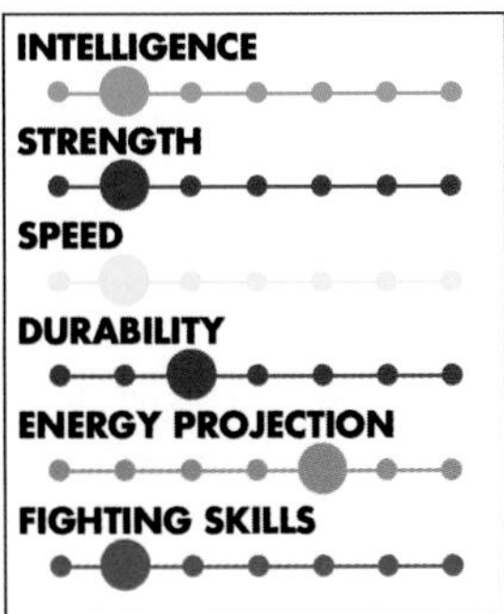

ESSENTIAL READING

- *Essential Spider-Man Vols. I & IV*
- *Spider-Man's Tangled Web Vol. II TPB*

Art by Gregg Schigiel

POWERS/WEAPONS

- Generation and storage of up to 1,000,000 volts of electrical energy
- Mental manipulation of electrical devices
- Ability to "ride" electricity

GREEN GOBLIN

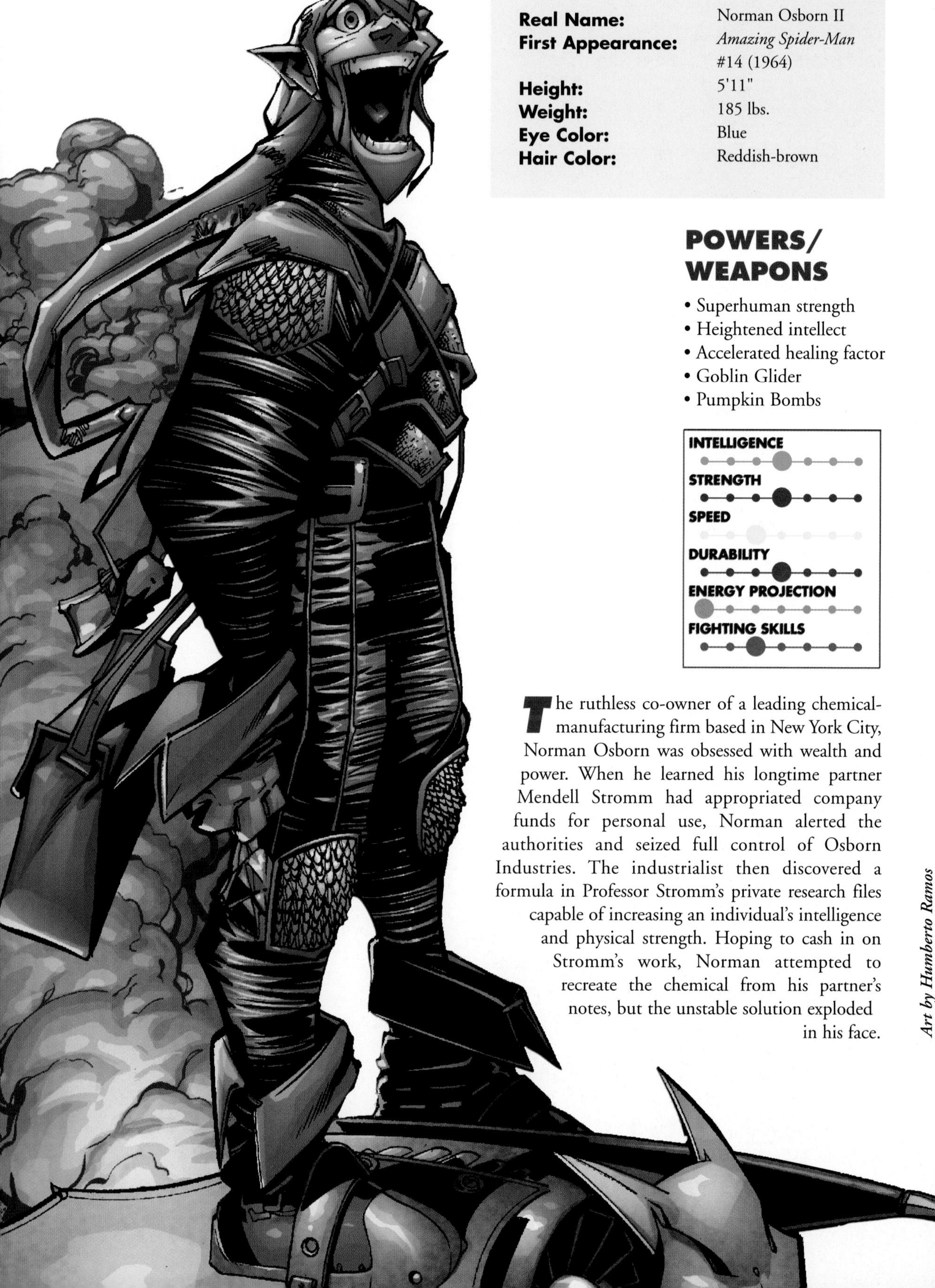

Real Name:	Norman Osborn II
First Appearance:	*Amazing Spider-Man* #14 (1964)
Height:	5'11"
Weight:	185 lbs.
Eye Color:	Blue
Hair Color:	Reddish-brown

POWERS/ WEAPONS

- Superhuman strength
- Heightened intellect
- Accelerated healing factor
- Goblin Glider
- Pumpkin Bombs

INTELLIGENCE
STRENGTH
SPEED
DURABILITY
ENERGY PROJECTION
FIGHTING SKILLS

The ruthless co-owner of a leading chemical-manufacturing firm based in New York City, Norman Osborn was obsessed with wealth and power. When he learned his longtime partner Mendell Stromm had appropriated company funds for personal use, Norman alerted the authorities and seized full control of Osborn Industries. The industrialist then discovered a formula in Professor Stromm's private research files capable of increasing an individual's intelligence and physical strength. Hoping to cash in on Stromm's work, Norman attempted to recreate the chemical from his partner's notes, but the unstable solution exploded in his face.

Art by Humberto Ramos

The serum did augment Osborn's intelligence dramatically, but at the price of his sanity. As a result, a second, even more sinister persona soon emerged—not unlike the green, goblin-like wraith that had haunted the nightmares of Norman's youth. His precarious mental state led him to arm himself with combustible projectiles and a gravity-defying glider. By killing Spider-Man, he hoped to attain instant credibility among the denizens of the underworld and set himself up as head of a worldwide crime syndicate.

Amazing Spider-Man #14, July 1964

After failing repeatedly to kill Spider-Man, the Goblin followed him and discovered his true identity: his son Harry's best friend and roommate Peter Parker. He then boastfully unmasked himself before Peter. In the ensuing battle, Norman was electrocuted and stricken with amnesia, which hid his memories of the Goblin and restored his original personality. Deciding Norman should not be punished for crimes he had committed while insane, and that Harry would be better off not knowing his father was the Goblin, Spider-Man elected not to expose his enemy's other identity.

Through the years, it became apparent that Norman favored Peter over his own son. An orphan, Peter was studious, inventive and industrious—a self-made success, like himself. Norman saw Harry as a good-for-nothing drug addict who would only go as far in life as his trust fund would take him. Likewise, Peter came to respect Norman, able to separate the driven businessman from the deranged psychopath who had attempted to kill Spider-Man on numerous occasions.

Art by Alex Ross

GREEN GOBLIN

Norman's sanity proved transitory, however, and the Goblin's personality and memories repeatedly resurfaced. Twice, Spider-Man managed to induce Norman into repressing the Goblin and returning to his normal state of mind in which he had no memory of his actions. But Peter's continued belief in the possibility of Norman's rehabilitation resulted in tragedy. To lure the web-slinger into a final showdown, the Goblin kidnapped Peter's first true love, Gwen Stacy. Despite Spider-Man's best efforts to save her, the Goblin took Gwen's life, hurling her from the top of the George Washington Bridge. Norman seemingly died, as well, impaled on his own glider as Spider-Man leapt from its path.

Mentally unbalanced following his father's death, Harry held Spider-Man responsible. Later discovering his friend's double identity, Harry became the new Green Goblin and set out to exact vengeance on Peter. His soul tainted by the touch of the Goblin, Harry slipped further into insanity and ultimately lost his life to the Goblin legacy.

The Goblin formula had actually delivered Norman from certain death, and he escaped to Europe, where he carved out a sprawling, secretive criminal empire. In the wake of Harry's failure to carry on the Osborn legacy, Norman attempted to mold Peter into a worthy heir. Poisoning him with a powerful hallucinogen, Norman caused Peter to strike at his own friends and loved ones in the guise of the Goblin. Nearly breaking Peter through physical and psychological torture, Norman offered him the chance to embrace the darkness within his soul. Even under extreme duress, Peter found the strength to reject Norman's offer, incurring his adversary's eternal wrath. Paralyzed by Norman's knowledge of his own identity, Peter has yet to expose him to the authorities. As a result, Norman remains a wealthy, respected industrialist.

Still stinging from Peter's rejection, Norman is finished waiting for sinister schemes to come to fruition. Striking at Spider-Man through his friends and loved ones, the Goblin won't rest until he has destroyed the wall-crawler's world. No games, no tricks—just a mad thirst for vengeance.

ESSENTIAL READING

- *Essential Spider-Man Vols. I-V*
- *Spider-Man: Blue HC*
- *Spider-Man: The Death of Gwen Stacy TPB*
- *Spider-Man: Revenge of the Green Goblin TPB*
- *Spider-Man: Return of the Goblin TPB*

Art by Humberto Ramo

Art by Jae Lee

KRAVEN

Real Name:	Alyosha Kravinoff	**Weight:**	220 lbs.
First Appearance:	*Spectacular Spider-Man* #243 (1997)	**Eye Color:**	Brown
Height:	6'3"	**Hair Color:**	Black

Alyosha Kravinoff's father—former Russian noble Sergei Kravinoff, the original Kraven the Hunter—came to America to hunt Spider-Man. His initial pursuit gave way to a yearslong battle between the two, but Kraven's repeated failures slowly drove him toward the brink of insanity. Their rivalry came to a head when Kraven buried Spider-Man alive and assumed his identity. Having proven he was his adversary's superior, Kraven at last experienced peace. Feeling that he had finally found true happiness, he took his own life. Alyosha, his youngest son, was devastated by the loss.

Alyosha had grown up in Africa, where he learned from his father the ways of the beast and the hunt, and how to be a proper and noble man. Following Sergei's death, Alyosha traveled to New York to test the web-slinger himself. He needed to understand what had compelled his father to pursue the hero with such fury, but the two came to an eventual understanding when Spider-Man finally made clear the circumstances surrounding the elder Kraven's last hunt.

Aloysha now recognizes that his father chose to walk a path likely to result in a violent death. Determined not to follow in his footsteps, Aloysha aims to become the first in his family to break from the Kravinoff legacy of madness and depravity. A true Renaissance man, "Al" possesses a deep, almost spiritual sense of right and wrong—along with a razor-sharp wit and a true concern for the people around him. One of those people is his girlfriend Timber, a struggling actress. Seeing her constantly rejected for roles by producers who lacked vision was more than Al could bear. He took Timber to Hollywood and set himself up as a producer. Al learned quickly Hollywood is a jungle in its own right, and that he'd need all his skills and cunning to survive.

INTELLIGENCE
STRENGTH
SPEED
DURABILITY
ENERGY PROJECTION
FIGHTING SKILLS

POWERS/ WEAPONS

- Superhuman strength, speed, agility and stamina
- Animalistic abilities and senses
- Communication with and control over animals
- Mastery of all hunting weapons

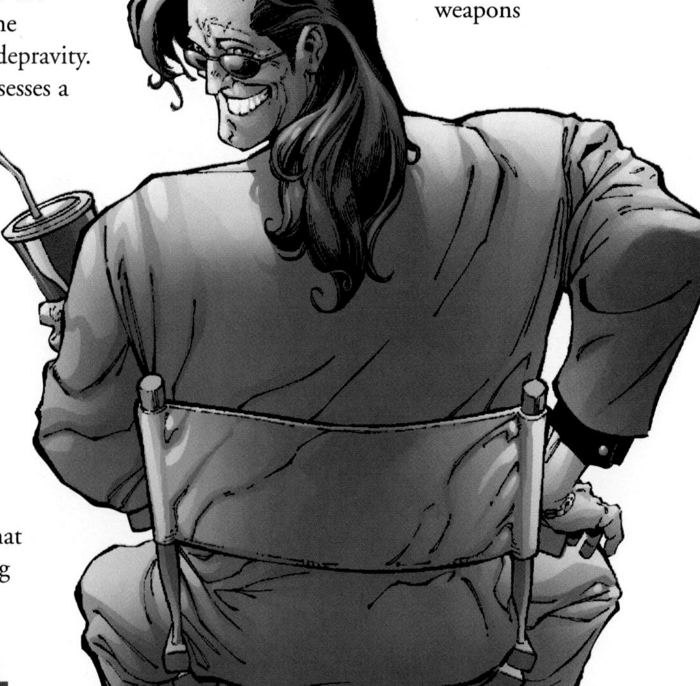

Art by Joe Quesada

ESSENTIAL READING

- *Essential Spider-Man Vols. II, III & IV*
- *Spider-Man: Kraven's Last Hunt TPB*
- *Spider-Man's Tangled Web Vol. III TPB*

LIZARD

Real Name:	Dr. Curtis Connors	**Eye Color:**	Blue as Connors, red as Lizard
First Appearance:	*Amazing Spider-Man* #6 (1963)		
Height:	5'11"	**Hair Color:**	Brown as Connors, none as Lizard
Weight:	175 lbs.		

Army surgeon Curtis Connors was honorably discharged after losing his right arm in the line of duty. Also a brilliant herpetologist, Dr. Connors studied the regenerative properties of reptiles, hoping he could somehow apply those abilities to humans and re-grow his lost limb. After years of study, Connors believed he had isolated the genes responsible for regeneration and injected himself with a formula of his own creation. The serum initially restored Connors' missing arm—but then quickly triggered a body-wide mutagenic change, transforming him into a lizard-like creature.

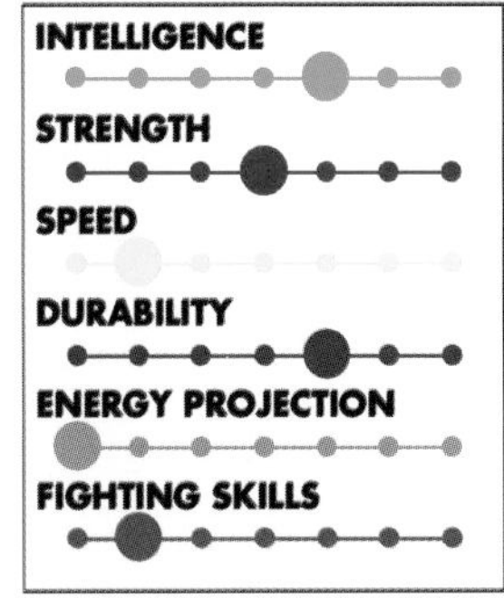

The Lizard soon came into contact with Spider-Man, who used his biochemical expertise to devise a treatment that temporarily reversed Connors' transformation. Over time, Connors and Spider-Man became friends and colleagues, each respecting the others' knowledge and scientific skill. Connors continues to revert into the Lizard when exposed to stress or specific chemical signals, however. Not wishing ill to come to his friend—and understanding all too well the danger posed by the Lizard—Spider-Man is always quick to respond and reverse the transformation.

Through the years, the formula has caused a schism in Connors' psyche as his more primitive, reptile side struggles for dominance. The Lizard has its own goals: notably, the destruction of the human race, which it sees as unfit to rule the planet. The sight of his wife and son can cause Connors' personality to reassert dominance, however, suggesting that some aspect of the scientist's psyche lives within the Lizard. Conversely, Connors has willingly transformed into the Lizard on occasion to achieve certain ends, hinting that a portion of the beast exists within him as well.

POWERS

- Superhuman strength and speed and the ability to scale sheer surfaces
- Limited invulnerability
- Mental communication with and control over reptiles in a one-mile radius
- Wields his tail as a weapon and can swing it at more than 70 mph.

Art by John Romita, Jr.

MORLUN

Real Name: Morlun
First Appearance: *Amazing Spider-Man* #30 (2001)
Height: 6'2"
Weight: 175 lbs.
Eye Color: Red
Hair Color: Black

Morlun is one of many beings who hunt individuals gifted with animal-based, totemistic powers, such as those possessed by Spider-Man. Driven by nature, Morlun must feed to survive. Like a vampire, he absorbs his prey's life force for sustenance. Through the centuries, his hunt has become a ritualized game of cat and mouse, with the confident hunter slowing closing in on his doomed quarry. Morlun is a creature of singular purpose: Nothing matters but his hunger.

After learning of Spider-Man's existence, Morlun traveled to America with his human assistant Dex to hunt the hero. Knowing that Spider-Man would rush to the rescue of those in danger, Morlun set a fire to lure the wall-crawler to him. During their first encounter, Morlun nearly beat Spider-Man to death, testing his adversary's abilities and worthiness as prey. Spider-Man barely escaped with his life.

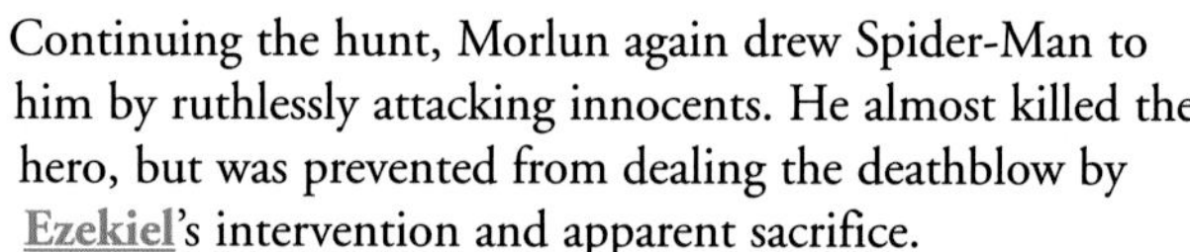

Continuing the hunt, Morlun again drew Spider-Man to him by ruthlessly attacking innocents. He almost killed the hero, but was prevented from dealing the deathblow by Ezekiel's intervention and apparent sacrifice.

After studying a sample of his predator's blood, Spider-Man determined that Morlun sought to feed on the spider in him because he thought it to be pure. Resorting to drastic measures, Spider-Man injected himself with a near-lethal dose of radiation and awaited Morlun's inevitable attack. When Morlun attempted to drain Spider-Man's life force, the creature was overcome by the radiation and severely weakened. Morlun had underestimated Spider-Man, viewing the hero simply as food rather than a worthy adversary. While begging for mercy from Spider-Man, Morlun was shot and presumably killed by Dex, who had suffered years of abuse at his master's hand.

POWERS/ WEAPONS

- Superhuman strength, reflexes, and speed
- Draws life force from victims

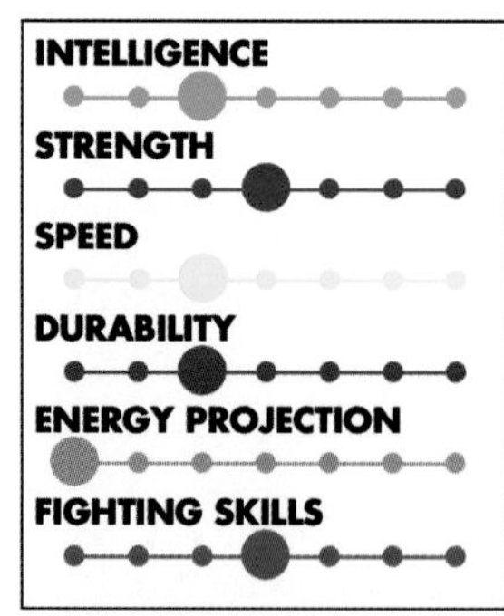

ESSENTIAL READING

- *Amazing Spider-Man Vol. 1: Coming Home TPB*

Art by John Romita, Jr.

MYSTERIO

Real Name:	Quentin Beck	**Weight:**	175 lbs.
First Appearance:	*Amazing Spider-Man* #13 (1964)	**Eye Color:**	Blue
Height:	5'11"	**Hair Color:**	Black

Quentin Beck was once one of Hollywood's most accomplished special-effects artists. Building upon his great strides, his peers in the field dominated the industry, earning accolades and Oscars. But Beck sought greater fame than his behind-the-scenes role allowed. While others tinkered with two-dimensional imagery, Beck chose to take the illusions off the screen. After committing a series of crimes dressed as Spider-Man, he adopted the guise of Mysterio, an adventurer who meant to capture the rogue wall-crawler. The would-be champion proved no match for the arachnid-like hero, however, and Beck was jailed for his attempt.

Humiliated, Beck's animosity toward Spider-Man grew. He felt the web-slinger had stolen the glory meant for him, forever relegating Mysterio to the role of second-class super-villain. Beck vowed to set things right. To gain an upper hand in his battles with the wall-crawler, he studied hypnosis, sleight of hand, psychology and brain chemistry. Beck also added psychoactive chemicals and state-of-the-art illusions to his arsenal. Mysterio continued to clash with Spider-Man for years, but even his expanded repertoire proved insufficient. Countless defeats at the hero's hands only served to stoke his anger.

Beck learned during a period of incarceration that he had brain and lung cancer, a result of exposure to the chemicals he had used as Mysterio. He was released from prison with less than a year to live. For his last act, Beck decided defeating Spider-Man physically was not enough: He would utterly destroy Spider-Man from the inside, driving him insane. Unable to exact final revenge upon Spider-Man at the time, Mysterio instead deemed Daredevil a suitable substitute. Launching an intricate, all-encompassing illusion, Beck sought to goad Daredevil into killing him, an appropriate end to his career as a villain. Mysterio misjudged Daredevil's will, however, and was beaten yet again. Utterly defeated yet ever the showman, Beck apparently committed suicide in front of the hero.

ESSENTIAL READING

- *Daredevil Visionaries: Kevin Smith TPB*
- *Essential Spider-Man Vol. 1*

POWERS/ WEAPONS

- Accomplished magician and hypnotist
- Skilled amateur chemist
- Holographic projectors
- Hallucinogenic gases

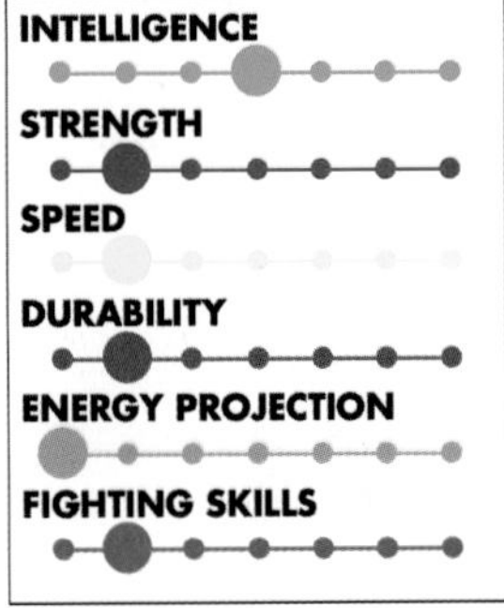

Art by Joe Quesada

RHINO

Real Name:	Alex O'Hirn	**Weight:**	710 lbs.
First Appearance:	*Amazing Spider-Man* #41 (1966)	**Eye Color:**	Brown
Height:	6'5"	**Hair Color:**	Brown

Seduced by promises of wealth and power, small-time enforcer Alex O'Hirn underwent months of chemical and radiation treatments to transform himself into a superhumanly powerful assassin. O'Hirn's newfound strength and speed carried a horrific price, however: a near impregnable, chemically and radioactively treated rhinoceros-like exoskeleton permanently bonded to his body. Ultimately turning on his backers, O'Hirn became a free agent in the world of super-powered criminals. Spider-Man handed the man-mountain his first defeat, virtually destroying the Rhino's armor with acid.

Given that the Rhino's preferred plan of attack is to run into things and knock them down, the super-hero community has always viewed him as more of a joke than a threat—a fact to which his lengthy arrest record readily attests. Easily outsmarted, the Rhino also is looked down upon by his fellow criminals, who often laugh at him behind his back. As a result, O'Hirn has undergone additional treatments to further augment his strength, seeking out more and more powerful Rhino suits with the failure of each successive hide.

All brawn and no brains, the Rhino may not be intelligent, but he's no fool. He knows that without his suit, he's just another muscle-bound thug—one most likely destined for a short life and violent death. With the armor, he isn't just a nobody; he's a threat not to be ignored. As such, the Rhino will never shed his hide, despite the medical and social complications it presents.

POWERS/WEAPONS

- Superhuman strength and stamina
- Virtually impenetrable hide
- Above-average speed

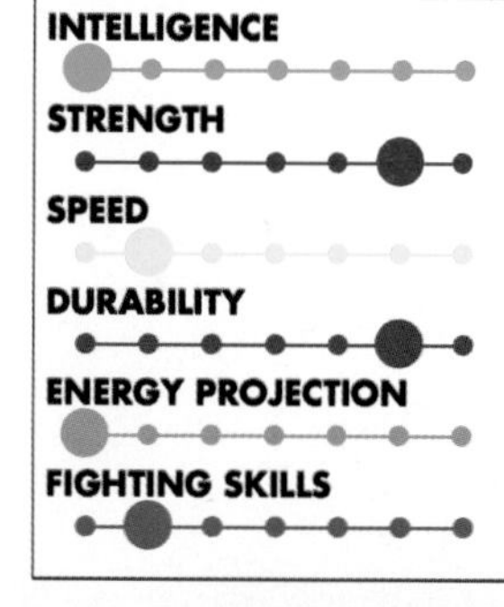

ESSENTIAL READING

- *Essential Spider-Man Vol. III*
- *Spider-Man's Tangled Web Vol. I TPB*
- *Spider-Man Visionaries: John Romita TPB*

Art by Duncan Fegredo

SANDMAN

Real Name:	William Baker, a.k.a. Flint Marko	**Weight:**	240 lbs in human form; 450 lbs. at maximum density and normal mass in "sand" form
First Appearance:	*Amazing Spider-Man* #4 (1963)		
Height:	6'1"		
Eye Color:	Brown		
Hair Color:	Brown		

Born and raised on the wrong side of the tracks, William Baker learned to steal at an early age. He cheated and bluffed his way through school, but excelled at football. Baker was expelled when he accepted a bribe to throw an important game. Landing steady work as a mob henchman, Baker adopted the underworld alias Flint Marko. Despite his success as a gangster, Marko entertained thoughts of reforming to marry his girlfriend Marcy Conroy. But when he was arrested for his crimes, he grew increasingly hostile. Upon his release, Marko discovered that Conroy had left him for another member of his gang, Vic Rollins. After exacting brutal revenge on Rollins, Marko embarked on a one-man crime spree. Narrowly evading the law, he made his way down the East Coast.

Marko sought refuge at a nuclear test site near Savannah, Georgia. He was lying on a nearby beach when an experimental reactor's steam system exploded, bombarding him with a massive dose of radiation. Afterwards, Marko found that he could transform his body into an animated, sand-like substance. Now able to elude the authorities with ease, Marko embarked on a criminal career, most often thwarted by Spider-Man.

The Sandman's need for validation swiftly overtook his greed and lust for power. Marko became determined to prove himself to the world at large as a formidable threat to Spider-Man. Marko knows he possessed the raw power to soundly defeat his enemies—but that knowledge is the source of bitter frustration, since he can never use his abilities effectively enough to win a decisive victory over the wall-crawler.

POWERS/WEAPONS

- Ability to transform any part of his body into a sand-like substance and alter his size and mass by incorporating nearby sand
- Superhuman strength
- Virtually indestructible

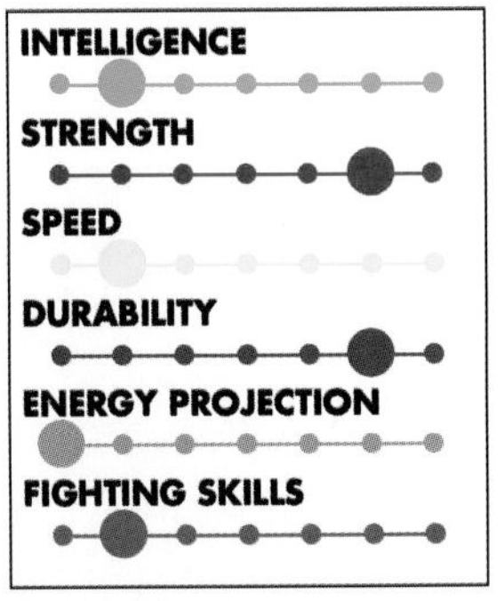

ESSENTIAL READING

- *Essential Spider-Man Vol. I*
- *Peter Parker, Spider-Man Vol. I: A Day In the Life TPB*
- *Spider-Man's Tangled Web Vol. IV*

Art by Mark Bagley

VENOM

Real Name:	Eddie Brock	**Weight:**	260 lbs.
First Appearance:	*Amazing Spider-Man* #299 (1988)	**Eye Color:**	Blue
Height:	6'3"	**Hair Color:**	Reddish-blond

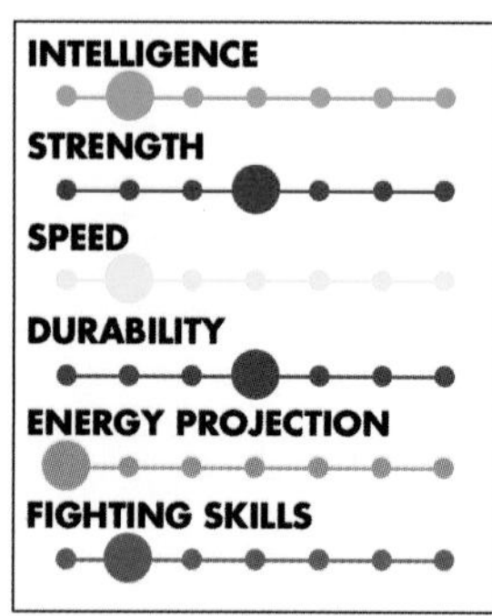

POWERS/ WEAPONS

- Superhuman strength and agility, as well as the ability to spin web-like strands and scale sheer surfaces
- Immunity to Spider-Man's early warning danger sense
- Mimicry of any individual's appearance

The homicidal embodiment of pure hatred and blinding rage, Venom is an amalgamation of two wildly disparate beings, each obsessed with Spider-Man. One half is Eddie Brock, an unethical former journalist whose meteoric career was cut short when Spider-Man revealed a story he had written to be false. The other is the alien symbiote that posed for a time as Spider-Man's black costume, attempting all the while to graft itself permanently to the wall-crawler.

Coincidentally arriving at the church where the creature had gone to ground, the devastated Brock's intense emotions attracted the empathic symbiote, which Spider-Man had rebuffed repeatedly and nearly destroyed. Brock gave himself fully to the alien, their mutual fixation fanned into an overwhelming animosity by the union. There is no more Eddie Brock, no more symbiote: There is only Venom.

Armed with the alien's intimate knowledge of Spider-Man, Venom embarked on a campaign of terror against Peter Parker, often tormenting the hero's friends and loved ones to cause him personal distress. On numerous occasions, Venom has targeted Mary Jane Watson, using her pain as a means to unsettle Spider-Man.

Utterly insane and totally without remorse, Venom is the antithesis of his adversary. Spider-Man understands that with great power, there must also come great responsibility. Driven entirely by a single base emotion, Venom comprehends only its all-consuming desire for revenge.

ESSENTIAL READING

- *Spider-Man vs. Venom TPB*
- *Spider-Man: Maximum Carnage TPB*
- *Spider-Man Visionaries: Todd McFarlane Vol. 1 TPB*

Art by John Romita, Jr.

VULTURE

Real Name:	Adrian Toomes	**Weight:**	175 lbs.
First Appearance:	*Amazing Spider-Man* #2 (1963)	**Eye Color:**	Hazel
Height:	5'11"	**Hair Color:**	None

A brilliant electronics engineer, Adrian Toomes devoted much of his life to the creation of an electromagnetic harness that would allow its wearer to fly like a bird. Bilked out of his life savings and the profits from his successful electronics firm by his business partner, Toomes invented the costumed identity of the Vulture to expose his associate's misdeeds.

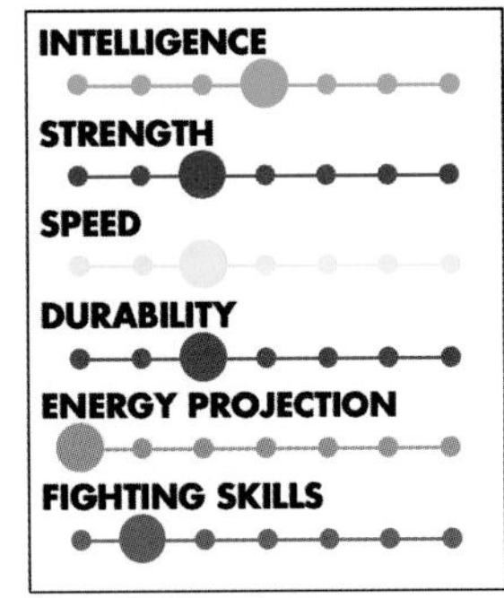

The Vulture's quest for justice dimmed as he began to revel in the illicit thrill of thievery and the ease with which he could commit crimes thanks to the power of flight. Seeking to steal enough money to live a life of luxury, the Vulture attracted the attention of Spider-Man. Ultimately, the hero captured Toomes, leaving him to stew in his hatred for Spider-Man and plan his revenge from jail.

Of all the web-slinger's foes, Toomes takes Spider-Man's incessant jokes and biting comments most personally; he has developed a deep hatred for the hero as a result. Unwilling to take responsibility for his lackluster criminal career, Toomes blames the wall-crawler's interference for his inability to attain a life of wealth and comfort. The Vulture continues to stalk the city from on high, hoping his next score will earn him the handsome reward so far denied him by his hated foe.

POWERS/ WEAPONS

- Superhuman strength and flight while in costume
- Variety of energy-based pistols and grenades

ESSENTIAL READING

- *Essential Spider-Man Vols. I-IV*
- *Daredevil: Love's Labors Lost TPB*

Art by John Romita, Jr.

X-MEN

CHANGE IS COMING. THE FUTURE OF EVOLUTION HAS EMERGED. THEY ARE MUTANTS,* HOMO SUPERIOR, *GIFTED WITH STRANGE AND FANTASTIC ABILITIES SIMPLY BY VIRTUE OF THEIR GENETIC MAKEUP.

Every day, mutants are born in greater numbers—and humanity's panic and paranoia increases exponentially. Mutants are called freaks. Genetic monstrosities. They are mocked, feared, spat upon and accused...of stealing human jobs, eating human food and taking human partners. But they are emerging in the inner cities, in the suburbs, in the deserts and in the jungles. They need teachers, people who can help them overcome their anger and show them how to use their strange gifts responsibly.

Under a cloud of increasing anti-mutant sentiment, Professor X created a safe haven at his Westchester mansion where he could train teenagers to use their unique genetic gifts for the betterment of all. Hated and feared by humanity, the outcast adventurers continued to hone their strange powers while defending the world from those mutants who would take advantage of their tremendous abilities to subjugate mankind.

Art by Frank Quitely

RIP
HOMO SAPIENS
33.000 BC - 2005 AD

AGENT X

Real Name:	Alex Hayden
First Appearance:	*Agent X* #1 (2002)
Height:	6'
Weight:	215 lbs.
Eye Color:	Brown
Hair Color:	None

POWERS/ WEAPONS

- Superhuman healing factor
- Above-average strength, speed and dexterity
- Proficient in the use of virtually any weapon, but especially guns

INTELLIGENCE

STRENGTH

SPEED

DURABILITY

ENERGY PROJECTION

FIGHTING SKILLS

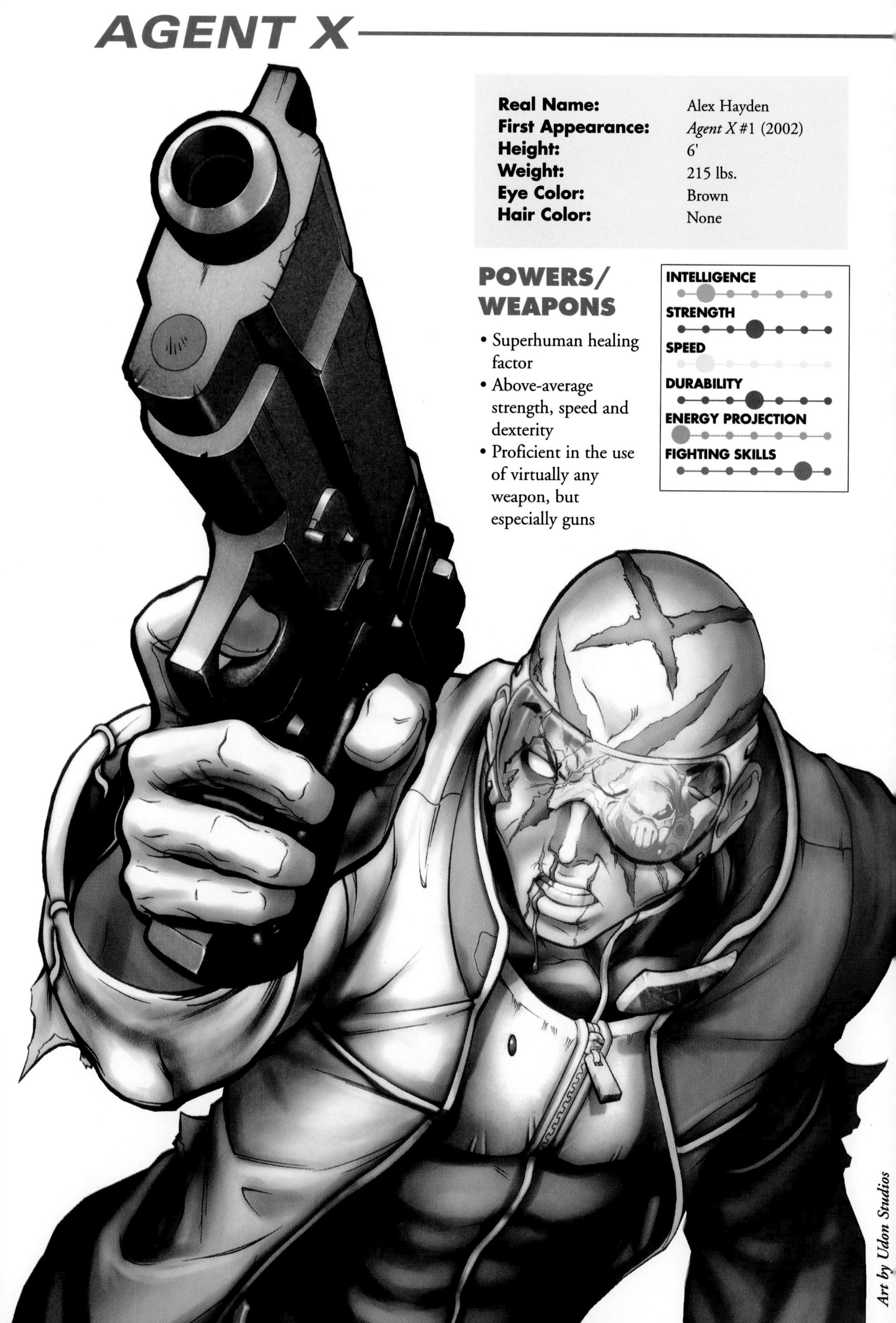

Art by Udon Studios

Agent X #1, August 2002

He knows nothing of his past—and he doesn't care; he just wants to become the world's greatest mercenary. Taking the name Alex Hayden, the man now called Agent X literally stumbled into the life of receptionist Sandi Brandenberg, who took him in because of his resemblance to an old friend and her fondness for hard-luck cases.

Appearing to have been grievously wounded, with the letter "X" carved into both his skull and face, Hayden was a blank slate. As far as he knew, he had come into existence only moments before he found Sandi. While Hayden recalled nothing of his previous life, he did know one thing, and with burning conviction: He wanted to become the world's best mercenary.

Sandi took compassion on Hayden and appealed to her boyfriend—the Taskmaster, a world-renowned mercenary—to train him. Taskmaster believed Hayden was merely an old colleague pretending to be stricken with amnesia, but his theory was refuted when Hayden denied under great duress approaching torture that he knew anything about his past.

The Taskmaster's training worked in ways neither Hayden nor his teacher had expected. The instruction awakened some innate abilities, and Hayden's skills grew exponentially with experience—even more so during times of stress.

Together, Hayden and Sandi formed Agency X, a no-questions-asked mercenary service. Armed with any number of weapons, a non-stop mouth and a bizarre sense of humor, Agent X seeks to make a name for himself as a soldier-for-hire.

Refusing to pause for even a moment of self-reflection, Hayden's singular ambition drives him ever onward. To what end, though, Hayden himself may never know. His total being is focused only on acquiring the skills he needs to be the best mercenary the world has ever seen. So far, he's succeeding. Agent X is very good at doing very bad things.

ARCHANGEL

Real Name:	Warren Kenneth Worthington III
First Appearance:	*X-Men* #1 (1963)
Height:	6'
Weight:	150 lbs.
Eye Color:	Blue
Hair Color:	Blond

Art by Kia Asamiya

ESSENTIAL READING

- *Essential Uncanny X-Men Vol. 1*
- *Uncanny X-Men Vol. I: Hope TPB*
- *X-Men: Fall of the Mutants TPB*
- *X-Men: Mutant Massacre TPB*

While attending a prestigious East Coast boarding school, Warren Worthington sprouted wings from his shoulder blades. Initially alarmed by his mutant gift, Warren soon grew to relish the freedom of flight. Still, he strapped the wings tightly to his back to avoid suspicion—and discrimination. Warren was forced into action, however, when fire struck his dormitory. Donning a long, blond wig and nightshirt to conceal his identity, he saved the students from certain death, appearing as an angel to onlookers.

Despite the obvious risks—exposure, loss of personal standing, even death—Warren would not be grounded. Shortly after saving his classmates, he took to the skies of New York City as a costumed crimefighter. Warren's nocturnal activities drew the attention of Professor X, who invited him to become a founding member of the X-Men. Warren accepted Xavier's offer.

Warren initially hid the secret of his double life with a mask, but later revealed his identity to the public. Besides serving as an example to other mutants, he naïvely hoped to dazzle humanity with the photogenic face of evolution. Tolerated only because of his family's vast wealth and impeccable standing, Warren quickly learned he would be embraced for who and what he truly is only if Xavier's dream for peaceful coexistence between man and mutant became reality. As such, he has fought for his mentor's vision in various capacities since his teens. But Warren was not always Xavier's prize pupil. For a time, he made more headlines for his social escapades and celebrity conquests than as the poster boy for human-mutant relations.

X-Men: Mutant Massacre TPB

Warren's carefree world came crashing down after dark forces conspired to clip his wings. When a squad of superhuman assassins descended on the Morlocks, New York City's subterranean mutants, the X-Men intervened. During the clash, one of the mercenaries impaled Warren's wings. The wounds became infected, and doctors were forced to amputate the crippled appendages.

Deeply depressed, Warren attempted to commit suicide by crashing his plane. Just before the explosion of his small aircraft, however, he was teleported to safety by Apocalypse. The mutant warlord offered to return Warren's ability to fly, but for a lofty price. Warren could regain what he had lost only by becoming Apocalypse's acolyte: the Fourth Horseman, Death. Warren was desperate and confused, and he surrendered himself to Apoclaypse completely. Born on razor-sharp wings of steel, the fallen hero fought his former teammates under his new master's thrall. Mentally unbalanced, Warren came to his senses only when tricked into believing he had killed his old friend Iceman.

Having reconciled himself to his short-lived servitude to Apocalypse, Warren finally molted the warlord's metallic wings to reveal his natural feathers underneath. Recovered from his brush with evil, Archangel again soars the skies alongside the X-Men. No longer a happy-go-lucky youth, Warren fully understands the price that must be paid for lasting peace between man and mutant. Now dedicated completely to Xavier's cause, he has used much of his sizeable inheritance to further the fight for a better tomorrow.

POWERS/ WEAPONS

- Flight via natural wings

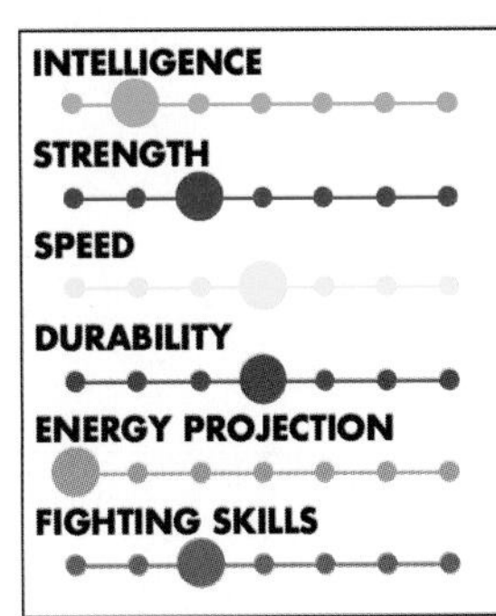

BEAST

Real Name: Dr. Henry McCoy
First Appearance: *X-Men* #1 (1963)

Height: 5'11"
Weight: 402 lbs.
Eye Color: Blue
Hair Color: Originally brown, bluish-black in furry form

ESSENTIAL READING

- *Essential Uncanny X-Men Vol. I*
- *New X-Men Vol. I: E Is For Extinction TPB*
- *New X-Men Vol. II: Imperial TPB*
- *Uncanny X-Men Vol. I: Hope TPB*
- *X-Treme X-Men Vol. I TPB*
- *X-Treme X-Men: Savage Land TPB*

Art by Kevin Sharpe

Henry McCoy was born with unusually large hands and feet, the first evidence of his mutant powers. As a youth, his superhuman agility and athletic prowess earned him recognition as a star football player. A big man on campus, Hank hid his mutation and growing thirst for knowledge in plain sight—until he was exposed as a mutant and asked to leave school. When Professor X learned of Hank's existence, he invited the teenager to enroll in his School for Gifted Youngsters. Hank excelled in the classroom, and the prestigious, private institution offered limitless academic opportunities and personalized study for the small, select student body.

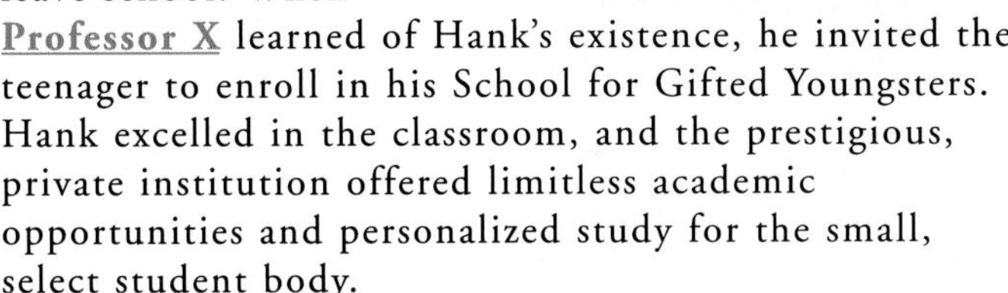

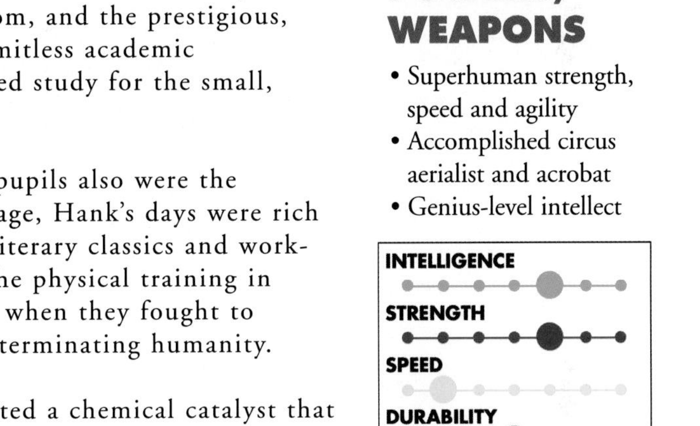

Art by Frank Quitely

POWERS/ WEAPONS

- Superhuman strength, speed and agility
- Accomplished circus aerialist and acrobat
- Genius-level intellect

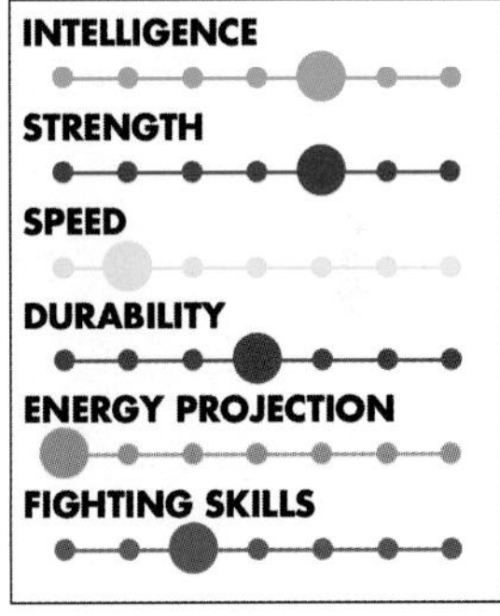

Few suspected Professor X's pupils also were the X-Men. Under Xavier's tutelage, Hank's days were rich with differential equations, literary classics and workouts in the Danger Room. The physical training in particular helped the X-Men when they fought to discourage Magneto from exterminating humanity.

After graduation, Hank isolated a chemical catalyst that triggered mutation. He sampled the serum himself, with unintended results. The formula caused him to grow fur, enlarged his canine teeth and amplified his already prodigious athletic abilities. He attempted at first to hide his condition, but Hank eventually learned to accept his blue, more bestial form. Following a second mutation into a catlike creature, however, he began to doubt his humanity.

Hank struggles to resist his feral urges, afraid others will come to see him as an animal rather than as a man. Although respected by the world's top minds, the Beast knows what it's like to be jilted by the proverbial Beauty, shunned by his longtime lover solely on the basis of his altered appearance.

Fighting his fear of loneliness and rejection, the Beast has dedicated himself to the creation of a better world for humans and mutants—a world in which Hank will be accepted for the brilliant, gentle man he truly is. The Beast is equal parts biochemist and activist, applying his physical gifts and vast intellect toward the fight for genetic equality.

BISHOP

Real Name: Lucas Bishop
First Appearance: *Uncanny X-Men* #282 (1991)
Height: 6'6"
Weight: 275 lbs.
Eye Color: Brown, sometimes red
Hair Color: Black

POWERS/ WEAPONS

- Energy absorption/emission
- Variety of energy-projecting firearms

INTELLIGENCE
STRENGTH
SPEED
DURABILITY
ENERGY PROJECTION
FIGHTING SKILLS

ESSENTIAL READING

- *X-Treme X-Men* Vols. I & II TPB
- *X-Treme X-Men: Savage Land* TPB

Art by Salvador Larroca

Lucas Bishop grew to adulthood roughly 70 years into Earth's future, a time and place governed by violence and ruled by fear—the exact world the X-Men have dedicated their lives to preventing. In this war-torn era, the heirs to the legacy of the X-Men have established the peacekeeping organization known as Xavier's Security Enforcers. Adherents to Professor X's dream for peaceful coexistence between *Homo sapiens* and *Homo superior*, the agency's founders believed mutants could police themselves. A homicide cop, Bishop patrolled the mean streets of a planet almost shattered by war, with one whole continent rendered uninhabitable by radiation. In pursuit of the mutant madman Trevor Fitzroy and an army of homicidal superhuman outlaws, Bishop and his XSE lieutenants traveled back to our present through one of the criminal's own time portals.

Stranded in the past, they tracked their mark into the midst of a fray between the X-Men and the Sentinels. Confronted with the legends of his youth, Bishop's first reaction was one of disbelief. He and his compatriots battled the X-Men ferociously, seeking to expose what they thought to be an uncanny deception. Their confrontation was cut short before Bishop could discover the error of his ways. Ultimately, Bishop's troops were slain by Fitzroy's forces during the deadly firefight. Only through the X-Men's intervention did the badly injured Bishop survive.

Finally coming to terms with his time-tossed condition, Bishop was honored when Professor X invited him to join the team whose members he had idolized since childhood. Bishop found new purpose with the X-Men, fighting alongside the mutant adventurers to avert the genetic war that was already history for him. Initially uneasy with Bishop's presence, the X-Men soon came to realize he was a devoted disciple of Xavier's philosophy.

Art by
Salvador Larroca

Although decades removed from his rightful jurisdiction, Bishop remains a police officer at heart. He stands steadfastly behind his badge and the oath he swore to it, and he won't rest until justice is served. A disciplined detective and battle-hardened soldier, Bishop relies on methodical analysis and thorough investigation to close most cases—but is willing to take extreme action when necessary, employing his mutant ability to absorb and rechannel energy to protect and serve a populace that hates and fears his kind.

CYCLOPS

Real Name:	Scott Summers
First Appearance:	*X-Men* #1 (1963)
Height:	6'1"
Weight:	185 lbs.
Eye Color:	Glowing red
Hair Color:	Brown

ESSENTIAL READING

- *Essential Uncanny X-Men Vol. 1*
- *Essential X-Men Vols. I-IV*
- *New X-Men Vol. I: E Is For Extinction TPB*
- *New X-Men Vol. II: Imperial TPB*
- *X-Men: Children of the Atom TPB*
- *X-Men: Vignettes TPB*
- *X-Men Visionaries: Jim Lee TPB*

The first X-Man, Scott Summers was the older of two sons born to Major Christopher Summers, a test pilot for the U.S. Air Force, and his wife Katherine. Major Summers was flying his family home from vacation when a midair accident crippled the Summers' plane. Katherine pushed Scott and his brother Alex to safety with the only available parachute. With Christopher and Katherine presumed dead, the authorities separated the two boys: Alex was adopted immediately, but Scott was injured in the fall and remained comatose in a hospital for a year. After recovering, he was placed in an orphanage. Years later, as a teenager, Scott began to suffer severe headaches and eyestrain. A specialist discovered that lenses made of ruby quartz corrected the problem.

Essential X-Men Vol. I

When Scott was in his mid-teens, his mutant power erupted in an uncontrollable blast of optic force that demolished a crane, causing it to drop its payload on a terrified crowd. Scott saved the onlookers' lives by obliterating the object with another blast. But the bystanders rallied into an angry mob, believing he had tried to kill them. Scott fled, escaping on a freight train. Shortly after, Professor X enlisted him as the first member of the X-Men, helping him harness his optic blasts. To call Professor X a mentor fails to express fully what he means to Scott. More than a teacher, Xavier is the father he never knew. Rather than merely educate Scott in the use of his superhuman powers, Professor X molded the young mutant into the honorable man he is today through precise instruction and unwavering example.

Scott would gladly lay down his life to make the Professor's dream of peaceful coexistence between humans and mutants a reality. As deputy leader of the X-Men, he acted as Xavier's second-in-command for years, through various roster changes. A natural-born leader, Scott's teenage social skills were nevertheless somewhat lacking. He fell in love with teammate Jean Grey, but his reserved demeanor at first prevented him from expressing his true feelings. Eventually, he overcame his anxieties, and the two entered into a romantic relationship. Following an adventure in space, Scott was unaware that Jean had been replaced and cast into suspended animation by the cosmic being called the Phoenix Force. Ultimately, the imprint of Jean's psyche compelled the power-mad entity to commit suicide, thus preventing it from destroying the universe. Scott believed the love of his life had died. Griefsticken, he left the X-Men, but his feelings for Jean endured.

Some time after the real Jean emerged from suspended animation, she and Scott married. She was his inspiration, a beacon lighting his soul with hopes and dreams. But through the years, Cyclops has demonstrated a tendency to put his personal life aside in favor of his responsibilities as leader of the X-Men. He has grown more comfortable shouting orders to Jean in the Danger Room than confiding in her his deepest feelings. Blessed and cursed as he is with concussive blasts that fire whenever he opens his eyes, Cyclops feels he must forever hold himself in check or risk destroying everyone and everything around him. As a

CYCLOPS

result of her husband's tunnel vision and stoicism, Jean has sought the support of others with increasing frequency, be it father figure Professor X or teammate Wolverine. At times, this has threatened to drive a wedge between the two, but Jean has always remained faithful to Scott.

The X-Men are much more than a team to Scott. They're his friends and his life. And when he was reunited with his brother Alex, who had begun to manifest mutant powers of his own, Cyclops brought him into his new family. As Havok, Alex trained with the X-Men to hone his ability to absorb and transmit cosmic energy.

Cyclops is blessed with the gift of vision: the ability to identify unique solutions to the unconventional problems often encountered by the X-Men. Scott believes in rigorous training and strict discipline, and rarely lets his guard down. Even Wolverine, who at first resisted Cyclops' leadership and openly feuded with him at every opportunity, has learned to trust his teammate's battlefield instincts.

POWERS/ WEAPONS

- Optic force blasts

INTELLIGENCE

STRENGTH

SPEED

DURABILITY

ENERGY PROJECTION

FIGHTING SKILLS

Art by Frank Quitely

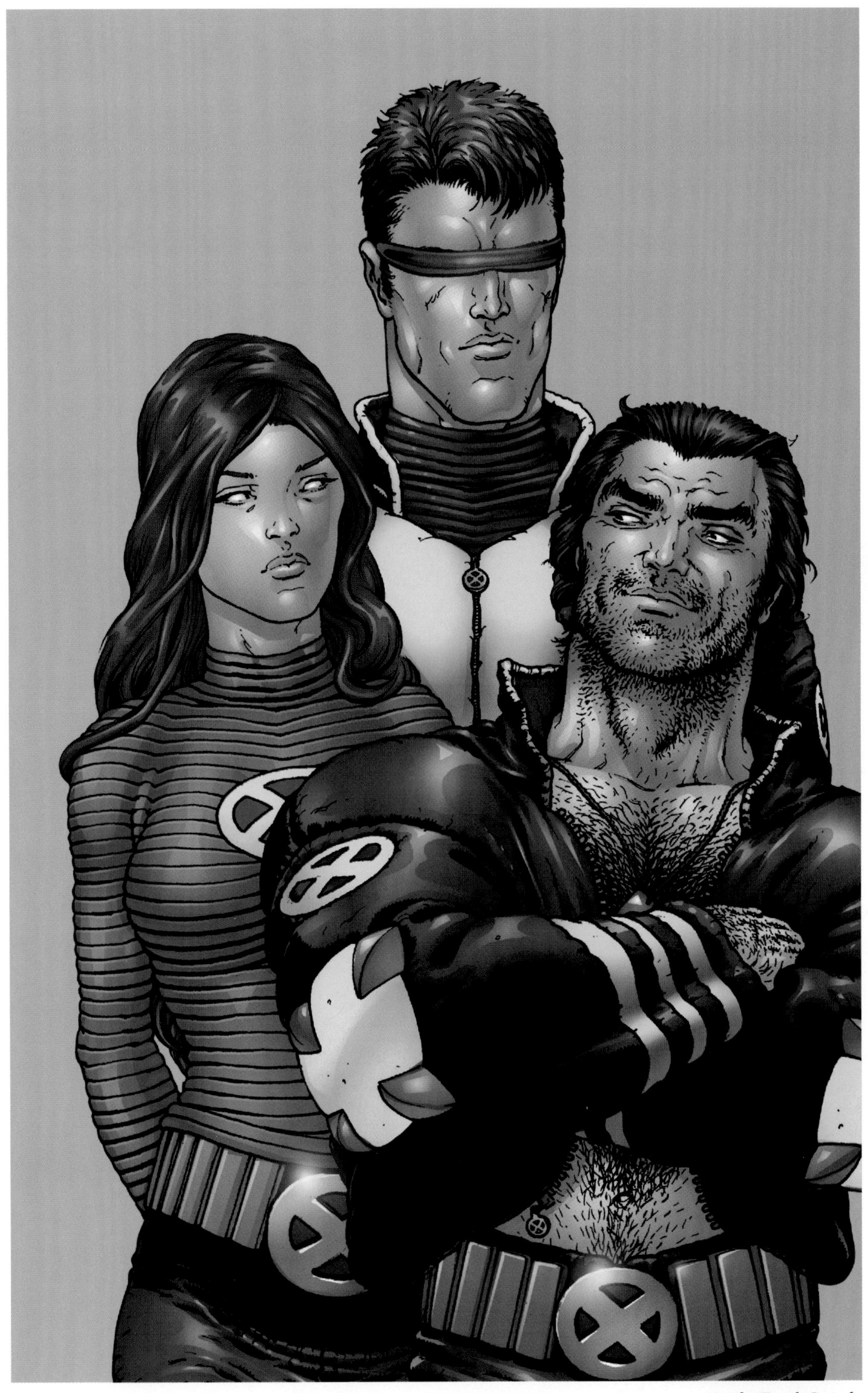

Art by Frank Quitely

EMMA FROST

Real Name:	Emma Frost
First Appearance:	*Uncanny X-Men* #129 (1979)
Height:	5'10"
Weight:	144 lbs.
Eye Color:	Blue
Hair Color:	Blonde

POWERS/ WEAPONS

- Diamond-hard, nearly indestructible skin
- Telepathy

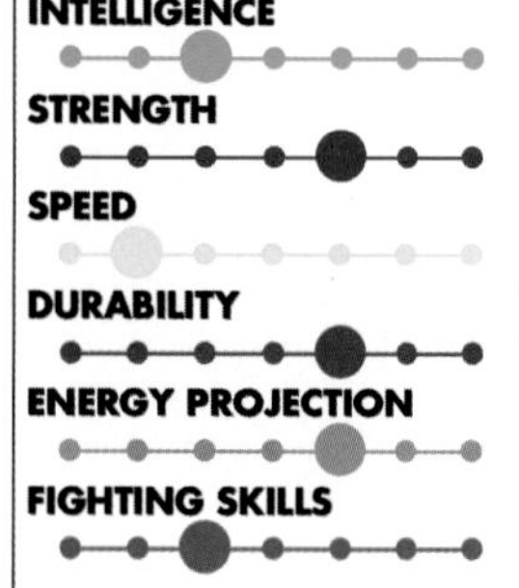

ESSENTIAL READING

- *The Origin of Generation X TPB*
- *New X-Men Vol. I: E Is For Extinction TPB*
- *New X-Men Vol. II: Imperial TPB*
- *X-Men: The Dark Phoenix Saga TPB*
- *X-Men: Vignettes TPB*

Born into a wealthy Boston mercantile family, Emma Frost ascended rapidly to the top of the corporate ladder on the strength of her intelligence, drive and personal charm—as well as her sex appeal and her secret psionic abilities. A hard-bodied seductress with the brains to back up her underhanded ambitions, Emma became majority stockholder of a multibillion-dollar conglomerate.

Despite her relative youth, Emma was named chairwoman of the board and chief executive officer of Frost International. She also became headmistress and chairwoman of the board of trustees of the Massachusetts Academy. For Emma, life is a battleground: Only the strong survive and the weak are doomed to become casualties of war. Unapologetic and uncompromising, Emma refuses to be counted among those killed in action.

Emma eventually attracted the attention of the planet's social elite, earning an invitation to join the world's wealthiest and most powerful individuals as a member of the exclusive Hellfire Club. Even among society's upper crust, the egoistic Emma felt surrounded by inferiors. Along with mutant ally Sebastian Shaw, Emma seized control of the club's Inner Circle to become its new White Queen.

As the Hellfire Club's White Queen, Emma's frequent power plays put her at odds with the X-Men. To fortify the organization's power base—and strengthen her own footing in particular—she recruited genetically gifted youngsters and helped them hone their abilities at her school. Emma was more than willing to put her protèges in harm's way, and the White Queen's Hellions clashed repeatedly with the X-Men. Ultimately, the Hellions sacrificed themselves to protect the severely injured Emma from time-traveling mutant terrorist Trevor Fitzroy, bluntly demonstrating the catastrophic effects of her unscrupulous machinations.

Hoping to ensure her students' welfare and the school's future, Emma had willed responsibility for the Massachusetts Academy to Professor X. During her psychic incapacitation following Fitzroy's attack, the school was added to the rapidly expanding Xavier Institute. Feeling she could succeed where Xavier had not, Emma resumed her role as headmistress of the Massachusetts Academy after her recovery and set out to train a new crop of young mutants: Generation X.

After the vast genocide in Genosha caused by Cassandra Nova and the Sentinels, Emma ultimately joined the X-Men, seeing the team as the only credible alternative to a world in which mutants are ghettoized, persecuted and exterminated. As a consequence of continued mutation, the White Queen has developed the ability to assume a diamond-hard, nearly indestructible form. In this state, Emma has no telepathic powers—and no empathy or compassion, just a cruel sense of humor and a cold, cold heart.

Art by Leinil Francis Yu

Art by Frank Quitely

GAMBIT

Real Name:	Remy LeBeau
First Appearance:	*Uncanny X-Men* #266 (1990)
Height:	6'1"
Weight:	175 lbs.
Eye Color:	Burning red
Hair Color:	Brown

Art by Georges Jeanty

ESSENTIAL READING

- *Wolverine/Gambit: Victims TPB*
- *X-Men: Mutant Genesis TPB*
- *X-Men: Mutant Massacre TPB*
- *X-Men Visionaries: Joe Madureira TPB*
- *X-Treme X-Men Vols. I & II TPB*

Always an outsider, Remy LeBeau was shunned as a youth because of his strange, burning-red eyes. Orphaned at birth, Remy spent his early years fending for himself on the hard streets of New Orleans. He survived by picking pockets, teaching himself the tricks of the trade through trial and error, eking out a modest living. But he had yet to learn the most important lesson of all: restraint. Remy unknowingly tried to pick the pocket of Jean-Luc LeBeau, head of the legendary Thieves Guild of New Orleans.

Jean-Luc took the boy under his wing and adopted him. In time, Remy mastered the ways of the clan—as well as those of its chief rival, the New Orleans Assassins Guild. To seal a peace pact between the organizations, Gambit married Bella Donna Boudreaux, granddaughter of the assassins' patriarch. But Bella Donna's brother, Julien, objected to the arranged union and challenged Gambit to a duel. Severely wounding his opponent, Remy was forced to flee New Orleans to prevent war between the guilds.

Art by Salvador Larroca

Gambit wandered the world and plied his skills as a master thief, aided by his mutant ability to charge inanimate objects with explosively released biokinetic energy. During his travels, he partnered with Storm of the X-Men, who had turned to thievery after being stricken with amnesia. When she regained her memories, Storm sponsored Gambit's admission to the team.

A lifelong transient, Remy had been banished from the only family he'd ever known. With the X-Men, he finally felt at home. Gambit's teammates accepted him for who he was, and forgave him the sins of his checkered past. Remy's charming façade masks a lifetime of pain, but rather than run from his inner demons, he has chosen to stand and fight for the future of mutankind. A valued member of the X-Men, Gambit has demonstrated his unswerving dedication to Xavier's cause.

As an X-Man, Gambit found true love in teammate Rogue, an outcast like himself. A thief by nature, Remy forever covets that which most would consider beyond reach. Blessed and cursed with the ability to absorb other mutants' thoughts and abilities through skin-on-skin contact, Rogue is the ultimate forbidden fruit—condemned never to touch her soulmate.

After Gambit stole Rogue's heart, she learned his deepest, darkest secret: Remy had unwittingly helped assemble a team of super-powered assassins, unaware his benefactor would dispatch them to annihilate the underground community of mutant outcasts called Morlocks. This damning revelation caused a rift between Rogue and Gambit, but the strength of their love has brought them together time and time again.

POWERS/ WEAPONS

- Charges inanimate objects, most frequently playing cards, with explosively released biokinetic energy
- Master thief

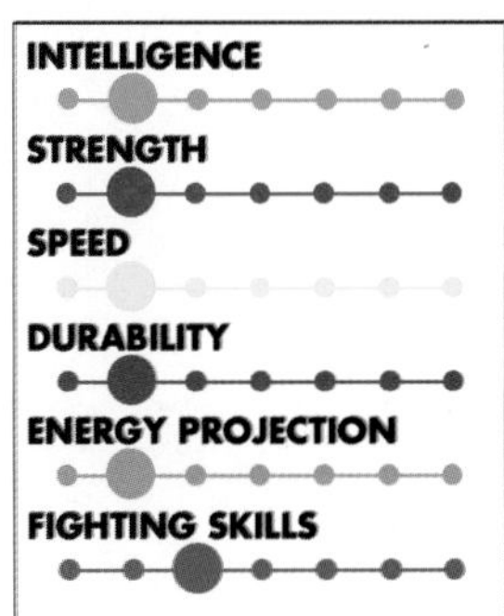

JEAN GREY

Real Name:	Jean Grey-Summers
First Appearance:	*X-Men* #1 (1963)
Height:	5'6"
Weight:	115 lbs.
Eye Color:	Green
Hair Color:	Red

ESSENTIAL READING

- *Essential Uncanny X-Men Vol. I*
- *Essential X-Men Vols. I & II*
- *X-Men: The Dark Phoenix Saga TPB*
- *X-Men: Phoenix Rising TPB*
- *New X-Men Vol. I: E Is For Extinction TPB*
- *New X-Men Vol. II: Imperial TPB*

When Jean Grey was 10 years old, she watched helplessly as a car struck her best friend. The strength of Jean's emotions awakened her latent telepathic powers, and she experienced the dying girl's feelings firsthand. Withdrawn and deeply depressed, Jean discovered she could not control her newly awakened mental abilities and was forced to isolate herself fromothers to keep hold of her sanity. Jean had been an average child; now, she could hear thoughts louder than voices.

Uncanny X-Men #137, September 1980

Jean's parents were referred to **Professor X**, who treated the young mutant for several years. Xavier erected psychic shields in Jean's mind so she wouldn't be able to use her telepathic abilities until she achieved the maturity necessary to control them. When Jean had attained a certain level of mastery with Xavier's aid, he recommended that her parents enroll her in his newly established School for Gifted Youngsters. As Marvel Girl, Jean became the fifth member of the **X-Men**. Following the removal of Xavier's psychic shields, she proved highly adept at using her telepathic powers. Through it all, Jean harbored strong feelings for fellow student **Cyclops**. For years, both were too shy to express their emotions. They eventually declared their true feelings for one another, and continued their romantic relationship.

When a rogue scientist unleashed a new generation of **Sentinels**, the androids abducted Jean and the X-Men and imprisoned them in an orbiting space station. The team escaped to Earth in a space shuttle but were forced to fly through a lethal solar-radiation storm. Because the pilot's cabin lacked sufficient shielding, Jean insisted on flying the shuttle, reasoning that her powers would protect her. The solar radiation, however, proved too great for her powers. Already succumbing to the agonizing effects of radiation poisoning, Jean was touched by the cosmic being known as the Phoenix Force. The entity created a body for itself that was identical to Jean's, duplicating her memories and personality and absorbing a portion of her consciousness. It then guided the shuttle to crash-land in Jamaica Bay off New York City. The Phoenix Force placed the real Jean in suspended animation within a cocoon-like pod resting on the bottom of the bay.

Eventually corrupted by its own limitless power, the Phoenix Force became a threat to all creation. Jean's persona ultimately regained dominance, and her psyche caused the entity to sacrifice itself to save the universe, committing suicide before Cyclops' horrified eyes. Months later, the **Avengers** discovered the pod and turned it over to the **Fantastic Four**. Finally breaking through the cocoon, the real Jean released herself. Fully healed, she reunited with the X-Men—and Scott, whom she later married.

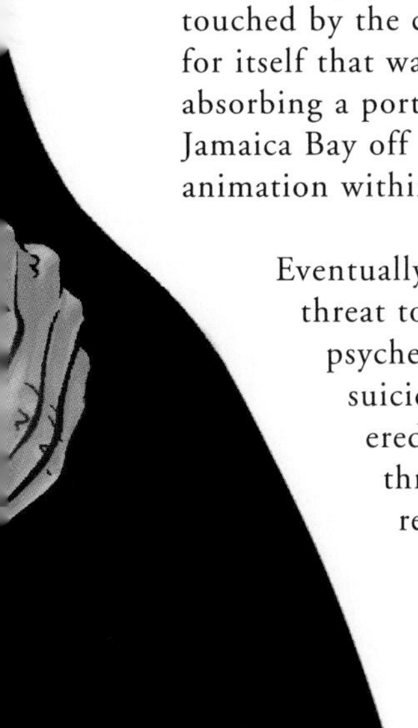

Art by Frank Quitely

JEAN GREY

Just as Jean hid her love for Scott as a teen, she must forever conceal her strong feelings for another X-Man: Wolverine. Tempering telepathy and telekinesis with warmth and compassion, Jean secretly hungers for an equally passionate partner. And while she remains faithful to her husband, part of her seeks something more than Scott's detached devotion. Wolverine is Cyclops' opposite in every way, matching Scott's stoicism and grace under fire with an animal passion and killer instinct that mask the heart of a poet. When Cyclops is worlds away, lost in his own agenda, Wolverine stands by Jean in the here and now. Logan shares Jean's feelings, but knows that Scott is the one for her. To the other X-Men, the unspoken attraction between Logan and Jean reads as a deep, binding friendship.

More than a costumed adventurer, Jean is mentor to a new generation of mutants. As headmistress at the Xavier Institute, she teaches a motley crew of troubled teenagers to survive in a world that hates and fears their kind, and hone their strange abilities in preparation for the day when mutants are Earth's dominant species.

POWERS/ WEAPONS

- Telepathy
- Telekinesis

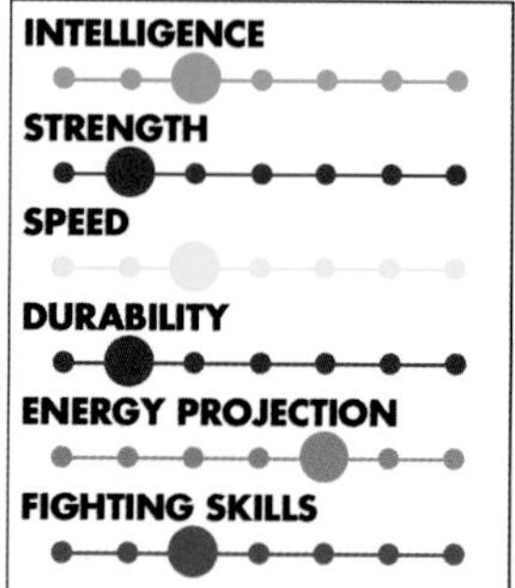

Art by John Paul Leon

Art by Adam Hughes

ICEMAN

Real Name: Robert Drake
First Appearance: *X-Men* #1 (1963)
Height: 5'8"
Weight: 145 lbs.
Eye Color: Brown
Hair Color: Brown

INTELLIGENCE
STRENGTH
SPEED
DURABILITY
ENERGY PROJECTION
FIGHTING SKILLS

POWERS/ WEAPONS

• Organic ice control

Art by Steve Uy

ESSENTIAL READING

- *Essential Uncanny X-Men Vol. I*
- *X-Men: Fall of the Mutants TPB*
- *X-Men: Inferno TPB*
- *X-Men: Mutant Massacre TPB*
- *Uncanny X-Men Vol. I: Hope TPB*

Bobby Drake discovered his mutant ability to control ice during his early teens, yet was encouraged to keep his condition hidden by his parents, who believed he would be hated and feared for what he was. But Bobby panicked when confronted by bullies. Revealing his powers for all to see, he temporarily encased the group's ringleader in ice.

News of the incident swept through his small Long Island community. Believing Bobby to be a menace, a mob of enraged townspeople broke into the Drakes' home. Bobby began using his powers to fight them off, but there were too many opponents for the young mutant to turn back on his own. The local sheriff took the teenager into custody for his own protection.

Art by Karl Kerschl

Learning of Bobby's plight, Professor X dispatched Cyclops to assess the situation. The first X-Man snuck into the jail as planned, but Bobby refused to accompany him. Cornered by the mob, the two teens were about to be hanged when Professor X used his psionic powers to halt the townspeople in their tracks and erase their memories of Bobby's abilities. Grateful, Bobby accepted Xavier's invitation to join the fledgling X-Men.

The team's youngest founding member, Bobby at first was unsure of himself and reluctant to use his abilities. Through training and experience, however, he learned to pull his weight in the field. On the surface, the easygoing Iceman appears irresponsible and undisciplined, constantly cracking jokes in the heat of battle. But his bravado masks a deep-seated sense of insecurity born of pain, prejudice and discrimination.

Though Bobby has flirted with normality—he even left the X-Men briefly to attend college and pursue a career in accounting—he is moved by a strong sense of responsibility to protect the very people who hate and distrust him. Fighting to fulfill the promise of peaceful coexistence between man and mutant, Bobby has also grown to love his life of adventure.

After years as a perceived lightweight, Iceman began experimenting with his abilities, adding mass to his slight frame and lifting himself high into the air without the aid of his customary ice slides. Once only able to sheathe himself with a protective layer of ice, he can now completely transform his entire body. No longer fearing the evolution of his abilities or intimidated by the enormity of his responsibilities, Bobby continues to explore the mutant experience to the fullest.

JUBILEE

Real Name:	Jubilation Lee
First Appearance:	*Uncanny X-Men* #244 (1988)
Height:	5'5"
Weight:	105 lbs.
Eye Color:	Blue
Hair Color:	Black

Art by Art Adams

ESSENTIAL READING

- *The Origin of Generation X TPB*
- *Essential Wolverine Vols. II & III*
- *X-Men Visionaries: Jim Lee TPB*

The daughter of prosperous Chinese immigrants, Jubilation Lee was born and raised in Beverly Hills, California. She attended an exclusive high school and blossomed into a talented gymnast, but the false security of her perfect world was shattered by the murder of her parents.

The Origin of Generation X TPB

Orphaned and impoverished, Jubilee learned to defend herself as a ward of the state, but also came to resent and defy authority. Fleeing custody, she sought shelter at the Hollywood Mall, where she survived as a petty thief. Cornered by mall security, a panicked Jubilee manifested her mutant powers in an explosion of energy bursts, startling the police and enabling her to escape.

From then on, Jubilee led a lonely life. Her outwardly hostile attitude masked a deeper fear and general mistrust. Jubilee continued to play cat-and-mouse with mall security until she was rescued from a squad of novice mutant hunters by the X-Men.

Initially distrustful of the outcast heroes, Jubilee followed the X-Men in secret for some time. She later learned to be a team player—serving as a valuable member of both the X-Men, who helped her hone her abilities, and Generation X, like-minded mutants her own age. For a time, Jubilee accompanied Wolverine on his globe-spanning adventures. The surly but goodhearted Logan became like a second father to her, helping the impatient, impetuous teenager channel her disposition for danger. Although polar opposites, Wolverine and Jubilee were a perfect match. Jubilee looked after Logan, preventing him from taking actions he might later regret. Wolverine protected her from the world, safeguarding what little remained of her innocence.

Despite her characteristically sarcastic remarks, Jubilee loves and trusts her teammates as family. With a fiery personality to match her explosive abilities, she is always any team's most outspoken member, but pulls her weight in the field. Jubilee's time among the world's most powerful beings has given her a better sense of her own destiny and provided her with the tools she needs to make her own way in a changing world.

POWERS/ WEAPONS

- Generation of explosive energy bursts, varying in power and intensity

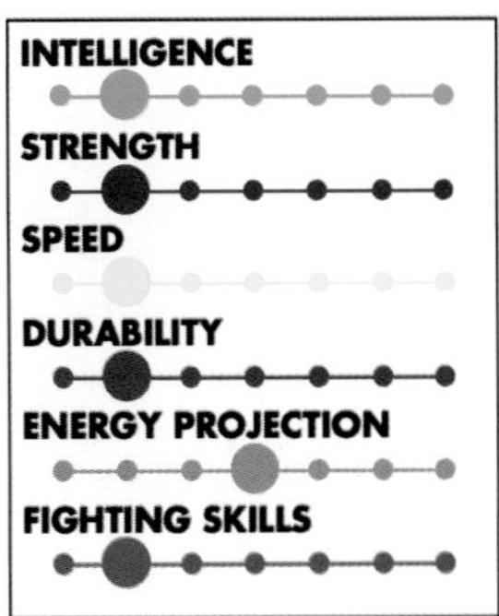

NIGHTCRAWLER

Real Name:	Kurt Warner
First Appearance:	*Giant Size X-Men* #1 (1975)
Height:	5'6"
Weight:	145 lbs.
Eye Color:	Yellow
Hair Color:	Black

ESSENTIAL READING

- *Essential X-Men Vols. I-IV*
- *Uncanny X-Men Vol. 1: Hope TPB*
- *X-Men: The Dark Phoenix Saga TPB*
- *X-Men: Days of Future Past TPB*
- *X-Men: From the Ashes TPB*
- *X-Men: Vignettes TPB*

Kurt Wagner has resembled a demon since birth. His unusual physical characteristics—indigo fur, a prehensile tail, pointed ears, fang-like teeth, three-fingered hands and two-toed feet—caused his mother Mystique to abandon her newborn son. Pursued by fearful villagers, she hurled Kurt over a waterfall to save her own life.

Kurt was discovered by a gypsy queen and raised in a traveling circus. Adopted by a motley crew of carnies who harbored no prejudice against so-called freaks, he learned that his mutant abilities and unique appearance were gifts to be celebrated. Long before his power of teleportation emerged, Kurt demonstrated tremendous natural agility. By adolescence, he had become the show's star acrobat and aerial artist. Assuming he was a normal human wearing a demon-like costume, audiences looked beyond his blue skin and saw him for the talented performer he was.

Art by Matt Smith

For a time, Kurt knew happiness and peace. But when a Texas millionaire, who sought to cast the young mutant in his American freak show, purchased the Bavarian circus, Kurt was forced to flee his ideal existence. He made his way to Winzeldorf, Germany, where the villagers thought he was responsible for a spate of recent murders. The townspeople were about to kill Kurt when they were psionically paralyzed by Professor X, who had come to recruit him for the X-Men.

Hated and feared for his strange powers and frightening appearance even more than most mutants, the blue-skinned swashbuckler is one of mutantkind's guardian angels, fighting the forces of bigotry and genetic terrorism. While many of his teammates can pass as human in public, Kurt is forever marked as an X-Man.

Blessed with friends and power, Nightcrawler is an idealist at heart. He learned long ago to look past appearances, and strives to see the humanity in those who refuse to recognize it in him. A man of faith, Nightcrawler holds dear to a dream that may be doomed to failure—universal acceptance and the peaceful coexistence of man and mutant—but still he believes in it with every fiber of his being. Kurt knows from painful experience how cruel the world can be, but he'll never stop trying to make it a better place.

POWERS/ WEAPONS

- Teleportation
- Accomplished acrobat
- Prehensile tail
- Limited invisibility

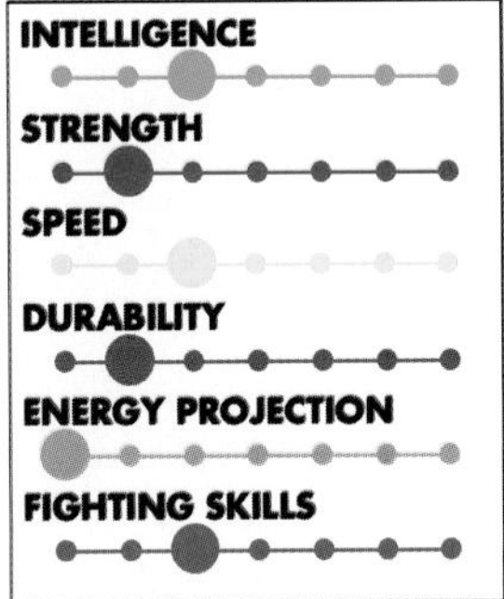

Art by Max Frezzato

PROFESSOR X

Real Name:	Charles Xavier	**Weight:**	190 lbs.
First Appearance:	*X-Men* #1 (1963)	**Eye Color:**	Blue
Height:	6'	**Hair Color:**	None

X-Men #1, September 1963

The world's most powerful telepath, Charles Xavier's crippled body serves as a constant reminder of his troubled past—one fraught with pain, loss and the bitter sting of oppression. The son of nuclear researcher Brian Xavier and his wife Sharon, Charles experienced the emergence of his telepathic powers while still a boy. Following her husband's accidental death, Sharon married Brian's colleague, Dr. Kurt Marko. Cain, Kurt's son by a previous marriage, came to live at the Xaviers' Westchester mansion shortly thereafter. A cruel and spiteful boy, he bullied his new stepbrother. As punishment, Cain's father beat him—and the untrained Charles felt his sibling's pain firsthand, since he could not yet control his fledgling abilities or terminate his contact with the boy's mind. As he grew older, Charles learned to rein in his burgeoning powers.

A brilliant student, Charles enrolled in the graduate studies program at Oxford University, where he met and fell in love with fellow student Moira Kinross. Their passionate discussions on the subject of genetic mutation gave way to an equally passionate romantic relationship, and the two planned to be married. Standing in their way was Moira's former boyfriend, Joe MacTaggert, a lance corporal in the Royal Marines—and a bully and thug, just like Cain. In Joe's eyes, Charles was an effete, good-for-nothing intellectual. To prove him wrong—and to validate himself in terms his rival would understand—Charles enlisted in the military after completing his studies at Oxford.

When Moira broke off their engagement without explanation, Charles left the Army to travel abroad. While in Cairo, Egypt, he clashed with the powerful mutant telepath Amahl Farouk. This experience inspired Charles to devote his life to protecting humanity from misguided mutants bent on world domination and safeguarding innocent mutants from human oppression. Charles next traveled to Israel, where he befriended fellow drifter Magnus, the mutant who would come to be called **Magneto**. Their powers were revealed to one another while battling terrorists. Charles espoused his optimistic belief that *Homo sapiens* and *Homo superior* could coexist, but Magnus foresaw mutants as the new minority to be persecuted and hunted because of their differences. Arriving in London, Charles renewed his friendship with Moira, who had since married Joe and was now a renowned geneticist; the two began to discuss the idea of founding a school for mutants. En route to the United States, Charles was involved in an accident that crippled his legs.

Despite this setback, he forged ahead and opened the school. Professor X's first student was 11-year-old **Jean Grey**, traumatized when she telepathically experienced the emotions of a dying friend. Charles helped Jean recover and taught her to use her telekinetic powers. Following his success with Jean, he embarked on his long-held plan to locate young mutants and enroll them in his School for Gifted Youngsters. Professor X even converted his mansion into a base from which he could train them to use their powers

Art by Adam Kubert and Richard Isanove

PROFESSOR X

for humanity's benefit. During the months that followed, Charles assembled a group of five students he dubbed the X-Men, because each possessed an "extra" ability normal humans lacked.

For years, Charles was widely regarded as an authority on genetic mutation, as well as an advocate of peaceful relations between man and mutant, but the general public was unaware he possessed superhuman powers. The situation changed when Cassandra Nova went on television while in possession of her brother's body and broke his decades-long silence. In hindsight, Charles believes Cassandra was right to expose him to the world. She took the step he knew he had to take. Charles always found an excuse not to put his reputation on the line. But Cassandra—in trying to do evil and expose Xavier to his enemies—freed him from his self-imposed exile. The world is finally listening, and all the X-Men had to do was take off their masks and step from the shadows.

POWERS/ WEAPONS

- Telepathy
- Astral projection

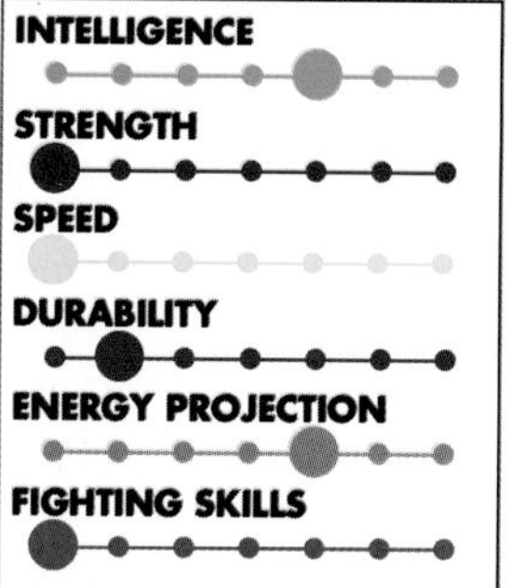

ESSENTIAL READING

- *Essential X-Men Vols. I-IV*
- *Essential Uncanny X-Men Vol. I*
- *New X-Men Vol. I: E Is For Extinction TPB*
- *New X-Men Vol II: Imperial TPB*
- *X-Men: Mutant Genesis TPB*

Art by Frank Quitely

Art by Adam Kubert and Richard Isanove

ROGUE

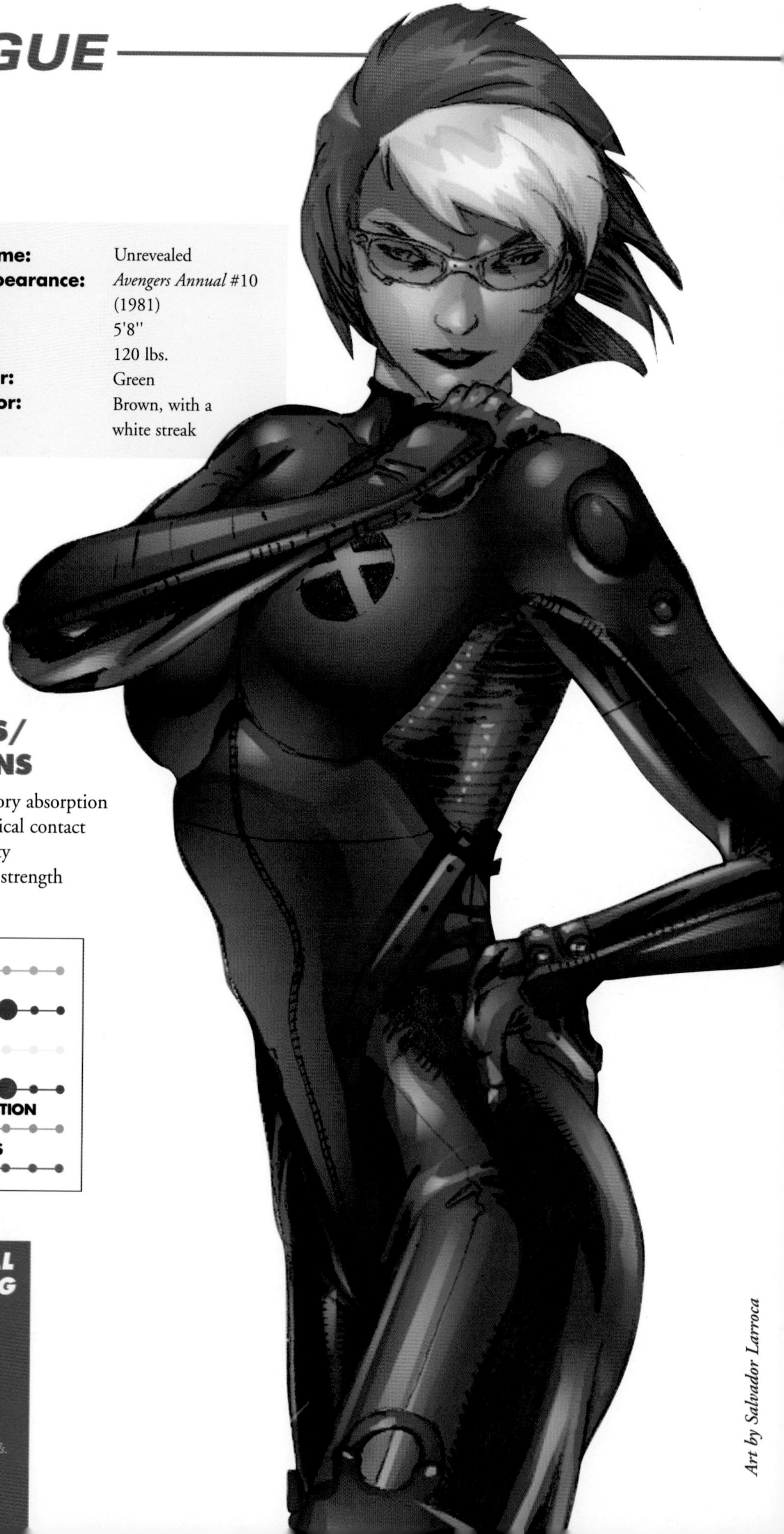

Real Name:	Unrevealed
First Appearance:	*Avengers Annual* #10 (1981)
Height:	5'8"
Weight:	120 lbs.
Eye Color:	Green
Hair Color:	Brown, with a white streak

POWERS/ WEAPONS

- Ability/memory absorption through physical contact
- Invulnerability
- Superhuman strength
- Flight

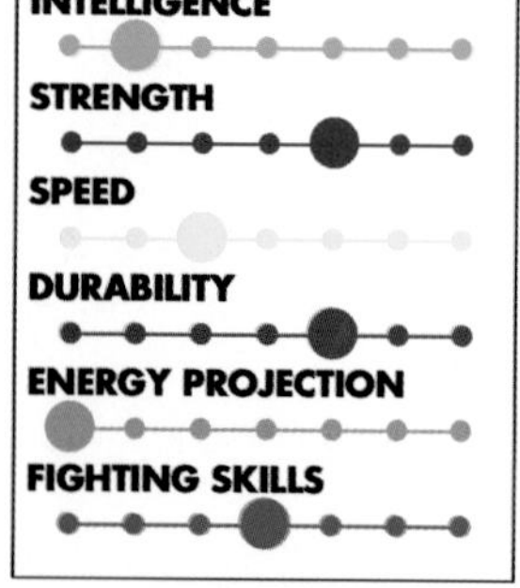

ESSENTIAL READING

- *Essential X-Men Vols. III & IV*
- *X-Men: From the Ashes TPB*
- *X-Men: Mutant Massacre TPB*
- *X-Men: Fall of the Mutants TPB*
- *X-Treme X-Men Vols. I & II TPB*
- *X-Treme X-Men: Savage Land TPB*

Little is known of Rogue's life before she manifested her mutant power, not even her real name. Raised in rural Mississippi, Rogue learned of her blessing and curse—the ability to temporarily absorb the psyches and abilities of others through skin-on-skin contact—when she first kissed her boyfriend Cody Robbins. When her lips met his, Rogue momentarily assimilated his identity and caused him to lose consciousness. In that instant, Rogue became Cody, his thoughts and feelings fighting for dominance in her mind, threatening to eradicate her individuality.

X-Treme X-Men Vol. I TPB

Terrified of what she had become, Rogue ran—as she would countless times in her young life, seeking safety in solitude. The slightest touch triggers the transfer, so she must remain on constant guard or risk injuring those around her and herself. Rogue was discovered by Mystique, who recognized the potential inherent in her mutant talents and adopted her. Manipulated by Mystique, Rogue engaged in terrorist activities as a member of the Brotherhood of Mutants, often coming into conflict with the X-Men. Rogue reluctantly participated in jailbreaks, assassination attempts and superhuman brawls—all the while anguishing over the fact that she could not control her abilities.

As her powers grew increasingly unstable and threatened to compromise her sanity, a desperate Rogue turned to Professor X for help. She had betrayed her surrogate mother by seeking sanctuary with Mystique's greatest adversary. Teacher and mentor to countless mutants, Xavier determined that the best way to aid the troubled teenager was to make her a member of the X-Men. The rest of the team resisted, until Xavier reminded his charges that only they could help her achieve her potential for good. With the X-Men, Rogue found a new life and a better purpose. She swiftly proved herself to be a loyal, brave and capable member of the team.

Through the years, Rogue has reveled in the freedom of flight, stood her ground against the planet's most powerful mutants and commanded the might of marvels. She's read minds with temporary telepathy, performed emergency surgery

ROGUE

using stolen skills and survived unscathed in the vacuum of space. But every time she uses her abilities to imprint the skills and psyche of another, she risks losing a little bit of her soul in the crush of unwanted memories and unrestrained thoughts.

Rogue's powers have been known to spasm out of control, and on those occasions, her mind becomes a battleground of residual psyches and strange memories. Every minute of every hour of every day—without repose, without a moment's peace—Rogue is haunted by the knowledge that if she gives in to the cacophony of voices, she'll be lost forever, a ghost in her own body.

Rogue's psyche is scarred, but she possesses greater strength than she knows. Thanks to the unflagging support of Xavier and the X-Men, she remains capable of great compassion and continues to fight for mutant rights, despite the danger inherent in the use of her powers.

As an X-Man, Rogue has known true friendship and unconditional love. Gambit stole the young mutant's heart, and their romance continues to flourish despite numerous stops and starts. Tragically, Rogue cannot act upon that love. Unable to master her powers, she cannot even touch her lover and is forced to keep him at arm's length.

Art by Salvador Larroca

Art by Kevin Sharpe

SHADOWCAT

Real Name: Katherine Pryde
First Appearance: *X-Men* #129 (1980)
Height: 5'6"
Weight: 110 lbs.
Eye Color: Hazel
Hair Color: Brown

POWERS/WEAPONS

- Ability to slide through solid objects by negotiating the spaces between atoms, walk on air and disrupt the inner workings of electrical devices.

INTELLIGENCE
STRENGTH
SPEED
DURABILITY
ENERGY PROJECTION
FIGHTING SKILLS

ESSENTIAL READING

- *Essential X-Men Vols. II-IV*
- *X-Men: From the Ashes TPB*
- *X-Men: Days of Future Past TPB*
- *Mechanix Vol. 1 TPB*

Art by Salvador Larroca

Way too smart for her own good but seemingly normal, 13-year-old Kitty Pryde grew up in suburban Deerfield, Illinois. Unaware she was a mutant, Kitty began suffering headaches of steadily increasing frequency, duration and intensity as a result of her emerging abilities. Lying on her bed one afternoon, she closed her eyes briefly, only to find herself moments later on the floor of the living room below. Unknowingly, she had used her power to pass through solid objects for the first time.

Uncanny X-Men #141, January 1981

Kitty's condition brought her to the attention of rival headmasters Professor X and Emma Frost, both advanced mutant telepaths. Kitty's parents chose the Xavier Institute, home of the X-Men, over Frost's dubious Massachusetts Academy, a front for the murderous Inner Circle of the exclusive Hellfire Club. Having distinguished herself by helping rescue a trio of X-Men abducted by Frost's operatives, Kitty soon became a member of team and fought for Xavier's dream of peaceful coexistence between man and mutant.

Ordinary no longer, the innocent, optimistic Kitty found herself surrounded by blue demons, faux goddesses, and telepaths who could read thoughts louder than words and lift weights with their minds. She should have been scared out of her wits, but Kitty was hardly in over her head. Faced with an uncertain future but full of potential, she came to embrace what she was, following the lead of the heroes whose world was now hers. When Kitty's parents filed for divorce, the X-Men became Kitty's surrogate family.

The X-Men were the bravest people she'd ever known, and Kitty was thrilled to be one of them. Living a life of fantastic adventure, she helped save the world and the universe—and fell in love with the steel-skinned Colossus, her literal knight in shining armor. Although their romance proved short-lived, they remained the best of friends.

Always industrious and eager, Kitty learned through the years not to rely solely on her phase-shifting abilities, honing her computer skills and technical expertise even as she perfected her fighting skills in the Danger Room. Over time, Kitty developed a close relationship with Wolverine, who became her mentor and taught her the martial arts.

Following the tragic death of Colossus and too many loved ones before him, a numb Kitty left the X-Men to find a new means of realizing Xavier's vision. At the University of Chicago, a world away from the front lines of genetic conflict, she soon discovered that even the campus community isn't safe from anti-mutant prejudice. Struggling to fit in, she remains a hero at heart—fighting for Xavier's dream her own way.

SOLDIER X

Real Name: Nathan Christopher Charles Summers
First Appearance: *New Mutants* #87 (1990)
Height: 6'8"
Weight: 350 lbs.
Eye Color: Blue
Hair Color: White

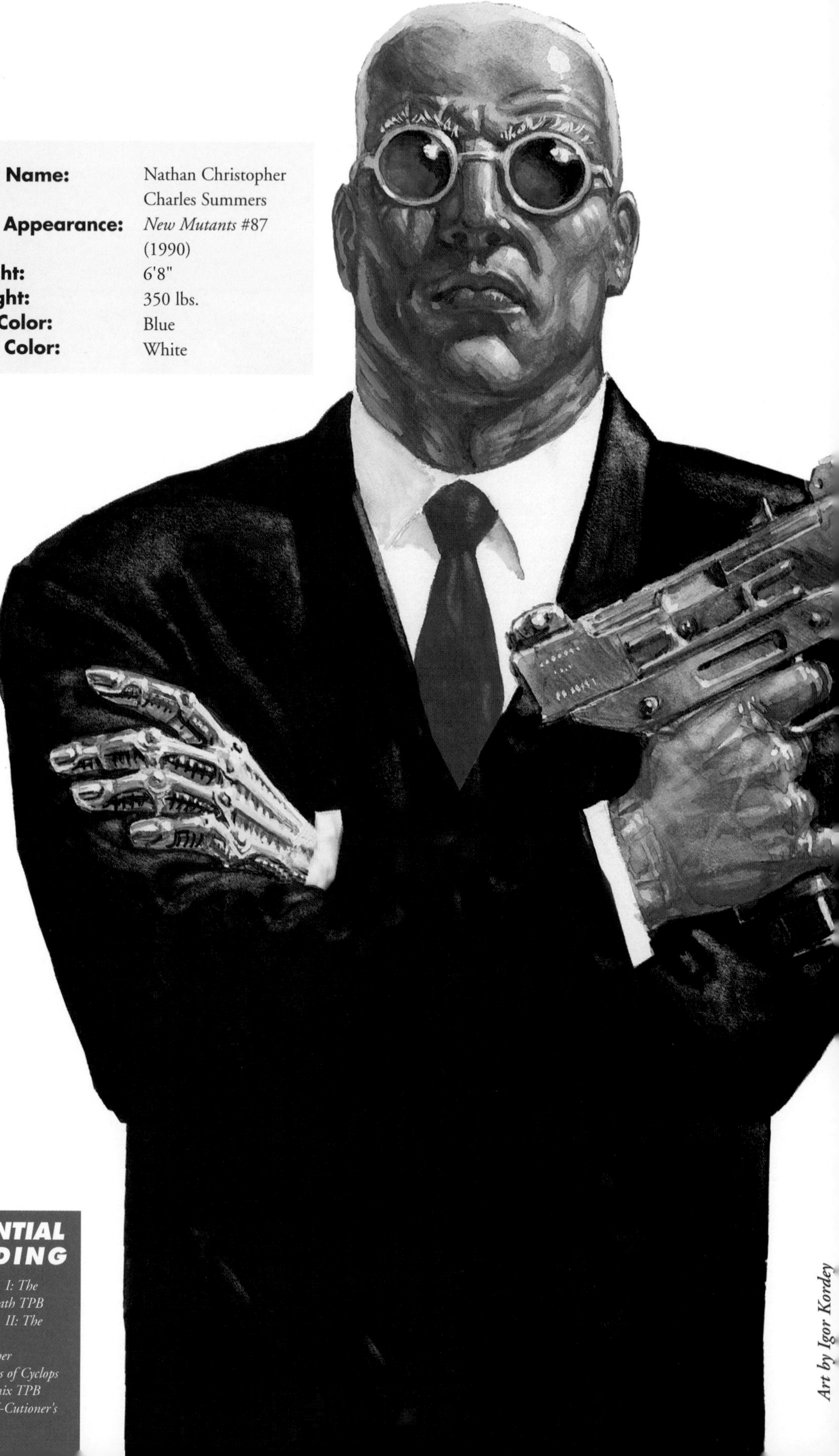

ESSENTIAL READING

- *Cable Vol. I: The Shining Path TPB*
- *Cable Vol. II: The End TPB*
- *The Further Adventures of Cyclops and Phoenix TPB*
- *X-Men: X-Cutioner's Song TPB*

Art by Igor Kordey

Always, mankind has feared what is different. In the future, that fear will explode into a bloody genetic war. Brother will battle brother, tearing society asunder, and the human race will wipe itself from the face of the Earth. Born in the present but sent 2,000 years into the future when an incurable techno-organic virus threatened his life, Nathan Summers was raised among the Askani, proponents of a practical belief system and way of life that focuses the psyche and brings inner peace. The clan taught him to use his telekinetic abilities to control the aggressive spread of the virus within his body, and tutored him in their spiritual and martial disciplines. Despite his control over the virus, half of Nathan's body became deformed during his teen years, taking on a metallic, robotic appearance.

Art by Igor Kordey

The Askani also taught Nathan that he was predestined to save the world from the bleak future in which they lived. Upon maturity, he was returned as a grown man to the 20th century to fulfill his destiny. Taking the name Cable, Nathan acquired a reputation in mercenary and intelligence circles as an extremely skilled soldier before ultimately joining forces with Professor X and his X-Men.

POWERS/ WEAPONS

- Telepathy
- Telekinesis
- Extremely proficient with any number of conventional weapons

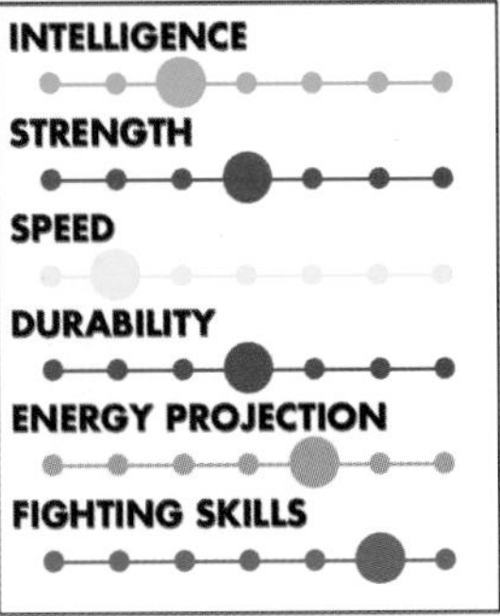

While allied with the X-Men, Nathan assumed leadership of a small group of Xavier's students. He forged the team into a proactive strike force, visiting retribution on those who would persecute their kind, rather than merely reacting to outbreaks of hostility like the X-Men. Ultimately, this proved to be the seed of a philosophical rift that would force Nathan to sever his ties with the X-Men and Xavier. Now he seeks his own fate.

In Nathan's eyes, Xavier's dream of peaceful coexistence between man and mutant through understanding and education is doomed to fail. He believes that the war between *Homo sapiens* and *Homo superior* has already begun, and that only he can stop it. A soldier fighting battle after battle in a war for the future, he travels the globe, forcibly intervening in world conflicts to target terrorism, ethnic cleansing and the oppression of any minority by a tyrannical majority.

Having finally purged the techno-organic virus from his body, Nathan is now more powerful than ever as a telepath and telekinetic, and uses both his mutant abilities and military skills to affect change on a global scale. Not content to enforce his will upon others, Nathan sows the seeds of peace in his wake, hoping that the Askani philosophy will help save the world from itself.

Despite seeking peace, Nathan is at heart a soldier, and is prepared to fight for what he believes in. The world is his battlefield, and he travels wherever he's needed. He will make a difference, or he will die trying.

STORM

Real Name:	Ororo Munroe
First Appearance:	*Giant-Size X-Men* #1 (1975)
Height:	5'11"
Weight:	127 lbs.
Eye Color:	Blue
Hair Color:	White

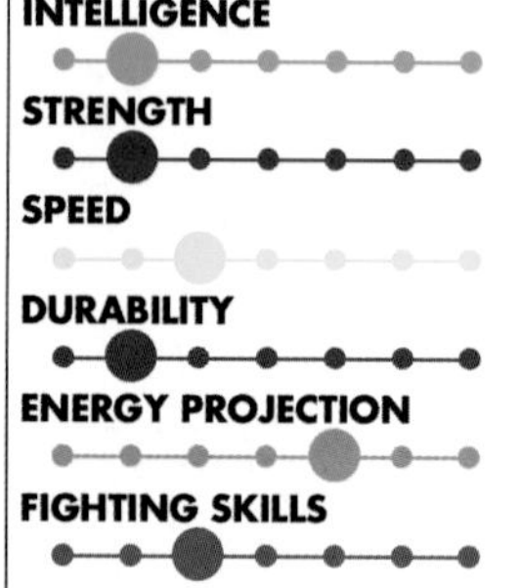

POWERS/ WEAPONS

- Weather control
- Flight

ESSENTIAL READING

- *Essential X-Men Vols. I-IV*
- *X-Men: The Dark Phoenix Saga TPB*
- *X-Treme X-Men Vols. I & II TPB*
- *X-Treme X-Men: Savage Land TPB*

Ororo Munroe is descended from an ancient line of African priestesses, all bearing the potential to wield magic. Her mother, the princess of a tribe in Kenya, married an American photojournalist and moved with him to Manhattan. When Ororo was 6 months old, she and her parents relocated to Cairo, Egypt. Five years later, a bomb destroyed their home during a Middle Eastern conflict. Ororo's parents were killed, but she survived, buried under tons of rubble near her mother's body. This traumatizing experience left Ororo with severe claustrophobia, which afflicts her still. Homeless and orphaned, she came under the tutelage of master thief Achmed el-Gibar. Ororo was his prize pupil, and she became the most accomplished pickpocket and thief in Cairo within a year.

Art Salvador Larroca

When she was 12, Ororo felt a strong urge to head south and reconnect with her familial roots, and journeyed alone across the Sahara Desert. Finally, she reached her ancestors' homeland: the Serengeti Plain, straddling the modern nations of Kenya and Tanzania. By adolescence, her mutant ability to manipulate the weather had emerged, and she used it to aid the local tribes, who worshipped her as the Storm Goddess. Professor X convinced her to abandon the sheltered world she had surrounded herself with so that she could use her great powers to benefit the entire world.

Hated and feared for her strange and frightening abilities—not revered, as she had been in Africa—Ororo has stood fast with the X-Men in their attempts to promote peaceful coexistence between man and mutant. Except for brief periods away from the team, she has remained a member ever since, even through the temporary loss of her mutant abilities.

Although a lifetime removed from her years in Africa, Storm's noble demeanor and selfless actions befit a young woman born of royalty. Self-assured and authoritative, she is also calm, gentle and understanding. A powerful presence among the X-Men, she is a classic beauty in every sense of the word. Storm bears a sense of responsibility for the safety of those she leads, and is deeply loyal to her friends and teammates.

While she commands Mother Nature's bountiful gifts, Ororo is capable of unleashing the catastrophic fury of the elements. One with the Earth, she truly understands the sanctity of life and feels a strong obligation to help preserve it in all its forms—man or mutant, plant or animal, good or evil.

Art by Chris Bachalo

WEAPON X

First Appearance: *Incredible Hulk* #180 (1974)

ESSENTIAL READING

- *Weapon X Vol. 1 TPB*
- *Wolverine/Deadpool: Weapon X TPB*

The original Weapon X program, a clandestine genetic-research organization sanctioned by the Canadian military, was designed to transform mutants into obedient and lethal super-soldiers—with or without their consent. The experimental division of Weapon X suffered a major setback, however, when the test subject code-named Wolverine escaped. As he fought his way to freedom, the feral mutant savagely killed and mauled scores of scientists and guards.

The program languished for years while funding was withdrawn and political factions within the Canadian government sought to dismantle it completely. Eventually, the official known publicly only as the Director, a former soldier attached to the program who was scarred in Wolverine's rampage, successfully lobbied for the relaunch of Weapon X under his leadership.

His injuries from that fateful night fueling his hatred for mutants, the Director uses desperate superhuman beings with nothing to lose to control and kill others of their species, commanding his forces in a personal war against all mutantkind.

Weapon X now recruits criminal or otherwise unsavory mutants, promising each his heart's desire—be it money, better control over his powers or permanent immunity from the law—in exchange for a prescribed term of service. The program provides a safe haven of sorts for mutants wanted by the authorities—such as Sauron, Mesmero and Sabretooth—as well as a semi-stable home for the likes of Kane, Wild Child and Aurora, all of whom have had difficulties adapting to normal society.

Sending his teams on sanctioned suicide missions or any variety of espionage-based tasks on behalf of his government, the Director also seeks to further his own agenda, one whose grand design only he knows. Most often, however, Weapon X teams are dispatched to deal with rogue mutants; those who cannot be recruited are terminated with extreme prejudice.

Viewing his operatives as means to an end, the Director is a dangerous puppetmaster, pulling strings and manipulating his team to create a world without mutants.

Art by Georges Jeanty

WOLVERINE

Real Name: Born James Howlett, currently known as Logan
First Appearance: *Incredible Hulk* #180 (1974)
Height: 5'3"
Weight: 195 lbs.
Eye Color: Brown
Hair Color: Black

POWERS/ WEAPONS

- Animal-keen senses
- Accelerated healing factor
- Adamantium-laced skeleton
- Retractable adamantium claws

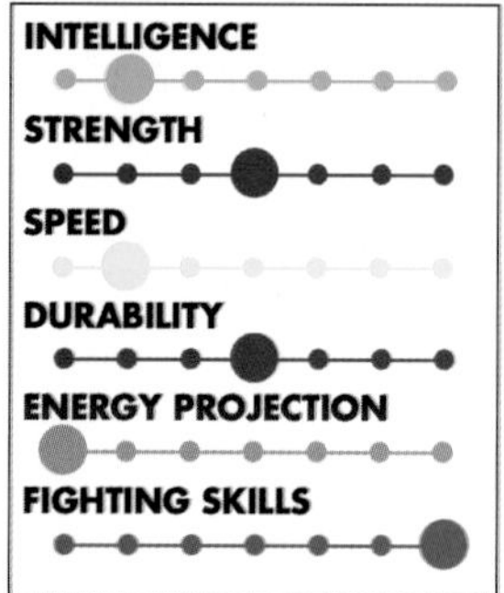

ESSENTIAL READING

- *Origin HC*
- *Weapon X TPB*
- *Wolverine TPB*
- *Essential Wolverine Vols. I-III*
- *Wolverine: The Best There Is TPB*
- *Wolverine/Deadpool: Weapon X TPB*
- *Essential X-Men Vols. I-IV*
- *New X-Men Vol. I: E Is for Extinction TPB*
- *New X-Men Vol. II: Imperial TPB*

Art by Esad Ribic

James Howlett, the mutant now known as Wolverine, was born into privilege in Alberta, Canada, during the late 19th century, the second son of John and Elizabeth Howlett. Young James' mother was distant and remote due to the untimely death of her first son. Growing up, the sickly James was close friends with the red-headed Rose, his companion and tutor, and "Dog," the son of the Howlett's cruel groundskeeper Thomas Logan.

The Incredible Hulk #181, November 1974

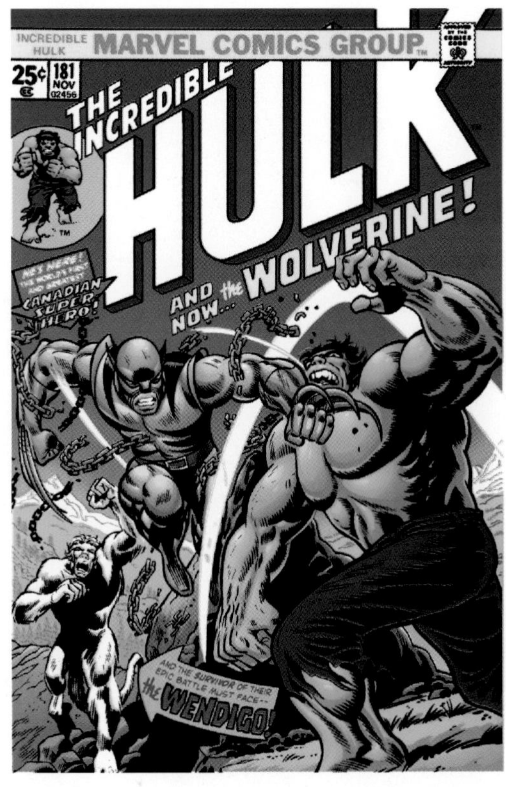

Dog's growing obsession with Rose finally prompted him to attack her, forcing James' father to fire Thomas and evict him and Dog from their home on the Howlett estate. The groundskeeper and his son stole into the mansion the next night and attempted to convince Mrs. Howlett to leave with them. Apparently, Thomas and Elizabeth Howlett had been engaged in an ongoing affair. When John Howlett interrupted them, Thomas shot and killed his former employer. At the shock of seeing his father murdered, James manifested his latent mutant abilities, and bone claws jutted from the back of each hand. The beast within the boy unleashed at last, James attacked and killed Thomas and slashed Dog's face. Completely unhinged by the violence, Elizabeth took her own life.

James suffered a severe breakdown; his mutant abilities "healed" his mind as well as his body, blocking all memories of his last months at the Howlett estate. Because Rose and James were blamed for the deaths at the mansion, she spirited him away to a British Columbia mining colony. Rose gave James the name "Logan," so that his real identity would remain unknown.

The frail Logan grew into a strapping young man at the mine and became known for his strength and ferocity. He spent a great deal of time among the wolves in the nearby wilderness, discovering he had more in common with the wild beasts than his fellow man. Bullied incessantly, Logan acquired the nickname "Wolverine" thanks to his tenacity and refusal to back down from a challenge.

Logan's happiness at the camp came to an end when Dog tracked him down. Finally remembering the night of his father's death, Logan fought Dog savagely. During the struggle, Logan accidentally impaled Rose on his claws, killing her. Wracked by grief over the death of the woman he truly loved, he fled into the woods. Logan was not seen again for many years, but the legend of the man called Wolverine had begun.

The rest of Logan's life is shrouded in mystery, peppered with half-truths and anecdotal reports of unconfirmed sightings. His healing factor seems to act against the

WOLVERINE

effects of aging—which would explain why, as a man of more than 120 years, he appears to be in his mid-30s.

In the latter half of the 20th century, the Canadian government subjected Logan to a bizarre battery of experiments intended to forge the ultimate killing machine. Weapon X scientists grafted the indestructible metal adamantium to Logan's skeleton and bone claws, and introduced memory implants that shaped his past to suit their ends. Combined with the earlier effects of his healing factor, these false memories have made it impossible for Logan to discern fact from fiction when recalling his former life. He now knows little of his past, save that it was fraught with pain and loss.

Wolverine was working as an operative for the Canadian government when he accepted Professor X's offer to join the X-Men. Logan chose to stay on partly out of his belief in Xavier's vision for the co-existence of humans and mutants, and partly because of his attraction to Jean Grey. During his time with the X-Men, Logan has worked to regain his lost memories, but virtually every answer leads him to even more new questions.

Although he would rarely admit it, Logan remains with the X-Men because he feels the team is the closest thing he has to a family in the world. Serving with the X-Men has given Logan what he had been missing for so long: a cause worth fighting for. Still somewhat uncontrollable and unpredictable in battle, and prone to an occasional berserker rage, Wolverine has proven to be a tremendous asset to the team; he continues to make his home in Xavier's mansion. Beneath his brutish exterior, Wolverine will always be the scared, insecure boy who lashed out at the world all those years ago, doomed never to make peace with his troubled past. Haunted by half-forgotten demons, he fights for those who can't fight for themselves.

Art by Frank Quitely

Art by Frank Quitely

THE XAVIER INSTITUTE

First Appearance: *X-Men* #1 (1963)

ESSENTIAL READING

- *Essential Uncanny X-Men Vol. I*
- *New X-Men Vol. I: E Is for Extinction TPB*
- *New X-Men Vol. II: Imperial TPB*

Art by Frank Quitely

Located on the grounds of Professor X's ancestral mansion, the Xavier Institute for Higher Learning is a secondary school where young mutants come to learn how to better understand and control their abilities. In addition to serving as base of operations for the X-Men, the institute is home to several dozen students, all unique in their own way.

Barnell Bohusk: Called the Beak due to his bird-like appearance, Barnell has demonstrated tremendous potential during his time at the school, most notably helping the X-Men defeat Cassandra Nova. One of the Beast's favorite students, Barnell is learning to fly by using the rudimentary wings on his back.

The Stepford Cuckoos: Individually, these quintuplets possess rudimentary mental powers. Uniting their minds to act in concert, they wield vast telekinetic and telepathic abilities and have potential for even more growth. Since coming under the tutelage of Emma Frost, the Cuckoos have begun to take on her aristocratic, snobbish attitude.

Angel: Able to spit acid and fly via insect-like wings, this troubled young mutant from the wrong side of the tracks was rescued by Wolverine when she was attacked by anti-mutant agents. Very much an individual, Angel has had a difficult time fitting in at the Xavier Institute. She has, however, bonded with Beak and the Cuckoos, with whom she helped the X-Men stave off an attack by the Shi'ar Imperial Guard and finally defeat Cassandra Nova.

Students displaying all forms of mutations, from morphological to psionic, attend the Xavier Institute. The school acts as a living laboratory, where the future of evolution can prepare to meet the present. Xavier and the X-Men serve as instructors, teaching a curriculum that covers both traditional subjects and those specific to mutants.

After years of secrecy, the public now knows the Xavier Institute houses mutants. This revelation has resulted in a certain amount of violence, but for the most part, residents of the surrounding towns have been tolerant of the school and its pupils. Although attending classes at the headquarters of the X-Men has created dangerous situations from time to time, students tend to take the excitement in stride, thrilling at the opportunity to see their mentors in action.

X-STATIX

First Appearance: *X-Force* #116 (2001)

ESSENTIAL READING

- *X-Force Vol. I: New Beginnings TPB*
- *X-Force Vol. II: The Final Chapter TPB*
- *X-Statix Vol. I TPB*

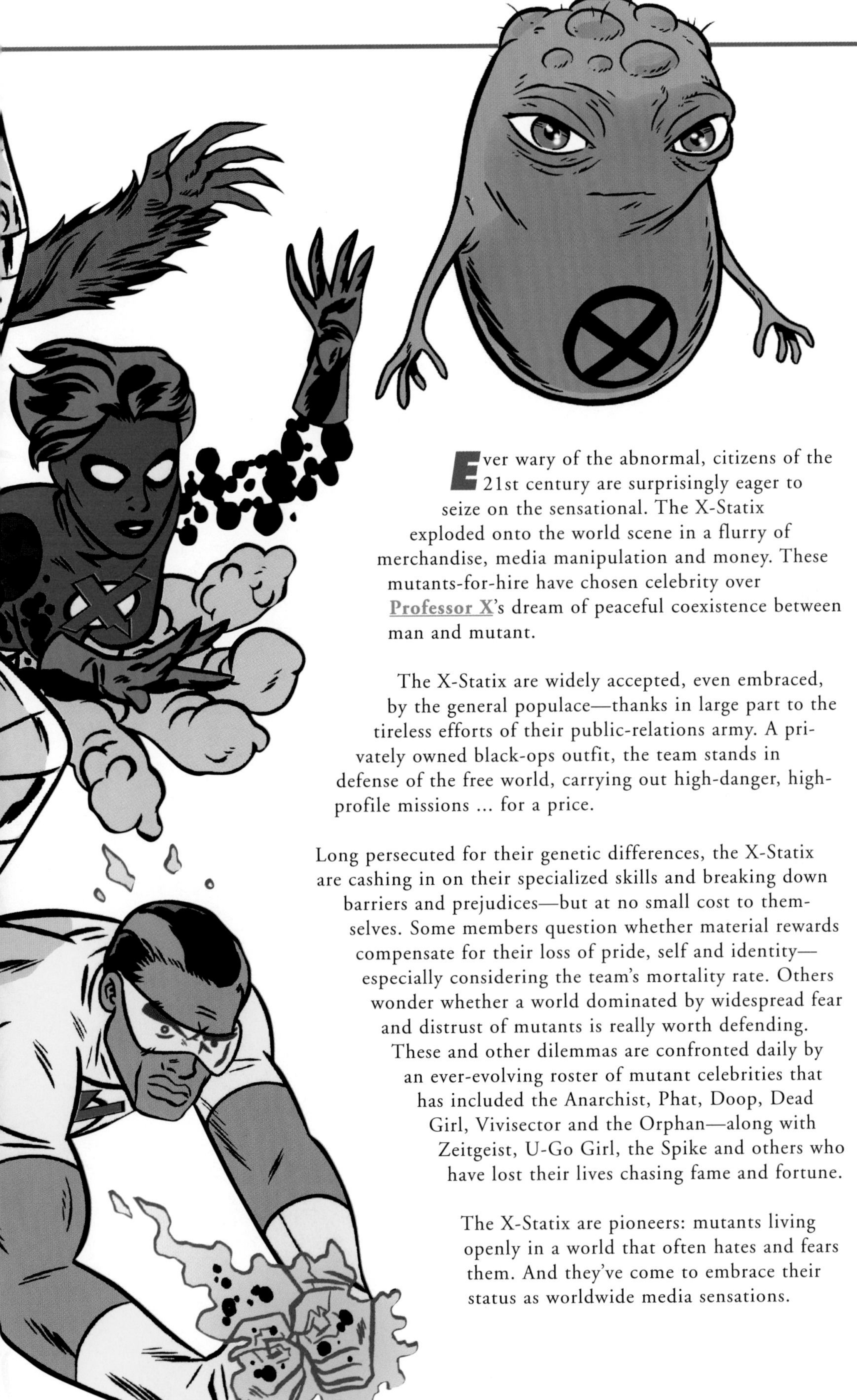

Ever wary of the abnormal, citizens of the 21st century are surprisingly eager to seize on the sensational. The X-Statix exploded onto the world scene in a flurry of merchandise, media manipulation and money. These mutants-for-hire have chosen celebrity over Professor X's dream of peaceful coexistence between man and mutant.

The X-Statix are widely accepted, even embraced, by the general populace—thanks in large part to the tireless efforts of their public-relations army. A privately owned black-ops outfit, the team stands in defense of the free world, carrying out high-danger, high-profile missions ... for a price.

Long persecuted for their genetic differences, the X-Statix are cashing in on their specialized skills and breaking down barriers and prejudices—but at no small cost to themselves. Some members question whether material rewards compensate for their loss of pride, self and identity—especially considering the team's mortality rate. Others wonder whether a world dominated by widespread fear and distrust of mutants is really worth defending. These and other dilemmas are confronted daily by an ever-evolving roster of mutant celebrities that has included the Anarchist, Phat, Doop, Dead Girl, Vivisector and the Orphan—along with Zeitgeist, U-Go Girl, the Spike and others who have lost their lives chasing fame and fortune.

The X-Statix are pioneers: mutants living openly in a world that often hates and fears them. And they've come to embrace their status as worldwide media sensations.

Art by Mike Allred

JUGGERNAUT

Real Name:	Cain Marko	**Weight:**	900 lbs.
First Appearance:	*X-Men* #12 (1965)	**Eye Color:**	Blue
Height:	6'10"	**Hair Color:**	Red

Art by Ron Garney

Cain Marko has wasted his entire adult life attempting to escape the shadow of his stepbrother, Professor X. Cain's father married Charles Xavier's widowed mother, presumably for her wealth, and took up residence in the family's Westchester mansion. A cruel and spiteful boy, Cain came to live with the family also.

Cain grew to hate his new stepbrother, mostly because his father favored Charles, and took to bullying the younger boy. As punishment, Cain's father beat him. Inexperienced at the use of his fledgling telepathic abilities, Charles could not control or terminate his contact with Cain's mind during these periods of pain. Somehow, Cain sensed that Charles had invaded his thoughts. Believing he had done so deliberately, Cain came to regard his stepbrother as an enemy. Over time, Cain grew increasingly resentful of Charles' scholastic and athletic achievements, and envious of his telepathic talents.

Art by Kia Asamiya

Drafted into military service, Cain served in the same unit as Charles. When Cain deserted under fire, Charles pursued his stepbrother, hoping he could convince him to return of his own accord. Charles followed Cain into a cave that housed the lost temple of Cyttorak, a powerful mystical entity. Motivated by greed and delusions of grandeur, Cain unearthed a large red ruby. Empowered by the gem, he was transformed into a superhuman being. Just then, an enemy bombardment caused a cave-in. Charles escaped, but Cain was buried under several thousand tons of rock. Eventually, he dug himself free with his newfound powers and made his way to America.

Lacking his stepbrother's moral fiber, Juggernaut turned his newfound strength against Charles and his X-Men. Each time they clashed, the heroes managed to beat back his bull rush. Often, Juggernaut worked with mutant terrorist Black Tom Cassidy, whom he befriended while in prison.

Cain remains little more than a super-powered thug. For all his physical strength, Juggernaut lacks strength of character. Despite his yearning for power, he has squandered his supernaturally enhanced abilities out of petty jealousy. Still, Charles holds out hope that Juggernaut will one day gain a better sense of understanding for the mutant plight, if not acquire a newfound respect for life and human dignity.

POWERS/ WEAPONS

- Supernatural strength
- Invulnerability
- Telepathy-blocking helmet

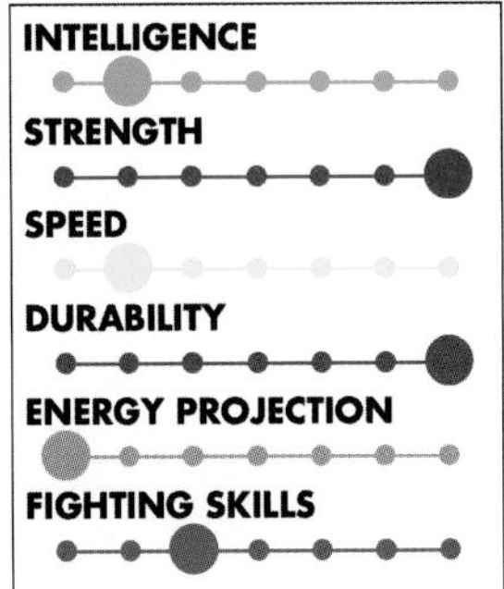

ESSENTIAL READING

- *Essential Uncanny X-Men Vol. I*
- *Essential X-Men Vol. I*
- *Uncanny X-Men Vol. I: Hope TPB*

MAGNETO

Real Name:	Magnus
First Appearance:	*X-Men* (Vol. 1) #1 (1963)
Height:	6'2"
Weight:	190 lbs
Eye Color:	Bluish-gray
Hair Color:	Silver

Art by Joe Madureira

Long before he learned of his mutant powers, Magneto felt the bitter sting of discrimination. He spent his youth interred at the Nazi death camp in Auschwitz, Poland, and was the only member of his family to survive the Holocaust. To Magnus, this experience bluntly and irrevocably demonstrated mankind's potential for inhumanity. After World War II, Magnus married Magda, a Gypsy girl he had rescued from Auschwitz. Their first child Anya was born several years later. When thugs prevented the couple from rescuing their young daughter from a fire, a helpless Magnus lashed out with his fledgling mutant abilities. In a white-hot moment of rage and pain, he killed his attackers and several onlookers. A terrified Magda fled before revealing that she was pregnant again.

X-Men: Mutant Genesis TPB

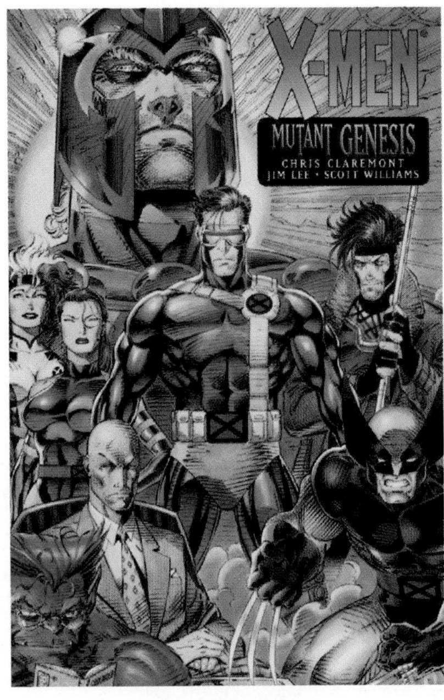

Traveling to Israel, Magnus worked as a volunteer helping treat Holocaust survivors. There, he befriended Charles Xavier, a young mutant telepath; the two were forced to reveal their powers to one another while battling terrorists. Xavier held fast to his optimistic belief that *Homo sapiens* and *Homo superior* could coexist, while Magnus foresaw mutants as the next minority to be persecuted for their differences. Magnus desperately tried to share his friend's hope, but was unwilling to stand by, powerless, while history repeated itself. Now calling himself Magneto, Magnus became determined to conquer the human race and thus prevent the oppression of his kind. Professor X's original students, the X-Men, thwarted his initial plot: the takeover of the Cape Citadel missile base. When next they clashed, Magneto had assembled the first Brotherhood of Evil Mutants, which included the Scarlet Witch and Quicksilver. Not until years later would Magneto learn they were his children.

POWERS/ WEAPONS

- Master of magnetism
- Skilled strategist

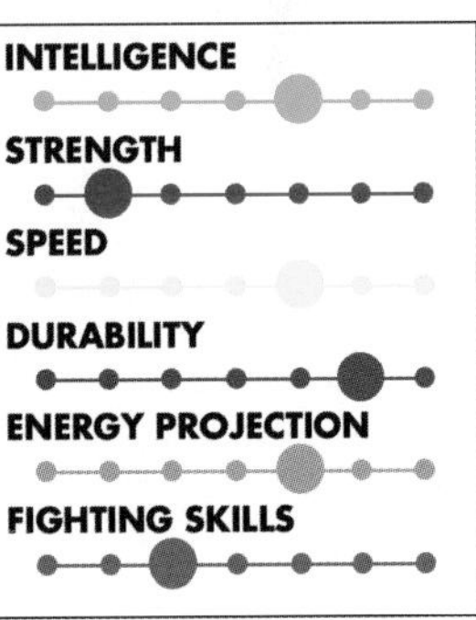

Rarely has Magneto hesitated to employ lethal force to advance his agenda. Xavier remained hopeful that he could convince his old friend to set aside his extremist beliefs—that is, until Magnus forcibly extracted the adamantium implants grafted to Wolverine's skeleton. To Xavier, this act proved Magneto to be irredeemable, and he telepathically lobotomized his one-time ally.

After recuperating from the wounds inflicted by Xavier, Magneto launched perhaps his most ambitious offensive to date: Holding the planet hostage with its own magnetic field, he demanded a homeland where mutants could govern themselves, free from oppression. Ultimately, the United Nations conceded. Members reasoned that granting the Master of Magnetism sovereignty over the island of Genosha would

ESSENTIAL READING

- *Essential X-Men Vols. I-III*
- *Essential Uncanny X-Men Vol. I*
- *Magneto: Rogue Nation TPB*
- *X-Men: Mutant Genesis TPB*

lead him to withdraw from the world stage. Magneto had rebuilt the war-torn country as a safe haven for mutants of all nationalities when a fleet of **Sentinels** controlled by **Cassandra Nova** decimated Genosha and slaughtered its inhabitants. Magneto's body was not found amid the wreckage of the island nation.

Whatever doubts surround the Master of Magnetism, one fact is certain: Magneto is a survivor. As he lived through the Holocaust, he will return to prevent the persecution of his people. Magneto has dedicated his life to the advancement of mutantkind, even if he must bring about humanity's downfall to ensure the ascendance of *Homo superior*. Arguably the most powerful being on Earth, Magneto believes mutants represent the next step in human evolution, and he's grown weary of waiting for *Homo sapiens* to cede control of the planet.

Art by Brandon Peterson

Art by Brandon Peterson

MYSTIQUE

Real Name:	Raven Darkholme	**Weight:**	125 lbs.
First Appearance:	*Ms. Marvel* #16 (1978)	**Eye Color:**	Yellow
Height:	5'10"	**Hair Color:**	Red

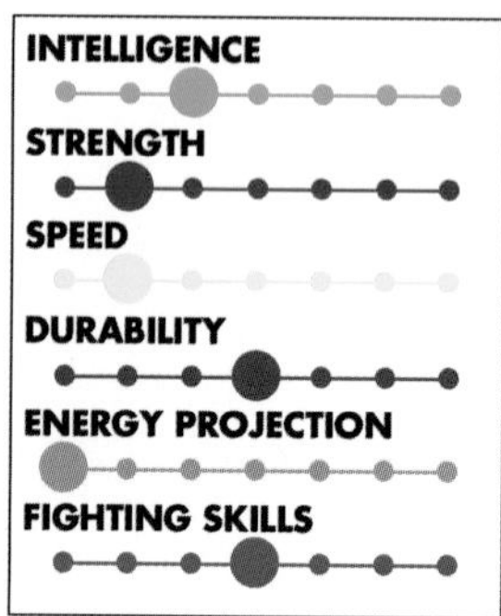

POWERS/WEAPONS

• Shapeshifting

Because she learned to control her powers at a very young age, Raven Darkholme was able to pass as a normal human being until she gave birth to Kurt Wagner, the blue-skinned mutant who would become Nightcrawler of the X-Men. Hounded by a mob of angry villagers, she was forced to abandon the demon-like infant to save her own life.

Unable to reveal her true face for fear of recrimination, Mystique attempted to manipulate people and events to bring about peaceful coexistence between man and mutant. But using her powers to shape the future proved far more difficult than she had imagined. Personal success was child's play; social engineering, however, proved next to impossible. The harder she tried, the more frustrated she became. With each new failure, Mystique grew more and more angry. The struggle made her what she is today: a sworn enemy of humanity.

Hoping to end the threat posed by humanity once and for all, Mystique established the second incarnation of the Brotherhood of Evil Mutants. Mystique's Brotherhood gained notoriety when it attempted to assassinate U.S. Senator Robert Kelly, an anti-mutant provocateur. The X-Men thwarted the Brotherhood's plans, as well as many other acts of terrorism perpetrated by Mystique and her cohorts. Perhaps feeling remorse for abandoning Nightcrawler, Mystique later adopted Rogue—but then forced the troubled teen to serve as a member of the Brotherhood. Mystique's fanatical pursuit of her genocidal goals caused a breach between the two, and Rogue left her adoptive mother's side to join the X-Men.

Whether operating undercover or fronting for a band of genetic extremists, Mystique possesses an almost pathological capacity for deception, and is willing to sacrifice her friends and allies to achieve her goals. Mystique is as determined as she is patient. In what she perceives as the inevitable war between man and mutant, she will not be a casualty.

ESSENTIAL READING

- *Essential X-Man Vols. II-IV*
- *X-Men: From the Ashes TPB*

Art by Salvador Larroca

CASSANDRA NOVA

Real Name:	Cassandra Nova	**Weight:**	115 lbs.
First Appearance:	*New X-Men* #114 (2001)	**Eye Color:**	Blue
Height:	5'4"	**Hair Color:**	None

Cassandra Nova began life as Professor X's twin sister, his utter opposite in mind and spirit. In the womb, Charles became self-aware first; sensing the other's malicious intent, he attempted to kill his twin. Cassandra was stillborn, but her psyche lived on. She spent 40 years clinging to a wall in the sewers under the hospital, copying Charles' cells to build a body.

A totally unique life form, Cassandra is what the alien Shi'ar call "Mummudrai," a sentient being's complete and total opposite. According to Shi'ar legend, every being must conquer its own spiritual or physical Mummudrai in the womb. Charles' antithesis, Cassandra lives only to kill and destroy mutants, while he seeks to unify and nurture them. In her first overt action, Cassandra unleashed a fleet of Sentinels on Genosha, decimating the island nation's exclusively mutant population while the world watched in horror.

After allowing herself to be captured, Cassandra attacked the X-Men at the Xavier Institute. During a pitched battle, she traded bodies with Charles, permitting her own to be severely damaged. The exchange occurred unknown to the X-Men. Wearing her brother's body, Nova next announced to the world that Charles was a mutant, placing Professor X and his students squarely under the media's microscope. Still inhabiting Charles' body, Cassandra later departed Earth in the company of Empress Lilandra of the Shi'ar, her brother's former lover. Cassandra quickly overtook Lilandra's intergalactic fleet and Shi'ar Imperial Guard and returned to Earth. She then compelled the Imperial Guard to annihilate the X-Men, while she prepared to use the super-computer Cerebra to telepathically coerce all mutants on the planet to kill one another. Nova's plan nearly succeeded, but she fell into a trap laid by the telepathic Jean Grey that virtually destroyed her brain and powers. Nova's psyche was trapped in the synthetic brain of a morphogenic alien, a prison in which the X-Men hope they can teach her to become human.

POWERS/ WEAPONS

- Telekinesis
- Telepathy

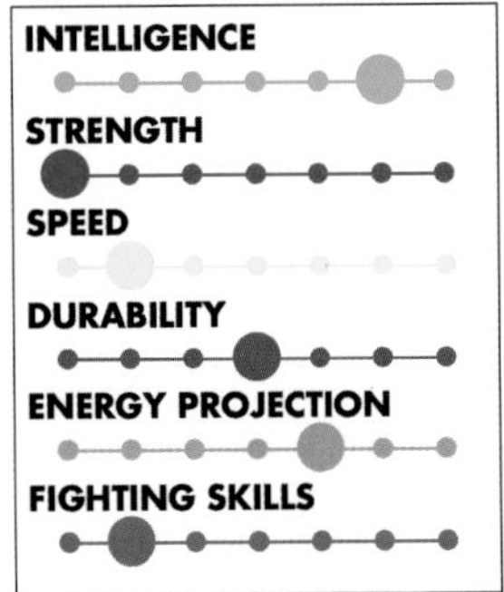

Art by Frank Quitely

ESSENTIAL READING

- *New X-Men Vol. I: E is For Extinction TPB*
- *New X-Men Vol. II: Imperial TPB*

SABRETOOTH

Real Name:	Victor Creed	**Weight:**	275 lbs.
First Appearance:	*Iron Fist* #14 (1977)	**Eye Color:**	Amber
Height:	6'6"	**Hair Color:**	Blond

ESSENTIAL READING

- *Weapon X Vol. I TPB*
- *Wolverine/Deadpool: Weapon X TPB*
- *X-Men: Mutant Genesis TPB*
- *X-Men: Mutant Massacre TPB*
- *X-Men Visionaries: Joe Madureira TPB*

POWERS/ WEAPONS

- Accelerated healing factor
- Superhumanly acute senses
- Indestructible Adamantium skeleton and claws

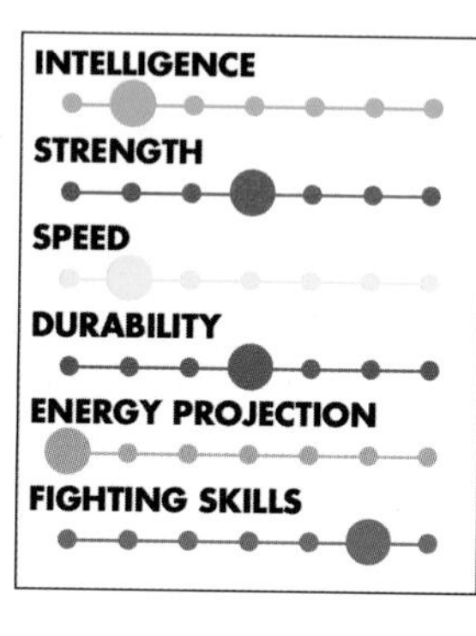

Sabretooth is the ultimate killing machine, driven by a psychotic need to hunt, fight and destroy. Little is known of Victor Creed's past before his time as a special operative for the CIA, but in that capacity, he worked closely with Wolverine, and both were products of the enigmatic Weapon X program. To ensure obedience, Weapon X scientists implanted false memories in their subjects, clouding Sabretooth's perceptions of his past.

Art by Georges Jeanty

Despite surface similarities, Wolverine and Sabretooth are polar opposites. Like Sabretooth, Wolverine is a lethal weapon, but his surly exterior hides the heart of a poet. Sabretooth has embraced the beast within; his unquenchable bloodlust only serves to exacerbate his feral fighting skills. Sabretooth has hated Wolverine from the day he waltzed into Weapon X with similar powers and fooled everyone into thinking he was top dog, earning Creed a reputation as a cheap imitation. Uneasy allies at best, the two had a falling out in the field due to Creed's reckless disregard for human life: Panicking under fire, Sabretooth snapped and murdered a double agent he considered baggage to facilitate his unit's escape. Wolverine and Sabretooth have been mortal enemies ever since.

Sabretooth's battles with Wolverine have been among his most ferocious. Adamantium claws, iron wills and two trained soldiers with accelerated healing factors—that either mutant makes it out alive is a testament to sheer toughness and a basic, animal instinct for survival.

A loner at heart, Sabretooth has been known to run with a pack on occasion. Creed has been a member of the Brotherhood of Mutants, a genetic terrorist organization; the Marauders, a team of superhuman assassins; X-Factor, a government-sponsored mutant strike force; and Weapon X, reconstituted under the leadership of a mysterious new director.

Women and children, the guilty and the innocent, mutants and humans, the weak and the strong—Creed is an equal-opportunity assassin with an all-consuming hunger for blood, provided the price is right or the situation suits his killer instincts. A relentless predator, Sabretooth stalks his prey with superhumanly acute senses. Once he has the scent, Creed closes in for the kill with the ferocity of a wild animal.

Art by Georges Jeanty

SENTINELS

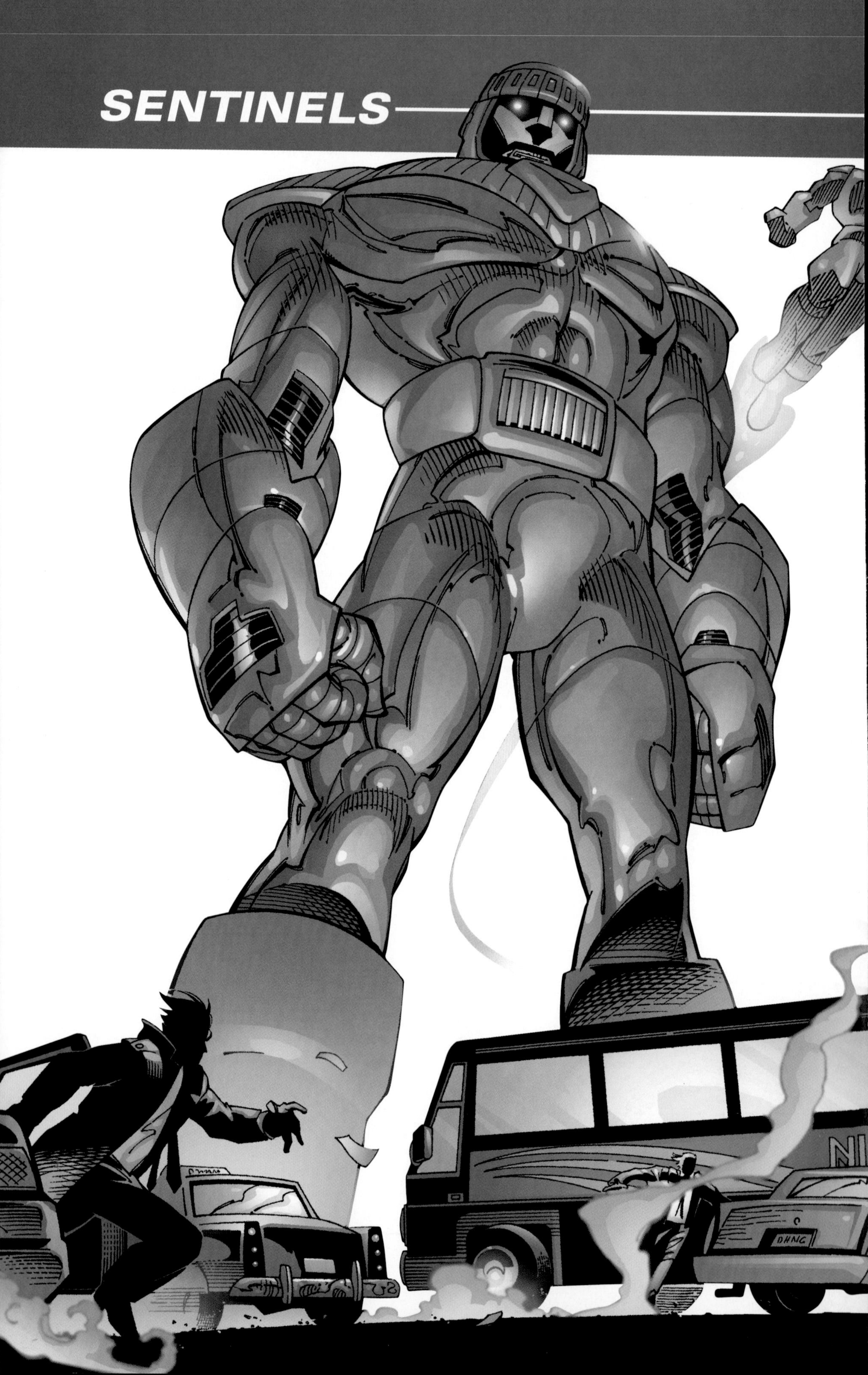

First Appearance: *X-Men* #14 (1965)

Art by Frank Quitely

Created by noted anthropologist Bolivar Trask, the first Sentinels were enormous robots designed to track and capture mutants, whom Trask saw as an emerging threat to humanity. Guided by humans or their own artificial intelligence, Sentinels are tireless embodiments of mankind's hatred and fear of change, a constant danger to every mutant the world over. Ultimately, Trask realized he was mistaken about the danger posed by mutantkind and gave his life to destroy his creations, which he now perceived as the greater threat.

The U.S. government later revived the Sentinel program, and secretly controls the bulk of Sentinel research and activity to this day. Most often, the androids have targeted the X-Men. Mystique's attempted assassination of anti-mutant Senator Robert Kelly unwittingly precipitated an alternate future in which the Sentinels were allowed free reign to eradicate that mutant menace. They succeeded only too well, wiping out not only most of the X-Men, but also every other superhuman being they deemed a threat to humanity.

Like their targets, the Sentinels began to evolve as a function of their programming and are no longer limited to humanoid form. Recent advances in Sentinel technology have yielded mutant-Sentinel hybrids and microscopic nano-Sentinels. Countless sanctioned and covert Sentinel bases exist around the globe, operated by both mutant-hunting humans and Sentinels themselves. Each Sentinel enclave may have a slightly different mission, but the androids' primary directive remains the destruction of mutants as a species. Their greatest success was the methodical extermination of Magneto and the 16 million citizens of his mutant haven Genosha.

Art by Adam Kubert

ESSENTIAL READING

- *New X-Men Vol. I: E Is For Extinction TPB*
- *Essential Uncanny X-Men Vol. I*
- *Essential X-Men Vols. I & II*
- *X-Men: Days of Future Past TPB*

SHI'AR IMPERIAL GUARD

Art by Jim Lee

First Appearance: *X-Men* #107 (1977)

Assembled from the far reaches of the Shi'ar empire, the Imperial Guard is a garrison of super-powered beings charged with the enforcement of galactic law. Due to their varied origins and disparate homeworlds, the members of the Guard collectively control virtually every form of matter and energy.

The Imperial Guard is responsible for maintaining peace among the thousands of worlds within the vast empire, as well as protecting and carrying out the decrees of Shi'ar Majestrix Lilandra. Led by Gladiator, the Guard is a collection of the empire's greatest warriors, including Electron, Starbolt, Titan, Astra, Manta, Smasher, Hussar and Warstar.

Because of the close relationship between Professor X and Lilandra, the Imperial Guard has encountered the X-Men and other Earth heroes on numerous occasions, both as allies and enemies. Gladiator alone battled the Fantastic Four to a standstill, and the Guard has soundly defeated the X-Men several times. When Jean Grey was imbued with the Phoenix Force and became a threat to the universe, Lilandra charged the Guard with the mutant's execution. Gladiator and his compatriots thrashed the X-Men, but Phoenix committed suicide before the Guard could complete its mission.

The Guard is also the Shi'ar's first line of defense, and has played important roles in the empire's military actions against both the Skrull and Kree. The Guard stood fast even when the empire suffered a serious blow at the hands of Cassandra Nova.

The members of the Imperial Guard are akin to legions of Roman soldiers who would sooner die than see their emperor injured. The Guardsmen would and have fought to the death to protect their ruler and ensure the empire's survival.

ESSENTIAL READING

- *New X-Men Vol. II: Imperial TPB*
- *Fantastic Four Visionaries: John Byrne TPB*
- *Essential X-Men Vol. II*

ULTIMATE MARVEL

IT ALL STARTED IN 1961, WITH THE CREATION OF THE FANTASTIC FOUR. MORE THAN FORTY YEARS AND THOUSANDS OF STORIES LATER, THE MARVEL UNIVERSE HAD EVOLVED INTO A RICH TAPESTRY OF 4,000-PLUS CHARACTERS WITH COMPLEX BACK-STORIES AND SHARED HISTORIES. MANY LOYAL FANS SAW THIS CROSS-TITLE CONTINUITY AS AN IMPORTANT DIMENSION OF THE STORIES THEY LOVED, BUT IT ALSO ACTED AS A DETERRENT TO CASUAL READERS. WITH MARVEL PULLING IN FEWER AND FEWER NEW FANS, DRASTIC MEASURES WERE REQUIRED.

In a bold move, President and COO Bill Jemas and Editor-in-Chief Joe Quesada set out to return Spider-Man and the X-Men to their roots. The fledgling *Ultimate* line would reinvent these and other classic Marvel characters from the ground up for a modern audience, cutting to the core of what made them compelling in the first place. Quesada and Jemas recruited the industry's best writers and artists to tell clear, compelling stories with fresh voices: Brian Michael Bendis and Mark Bagley on *Ultimate Spider-Man*, and Mark Millar and Adam Kubert on *Ultimate X-Men*.

Bold, innovative versions of iconic heroes, *Ultimate Spider-Man* and *Ultimate X-Men* attracted old fans and new readers alike, and the media took note. Sales started high and kept growing. Hundreds of thousands of people discovered Spider-Man and the X-Men for the first time—again.

In the *Ultimate* titles, anything can happen. Freed from the constraints of continuity and completely accessible to new readers, every character is new, every relationship is fresh, and every vista is open for exploration.

Art by Bryan Hitch

ULTIMATE SPIDER-MAN

Art by Mark Bagley

ESSENTIAL READING

- *Ultimate Spider-Man Vols. I-IV TPB*
- *Ultimate Spider-Man Vol. I HC*
- *Ultimate Marvel Team-Up HC*

Peter Parker has all the worries of your average 21st-century teen: grades, girls and peer pressure. Peter is a bookish, introverted whiz, more comfortable with computers than among his classmates. Raised by his Aunt May and Uncle Ben, Peter learned responsibility at an early age. Shunned by the "in crowd," he also learned to rely on himself.

Gaining amazing abilities from the bite of a genetically altered spider didn't make things any easier. Beginning with the murder of his uncle, Peter's already-complicated life became a balancing act between his heroic responsibilities as Spider-Man and his high-school career. Now, no matter which role he chooses, he can't win. If he spends more time as Spider-Man, Peter's personal life suffers. Less, and he puts innocent people at risk from foes such as the Green Goblin, Doctor Octopus and the Kingpin.

Ultimate Spider-Man Vol. II: Learning Curve TPB

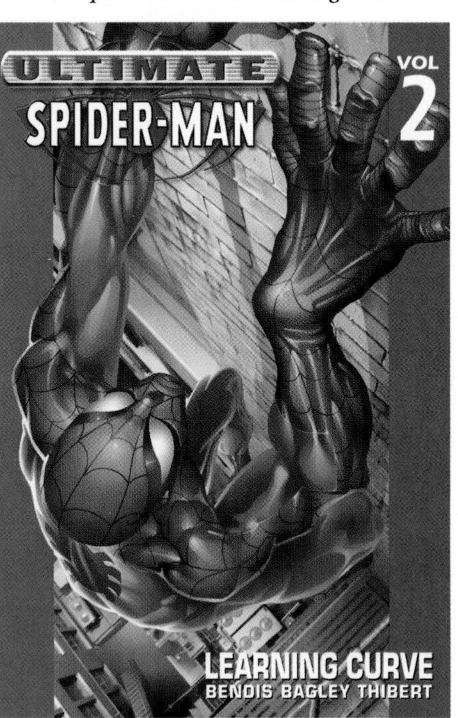

The Green Goblin once was industrialist Norman Osborn, father of Peter's best friend Harry. Driven by ambition, Osborn transformed himself into a barely human beast of a man when he set out to duplicate the accident that gifted Peter with amazing abilities.

Injured in the laboratory explosion that gave birth to the Goblin, Dr. Otto Octavius awoke from a coma to find his body fused to the mechanical appendages he was using at the time. His mind irrevocably altered, Doctor Octopus began a campaign of bloody revenge against all associated with the accident—including Spider-Man.

With his fingers in every pie, Wilson Fisk is New York City's so-called Kingpin of Crime. Ruling the underworld with a massive iron fist, the Kingpin pulls strings Peter never even knew existed.

Kraven, Electro, the Enforcers and dozens of other flamboyant criminals have sought to make names for themselves by defeating Spider-Man, and the misunderstood hero is currently wanted for questioning by the NYPD.

Despite the headaches and heartaches of his costumed life, there are days Peter prefers fighting enemies he can see as Spider-Man over lying to Aunt May about his whereabouts, juggling the attention and affections of Mary Jane Watson and Gwen Stacy, and standing up to school bully Flash Thompson.

There are days he doesn't know whose life is more difficult: Peter Parker's or Spider-Man's.

ULTIMATE X-MEN

Art by Salvador Larroca

ESSENTIAL READING

- *Ultimate X-Men Vols. I-III TPB*
- *Ultimate X-Men Vol. I HC*
- *Ultimate Marvel Team-Up HC*

They are the Tomorrow People—*Homo superior*. Through evolution, these mutants have developed powers and abilities far beyond the faculties of normal humans.

In pursuit of peaceful coexistence between humanity and mutantkind, Professor Charles Xavier has molded his teenage students into a highly trained task force. The X-Men use their unique genetic gifts to protect a world that fears and hates them. Starting with Marvel Girl and Cyclops, Professor X brought together Storm, weather-manipulating car thief; Beast, reclusive loner with genius-level intelligence and the agility of an ape; Colossus, steel-skinned enforcer for the Russian Mafia; and Iceman, a runaway teen terrified of his power.

The wildcard in the mix is Wolverine, a mercenary in every sense of the word. A minion of the genetic terrorist Magneto, he joined the X-Men as a mole. Wolverine was ready to kill the young mutants at his master's whim before being swayed to fight on their side—partly due to Xavier's philosophy, but mostly because of his attraction to Marvel Girl.

Xavier's mission is a timely one. Anti-mutant sentiment is sanctioned by the government and enforced by mutant-hunting robots called Sentinels. Standing in opposition to Xavier's non-violent methods and humanity's attempts to persecute mutants are Magneto and his Brotherhood, disenchanted souls who believe that *Homo superior* is humanity's true heir apparent.

Once allies, Magneto and Xavier now stand on opposite ends of the battlefield. Xavier steadfastly believes that a genetic war between mutants and humans will result in the extinction of both species, and has endeavored for years to encourage better understanding between the two.

Thanks to the power they embody, the X-Men have become unwilling players in the global political picture. They've had run-ins with the U.S. government, S.H.I.E.L.D. and even the enigmatic Weapon X program, which kidnapped the mutants and forced them into covert military service.

Fiercely independent, the X-Men are ready and willing to stand and fight for a better tomorrow.

Art by Adam Kubert

THE ULTIMATES

Art by Bryan Hitch

ESSENTIAL READING

- *Ultimates Vol. 1: Super-Human TPB*

It's the 21st century, and the world has changed. The established order has proven ineffective, and ordinary people are scared. Who will protect them from the newly rising threats to mankind?

Funded by S.H.I.E.L.D. and overseen by General Nick Fury, the Ultimates are a super-powered strike force backed by five thousand technicians and ten thousand support troops. They are S.H.I.E.L.D.'s very public face, seen as both super-soldiers and super-celebrities.

Art by Bryan Hitch

The team's field commander is Captain America, the original World War II Super Soldier, recently thawed from accidental suspended animation in a block of ice. Adjusting to life in the new millennium, Captain America is a soldier's soldier, a born leader with unwavering loyalty to the flag and his cause.

Billionaire inventor Tony Stark, known to the world as Iron Man, spends as much time cavorting with celebrities as he does in his high-tech armor. Thor, self-proclaimed Norse Thunder God, may be merely a delusional, super-powered human.

S.H.I.E.L.D. agent and scientist Janet Van Dyne—better known as the Wasp—can shrink to the size of an insect at will, thanks to her husband Hank Pym's experiments. Capable of growing to a height of sixty feet, Pym is better known to the world as Giant Man. He has been working with Dr. Bruce Banner for several years to replicate the Super-Soldier Serum that created Captain America.

A semi-neurotic, scrawny scientist, Bruce Banner was demoted after several disastrous attempts to duplicate the formula. Banner tested the serum on himself, transforming into a green giant that went on a rampage through Manhattan and was dubbed the Hulk. As a result, Fury and the other members of the team keep Banner at arm's length.

The Ultimates function as smoothly as a crack military unit, falling together under Captain America's command. They are America's first, best line of defense.

THE CALL OF DUTY

THE WORLD CHANGED FOREVER ON SEPTEMBER 11TH, 2001— AND SO DID THE MEANING OF THE WORD "HERO."

Inspired by thousands of stories of selfless courage on that tragic day and in the weeks that followed, Marvel Editor-in-Chief Joe Quesada and President and COO Bill Jemas recognized that the paradigm of heroes and heroism had shifted toward real men and women. The true heroes of that day and our world are police officers, firefighters and EMTs.

Marvel Comics honors these brave individuals in *The Call of Duty*. Receiving nationwide press coverage, initial releases *The Brotherhood*, *The Precinct* and *The Wagon* have captivated scores of new fans, many of whom had never picked up a comic before.

The Brotherhood's Lieutenant James MacDonald of the FDNY, *The Precinct*'s Sergeant Frank Gunzer of the NYPD and *The Wagon*'s EMT Jennifer Montez serve New York and its people out of loyalty and responsibility. All three share common battle scars: old wounds, broken relationships and tortured consciences.

Each is shaken when a little girl impossibly appears before them in the most harrowing of situations, warning of great death and destruction.

MacDonald is a lieutenant fireman, stationed in Brooklyn, directly across the river from where the Twin Towers once stood. He has never allowed fear to overwhelm his responsibilities as a firefighter, despite the risks. Yet in all his years on the job, MacDonald has never faced a danger like this, one that seems to stretch the bounds of normal human experience. Will his bravery be enough to extinguish this seemingly supernatural threat?

Gunzer is an ordinary New York City cop. Yet in the last 24 hours, his world has been turned upside down by a girl who doesn't exist, a brother he no longer knows and a wife who decides she can't be part of his life. He now has a new call to duty—not just to uphold the law, but to save all humanity.

It's tough enough to drive a speeding ambulance through the crowded concrete canyons of New York. Imagine having to do it in the Marvel Universe—a city teeming with powerful heroes, deadly villains and medical emergencies around every corner. It's all in a day's work for Montez. But now, an even deadlier threat looms.

MacDonald, Gunzer and Montez must overcome their inner voices that tell them they don't believe in ghosts or the supernatural. Once they do, they quickly realize they've become part of something much larger than any emergency they've ever faced.

Art by David Finch and Richard Isanove

ESSENTIAL READING

- *The Call of Duty Vol. I: The Brotherhood & The Wagon TPB*
- *The Call of Duty Vol. II: The Precinct TPB*

MARVEL ENCYCLOPEDIA

INDEX

POWER RATINGS

STRENGTH
Ability to lift weight

1 Weak: cannot lift own body weight
2 Normal: able to lift own body weight
3 Peak human: able to lift twice own body weight
4 Superhuman: 800 lbs-25 ton range
5 Superhuman: 25-75 ton range
6 Superhuman: 75-100 ton range
7 Incalculable: In excess of 100 tons

INTELLIGENCE
Ability to think and process information

1 Slow/Impaired
2 Normal
3 Learned
4 Gifted
5 Genius
6 Super-Genius
7 Omniscient

ENERGY PROJECTION
Ability to discharge energy

1 None
2 Ability to discharge energy on contact
3 Short range, short duration, single energy type
4 Medium range, medium duration, single energy type
5 Long range, long duration, single energy type
6 Able to discharge multiple forms of energy
7 Virtually unlimited command of all forms of energy

FIGHTING ABILITY
Proficiency in hand-to-hand combat

1 Poor
2 Normal
3 Some training
4 Experienced fighter
5 Master of a single form of combat
6 Master of several forms of combat
7 Master of all forms of combat

DURABILITY
Ability to resist or recover from bodily injury

1 Weak
2 Normal
3 Enhanced
4 Regenerative
5 Bulletproof
6 Superhuman
7 Virtually indestructible

SPEED
Ability to move over land by running or flight

1 Below normal
2 Normal
3 Superhuman: peak range: 700 MPH
4 Speed of sound: Mach-1
5 Supersonic: Mach-2 through Orbital Velocity
6 Speed of light: 186,000 miles per second
7 Warp speed: transcending light speed